500 Years [of Reformation:]
Tensions betwee[n Mission and Cultu]re

500 años de Reforma:
Tensiones entre Misión y Cultura

500 Jahre Reformation:
Spannungen zwischen Mission und Kultur

*Journal of the European Society of Women
in Theological Research*

*Revista de la Asociación Europea de Mujeres
en la Investigación Teológica*

*Jahrbuch der Europäischen Gesellschaft
von Frauen in theologischer Forschung*

Volume 25

ESWTR

Bibliographical information and books for review
in the Journal should be sent to:
Sabine Dievenkorn
HaOranim 2, Kiryat Tivon, Israel 3604302

Articles for consideration for the Journal
should be sent to:
Sabine Dievenkorn
HaOranim 2, Kiryat Tivon, Israel 3604302

500 Years of Reformation:
Tensions between Mission and Culture

500 años de Reforma:
Tensiones entre Misión y Cultura

500 Jahre Reformation:
Spannungen zwischen Mission und Kultur

Editors:
Sabine Dievenkorn, Teresa Toldy

PEETERS
LEUVEN – PARIS – BRISTOL, CT
2017

Journal of the European Society of Women
in Theological Research, 25

A catalogue record for this book is available from the Library of Congress.

© 2017, Peeters Publishers, Leuven / Belgium
ISBN 978-90-429-3551-8
ISSN 1783-2454
eISSN 1783-2446
D/2017/0602/133
Cover design by Margret Omlin-Küchler

All rights reserved. No part to this publication may be reproduced, stored in a retrieval system, or transmitted, in any form of by any means, electronic, mechanical, photocopying, recording or otherwise, without the prior permission of the publisher.

CONTENTS – INHALT – ÍNDICE

Editorial

Sabine Dievenkorn
Reformation und Eroberung in der Spannung von Mission, Kultur und Political Correctness 1

Reformation and Conquest in the Tension of Mission, Culture and Political Correctness 5

Reforma y Conquista en las tensiones de misión, cultura y corrección política 9

Theme – Thema – Tema

Maaike De Haardt
Transformation and the Virtue of Ambivalence 13

Marta María Zubia Guinea
Ecclesia semper reformanda. Hacia una Iglesia laica, al estilo del movimiento de Jesús 31

Gotlind Ulshöfer
Aus der Reformation lernen? Impulse im Zeitalter der Digitalisierung 47

Ninna Edgardh
Embracing the Future: The Church of Sweden in Continuous Reformation 67

Thalia Gur-Klein
21st Century Anti-Judaism in Feminist Theology 81

Elisabeth Schneider-Böklen
Elisabeth Cruciger – Nun, Minister's Wife and First Lutheran Poetess 117

Natalia Salas Molina
Liderazgo protestante femenino, un desafío desde la Reforma .. 131

Silvia Martínez Cano
Mujeres creyentes, culturas e Iglesias: Reformas para comunidades católicas vivas y en acción 143

Teresa Toldy
Someone is Missing in the Common House: The Empty Place of Women in the Encyclical Letter "Laudato si'" 167

Forum – Fórum

Silke Petersen
„Luther 2017" – ein erster Blick in die neue Lutherbibel 191

Ida Raming (traducido por Sabine Dievenkorn, Teresa Toldy, Montserat Escribano Cárcel)
Carta abierta a Cardinal Gerhard Ludwig Müller 197

Isabel Gómez Acebo
Comunidades de la Reforma pioneras en la concesión de ministerios a las mujeres: La tradición común 203

Book Reviews – Rezensionen – Recensiones 219

Vanessa Götz-Meiners, *Treue und Untreue in der Partnerschaft. Historische Entwicklungen – Moraltheologische perspektiven*, (Aschendorff Verlag: Münster 2016) 219

Carol P. Christ and Judith Plaskow, *Goddess and God in the world. Conversations in Embodied Theology*, (Fortress press: Minneapolis 2016) 222

Sabine Dievenkorn

Reformation und Eroberung in der Spannung von Mission, Kultur und Political Correctness

Dass Frauen als Theologinnen ihre Stimme erst etwa 500 Jahre nach der Reformation erheben konnten, liegt nicht zuletzt daran, dass die Reformation evangelische Theologinnen nicht hervorbrachte, nicht hervorbringen konnte und nicht hervorbringen wollte. Erst durch die Politik der Universitäten im 20 Jahrhundert wird sich das ändern.

Die Reformation hat eine weitreichende missionarische Dimension. Martin Luther leistete mit seiner Bibelübersetzung nicht nur einen Beitrag zur Verschriftlichung der deutschen Sprache. Übersetzend initiierte er einen theologischen Prozess der Translation und Transkulturation der Bibel. Patriarchal geprägtes kulturhistorisches und sozialpolitisches Umfeld erfuhren eine theologische Würdigung und entfalteten große Wirkung in ihrer politisch missionarischen Geschichte. Die Frau, in einer Ambivalenz zwischen Hexe, Hure und Heiliger, wird als „protestantischer Dienstleib" ins patriarchale Referenzsystem reduziert. In der Spannung zwischen Exegese und Eisegese übertrug der protestantisch werdende Ordensbruder die Bibel in die Alltags- und Gegenwartssprache des deutschen Mittelalters. Als ein, modern gesagt, agency-oriented Mediator versprachlichte er in seiner Übersetzung seine reformatorische Theologie. Oszillierend zwischen Autor und Leser, Quell- und Zieltext, verlieh er dem biblischen Wort die Interpretation, die er als politisch korrekt und theologisch geboten erachtete. Die so reformierte Bibel war eine Innovation für die patriarchale europäische Theologie und Wissenschaft. Männlicher Fortschritt als Individualismus und nationale Demokratien und Staaten waren eine Folge. Eine historische Chance für die protestierenden katholischen Theologinnen und protestantisch gewordenen Ordensfrauen eröffnet sich nicht. Mit der Beendigung des Klosterlebens in der evangelischen Kirche werden formal Lebensentwürfe und Bildungsmöglichkeiten für Frauen eingeschränkt.

Eine eben erscheinende, neue deutsche, protestantische Bibelübersetzung in der Tradition Martin Luthers illustriert aktuell die alten Problemfelder, Positionen und Perspektiven christlicher Bibelhermeneutik zwischen Tradition und

Transgression. Im Rekurs auf den Reformator werden hermeneutische Kategorien von Urtext und Original mit einem neopatriarchalen Verständnis von Normativität traditioneller Schriften ins Verhältnis gesetzt. Als Referenz an feministisch theologische Diskurse darf die partielle Visualisierung des Weiblichen gesehen werden. Ausreichend ist sie nicht.

Ein anderer Aspekt der Reform und der Reformation ist die kolonialisierte und missionierte sogenannte „Neue Welt". Der transferierte und tradierte Kultur- und Religionsexport bzw. -import patriarchaler und misogyner Strukturen, wird dem reformatorischen Dogma des Selbstverständnisses der Kirche als *„ecclesia semper reformanda"* nicht gerecht. Die Position von Frauen in Sprache, Kultur und Gesellschaft ist dafür ebenso Zeugnis wie feministische Implikationen in Politik und Wissenschaft, sei ihr Kontext theologisch oder säkular.

Der hermeneutische Konflikt von Übersetzung und Interpretation manifestiert theologisch die Vernetzung von Politik und Kultur im Beziehungsgeflecht von Theologie und Mission – innerer und äußere. In seiner ideologischen Verstrickung im Gefälle patriarchaler Strukturen hat das Auswirkungen in die politische Moderne hinein und ist in Ost und West ebenso präsent wie in Nord oder Süd. Ein Phänomen, das die Kultur- und Theologiegeschichte der Reformation über Raum und Zeit hinweg dem modernen Begriff des Neopatriarchalismus als Teil des globalen Kulturtransfers verbindet. Das vorliegende Jahrbuch ist dafür ein beredtes Zeugnis.

Im Zusammenspiel der femininen Stimmen aus dem katholischen Spanien und dem evangelikalen Chile zeigen sich Brüche in Tradition und Theologie für das Stichwort Reformation eine Chiffre ist, die in gemeinsamer spanischer Sprache das fundamental Trennende sichtbar macht.

Das moderne, europäisch protestantisch-kirchliche Erbe scheint mit allen damit einhergehenden Herausforderungen das Mutterland der Reformation verlassen zu haben. Auf der ganzen Welt hat man die Ereignisse des 31. Oktober 2016 im schwedischen Lund verfolgt, als zum ersten Mal in ökumenischer Gemeinschaft an die Reformation erinnert worden. In einer gemeinsamen Veranstaltung des Lutherischen Weltbund und der römisch-katholischen Kirche entstand es, das Foto, auf dem sich Papst Franziskus und die Erzbischöfin der Kirche von Schweden, Antje Jackelén, umarmen. Als Zeichen der Hoffnung und auch der Spannung, ist um die ganze Welt gegangen. Die lutherische Kirche von Schweden versucht eine Vorreiterrolle im Blick auf Fragen von Gender und Sexualität, Freiheit und Norm. Sie ist Partnerin in einer Gesellschaft, in der Glaube heute eine freiwillige Option darstellt. Die ehemalige Staatskirche ist mit neuen Herausforderungen konfrontiert sowohl im Blick auf religiöse als auch auf kulturelle Diversitäten. Die Kirche von Schweden hält diese unterschiedlichen Spannungen durch den reformatorischen Ansatz, der Programm ist, zusammen: eine Kirche zu sein, die ständig Reform braucht.

Die Pluralität einer translatorischen Kommunikation des Evangeliums eröffnen kritische Perspektiven auf die Moderne. Ein feministisch, gestalttheologischer Dialog der Weltreligionen entfaltet sich jenseits der binären Dichotomie von Zentrum und Peripherie. Epistemologisch und hermeneutisch kreative Strategien verknüpfen sich innovativ im Ringen um historisch kanonischen Schriften als die uns heute Heiligen Texte vertraut sind. Ihr Erbe entfalten sich im Spannungsfeld der Machtfaktoren und Intersektionalitätskriterien: *ecclesia semper reformanda*.

Das Geschlecht spielt in den medialen und sozialen Prozessen der Deutung, und der translatorischen Erklärung und Auslegung religiöser Schriften eine signifikante Rolle. Misogyne Auslegungstraditionen waren mit der Reform keineswegs beendet.

Katholischen Theologinnen ist noch heute, 500 Jahre nach Katharina von Bora, nach wie vor der Zugang zum Amt verwehrt. Reglementiert und reduziert auf ein fremdbestimmtes postfaktisches Bild, werden weibliche Räume und Möglichkeiten begrenzt. Gut drei Monate vor dem reformationsgedenkenden, versöhnlichen Bild aus Schweden beschloss die lettische Evangelischlutherische Kirche die Abschaffung der Frauenordination.

Als hätte es nie eine Reformation in Europa gegeben, entzündet sich noch immer jede kulturtheologische, sozialrelgiöse Debatte in Zeit und Raum am Verhaltenskodex der Frauen. Ihre Kleidung und ihr Körper, ihr Verhalten und ihr Freiraum werden patriarchal determiniert. Nicht selten sind sie dabei kooptierende Agentinnen, sich selbst verlierend zwischen den Ansprüchen des so genannten modernen und unverklemmten Zeitgeistes in Kultur, Religion und Gesellschaft.

Die Spannung zwischen Gender und Theologie spiegelt sich der Verortung zwischen vertikaler und horizontaler religiöser Autorität. Abzuwarten bleibt, wie sich das Phänomen der Autorität in den Religionen weiterentwickelt und wie und ob Visionen einer interreligiösen medial- und kontextorientierten Hermeneutik Gestalt annehmen kann. Kategorisierungen und Postulationen von Wahrheit, Autorität und Heiliger Schrift fordern heraus, wollen sie horizontal statt vertikal kommuniziert werden. Moderne neopatriarchale Spannungsfelder wie Fundamentalismus und Säkularisierung, Dekonstruktion und

Konstruktion engen die Sichtweise auf Migration und Translation oft erheblich ein. Hegemonialbestrebungen von Macht und Identität tragen wesentlich dazu bei, Fremdheit untereinander auszubauen. Dem gilt es theologisch entgegenzutreten.

Sabine Dievenkorn studierte Theologie, Mathematik, Physik und Germanistik. Sie ist Bildungs- und Übersetzungswissenschaftlerin, promovierte Theologin und evangelische Pfarrerin. Als Mitbegründerin der Academía de Teología Femenina "Maria Magdalena" in Santiago de Chile arbeitet sie dort als akademische Direktorin. Sie ist Professorin für Praktische Theologie, Gender und Translation Studies. Zurzeit ist sie im Sabbatical in Israel.

Sabine Dievenkorn

Reformation and Conquest in the Tension of Mission, Culture and Political Correctness

That women could raise their voices as theologians only 500 years after Reformation is due not least to the fact that the Reformation was not able to produce female evangelical theologians, nor had it wanted to, nor could it do so. This would change only with the transformation in universities' politics in the 20th century.

The Reformation has a far-reaching missionary dimension. Martin Luther, with his translation of the Bible, had not only contributed to the transcription of the German language. He initiated a theological process of translation and transculturation of the Bible. Patriarchally-coined cultural-historical and socio-political contexts have undergone a theological evaluation and have had a great effect in the history of political mission. The woman, ambivalently seen as the witch, the whore and the saint, is reduced into a "Protestant serving-body" in the patriarchal reference system. In the tension between exegesis and eisegesis, the Protestant-becoming monk transferred the Bible into the everyday language of the German Middle Ages. As an agency-oriented mediator – to use current day terminology – he inscribed, in his translation, his theology of Reformation. Oscillating between author and reader, source and target text, he gave the biblical word the interpretation that he regarded as politically correct and theologically viable. The so-reformed Bible was an innovation for patriarchal European theology and science, facilitating male progress in the form of individualism and national democracies and states. Protesting Catholic women theologians and Protestant-becoming nuns had no historical opportunity. With the termination of monastic life in the Protestant Church, formal life options and education possibilities for women had become restricted.

A newly-published, current-day German Protestant Bible translation in the tradition of Martin Luther illustrates the old problems, positions and perspectives of Christian biblical hermeneutics between tradition and transgression. In going back to the Reformer, hermeneutical categories of source text and originality are juxtaposed with a neopatriarchal understanding of the normativity attributed to traditional writings. The partial visualisation of the feminine in the translation may be seen as reference to feminist theology. However, this is far from sufficient.

Another aspect of reform and Reformation is the colonialised and missioned so-called "New World". The export or import of transmitted culture and religion, including patriarchal and misogynistic structures, does not meet the reformist dogma of the Church's self-description as *"ecclesia semper reformanda"*. The position of women in language, culture and society is as much a proof of this as are feminist implications in politics and science, be their context theological or secular.

The hermeneutic conflict of translation and interpretation theologically manifests the networking of politics and culture in the interrelatedness of theology and mission – internal and external. In its ideological involvement in the gradient of patriarchal structures, this has had an impact on political modernity – east and west, north and south. This phenomenon connects the cultural and theological history of the Reformation over space and time with the modern concept of neopatriarchalism as part of global cultural transfer. The present yearbook is an eloquent testimony of this.

In the interplay of feminine voices from Catholic Spain and evangelical Chile, breaches in tradition and theology are visible, where the term Reformation finally represents the fundamental distinctions more than the common denominators of the shared Spanish language.

The current, European-Protestant-ecclesiastical heritage seems to have left the motherland of Reformation with all its concomitant challenges. Throughout the world, the events of 31 October 2016 in Lund, Sweden, have been hailed as the first ever ecumenical commemoration of the Reformation. The joint event, organised by the Lutheran World Federation and the Roman Catholic Church, was the stage for Pope Francis' embrace with Antje Jackelén, the Archbishop of the Church of Sweden. The photo, a sign of hope as well as tension, has gone around the world. The Lutheran Church of Sweden strives to be a pioneer in questions of gender and sexuality, freedom and norm. It is part of a society where faith is now a voluntary option. The former state church is faced with new challenges concerning religious and cultural diversity. The Church of Sweden holds these different positions together through its program of Reformation, whereby it views itself as a church in need of constant reform.

The plurality of translatorial communication of the gospel opens up critical perspectives on our times. A feminist, gestalt theological dialogue of world religions unfolds beyond the binary dichotomy of centre and periphery.

Epistemologically and hermeneutically creative strategies link innovatively in the struggle for historically canonical scriptures as today's holy texts; and their inheritance reverberates in the tension field of power factors and intersectionality: *Ecclesia semper reformanda.*

Gender plays a significant role in the social processes and media of interpretation and in the translational explanation and interpretation of religious writings. Misogynist traditions of interpretation were by no means gone with the reform.

Catholic female theologians are still denied access to the office, even today, five hundred years after Katharina von Bora. Regulated and reduced to an externally determined post-factual image, female spaces and possibilities are limited. Just three months before the reformation-minded, conciliatory photo from Sweden, the Latvian Evangelical Lutheran Church decided to abolish women's ordination.

As if there had never been a Reformation in Europe, every cultural-theological, social-religious debate in time and space still puts at its focus women's code of conduct. Their clothes and their bodies, their behaviour and their freedom are patriarchally determined. Not infrequently, they become co-opted agents, losing themselves among the claims of the so-called modern and uninhibited *zeitgeist* in culture, religion and society.

The tension between gender and theology is reflected in the location amidst vertical and horizontal religious authority. It remains to be seen how the phenomenon of authority in religions can be further developed and how visions of an interreligious medium- and context-oriented hermeneutics may take shape. Categorisations and postulations of truth, authority, and Holy Scripture pose a challenge if they are to be communicated horizontally rather than vertically. Modern neopatriarchal fields of tension, such as fundamentalism and secularisation, deconstruction and construction, often significantly limit the way in which migration and translation are viewed. Hegemonic endeavours of power and identity contribute substantially to the expansion of foreignness. Theologically, this must be countered.

Sabine Dievenkorn

Reforma y Conquista en las tensiones de misión, cultura y corrección política

Si las mujeres pueden hacer oír su voz como teólogas recién 500 años después de la Reforma, ello se debe en gran medida a que la Reforma no produjo teólogas, ni podía ni quería producirlas. Esto va a cambiar recién gracias a la política universitaria del siglo XX.

La Reforma tiene una dimensión misionera de alcance mundial. Con su traducción de la Biblia, Martín Lutero no sólo hizo una aportación al idioma alemán escrito, sino que echó a andar un proceso teológico de traslación y transculturación de la Biblia. En el ámbito histórico-cultural y político-social marcado por el patriarcado, esa traducción obtuvo grandes resultados en su historia político-misionera. La mujer, en su ambivalencia como bruja, prostituta y santa, quedaba reducida a no ser más que "el cuerpo de servicio protestante" dentro del sistema patriarcal de referencias. En la tensión entre *exégesis* y *eiségesis*, el fraile que se volvía protestante traspuso la Biblia en el lenguaje del diario vivir contemporáneo del medioevo alemán. Al traducir, puso en palabras su propia teología reformadora, como lo haría hoy, para decirlo en términos modernos, un *agency-oriented mediator*. Así, oscilando entre la actividad del autor y la del lector, entre un texto que podía ser fuente, pero también objetivo, le dio al escrito bíblico la interpretación que él consideraba políticamente correcta y teológicamente requerida. La Biblia quedaba así reformada, y ella fue una innovación para la teología y la ciencia europea patriarcal. Las consecuencias fueron el progreso, masculino e individualista, la democracia nacional y los estados. No se abrió ninguna oportunidad histórica para que las teólogas católicas protestaran, ni para las religiosas que se volvieron protestantes. Al terminarse en la iglesia evangélica la vida de monjas enclaustradas, los proyectos de vida y las posibilidades de formación de las mujeres quedaron formalmente restringidas.

Una nueva traducción de la Biblia acaba de aparecer. Sigue la tradición de Lutero, es alemana y protestante. Ella viene a ilustrar hoy de nuevo el alcance del antiguo problema. Se toman allí posiciones y perspectivas de la hermenéutica cristiana de la Biblia en un vaivén entre tradición y transgresión. Recurriendo al reformador, se relacionan categorías hermenéuticas de texto primitivo y original con una forma neo-patriarcal de entender la normatividad de los escritos tradicionales. Se puede ver una referencia al discurso teológico feminista en la visualización parcial que se hace de lo femenino. Pero es una referencia que queda corta.

Otro aspecto de la Reforma es lo que se llama el "nuevo mundo". La exportación de cultura y religión, así como la importación de estructuras patriarcales y misóginas son hechos que no se condicen con la autoconciencia de la iglesia como *"ecclesia semper reformanda"*. Testigo de ello son tanto la posición de las mujeres en la lengua, la cultura y la sociedad, como las implicaciones en la política y la ciencia, sea en un contexto teológico o en uno secular.

El conflicto hermenéutico de traducción e interpretación pone teológicamente de manifiesto la implicación mutua de política y cultura en el tejido de relaciones entre teología y misión – tanto interna como externa. En el enredo ideológico de las estructuras patriarcales, esto repercute en la modernidad política, tanto en oriente como en occidente, e igual en el norte que en el sur. Es éste un fenómeno que, saltándose los tiempos y los espacios, vincula la historia de la cultura y la teología de la reforma con el concepto moderno de neo-patriarcado como parte de la transferencia cultural global. El anuario de referencia es de ello un testigo elocuente.

En el concierto de voces femeninas de la católica España y del Chile evangélico se advierten rupturas en la tradición y la teología, para las cuales la palabra "Reforma" viene siendo una clave que torna visible lo que, dentro de la lengua común, las separa de fondo.

La herencia moderna y europea, que eclesialmente es protestante, parece haber abandonado la patria de la Reforma con todos los desafíos que de ella dimanan. Todo el mundo pudo seguir y ver lo que sucedió el 31 de octubre 2016 en la ciudad sueca de Lund, cuando se conmemoró a la Reforma por primera vez en una comunidad ecuménica. En un acto común de la Federación Luterana Mundial y de la Iglesia Católica de Roma sucedió que el Papa Francisco y la Arzobispa de la Iglesia de Suecia, Antje Jackelén, se abrazaron. La fotografía del hecho dio la vuelta al mundo como signo de esperanza y también de tensión. La Iglesia de Suecia trata de tener un rol protagónico en cuanto a los temas de género y sexualidad, libertad y norma. Es parte de una sociedad donde la fe es hoy una opción libre. La antigua iglesia estatal se ve confrontada a nuevos desafíos en lo que se refiere a la diversidad tanto religiosa como cultural. La Iglesia de Suecia logra sostener estas distintas tensiones mediante el proyecto reformado de un programa según el cual se es iglesia necesitada de continua reforma. La pluralidad de una comunicación capaz de trasponer el evangelio inaugura una perspectiva crítica ante la modernidad. Un diálogo feminista y teológicamente constructivo de las religiones universales se está desarrollando por encima de la dicotomía binaria de centro y periferia. Estrategias creativas en lo epistemológico y lo hermenéutico se anudan en forma innovadora en una lucha en torno a escritos históricos canónicos que nos son hoy familiares como textos sagrados. Su herencia se desenvuelve en el campo tensional de los factores de poder y de los criterios de interseccionalidad: *ecclesia semper reformanda*.

El sexo juega un papel significativo en los procesos mediales y sociales de significación y explicación e interpretación translaticia de escritos religiosos. Las tradiciones de interpretación misógena no se acabaron con la Reforma.

500 años después de Catalina de Bora, el ministerio les sigue estando prohibido a las teólogas católicas. Se reglamentan y recortan los espacios femeninos hasta no quedar más que una imagen post-fáctica manipulada por extraños. Tres meses antes de la figura reconciliadora de la conmemoración sueca de la Reforma, la Iglesia Evangélica-Luterana de Letonia decidió abolir la ordenación de mujeres.

Como si la Reforma no hubiera nunca tenido lugar en Europa, se sigue encendiendo el debate cultural-teológico y socio-religioso sobre el código de conducta de las mujeres. Su vestido y su cuerpo, su comportamiento y su libertad siguen estando determinados por el patriarcado. Así se vuelven agentes de co-optación que se pierden en la cultura, la religión y la sociedad, entre las pretensiones del así llamado espíritu moderno y liberado de la época.

La tensión entre género y teología se refleja en la discusión sobre autoridad religiosa vertical y horizontal. Hay que esperar cómo se desarrolle el fenómeno de la autoridad en las religiones y si puede adoptar la forma de una hermenéutica interreligiosa orientada medialmente en sus contextos respectivos. Al categorizar y postular la verdad, la autoridad y la Sagrada Escritura, se plantea el desafío de comulgar con ellas en forma horizontal y no vertical. Nuevas polarizaciones neo-patriarcales, como entre fundamentalismo y secularización, des-construcción y construcción, estrechan notablemente la mirada hacia migración y traslación. Las pujas hegemónicas por poder e identidad contribuyen fuertemente a aumentar la alienación recíproca. Hay que enfrentarlas teológicamente.

Maaike De Haardt

Transformation and the Virtue of Ambivalence

In this paper, delivered as key-note lecture at the Feminists Association's Colloquium on transformation and the Church at Lisbon, 2015, it is argued that contrary to the suspicion of both secular and post-Christian feminists and the anti-gender movement in the churches, feminist theologies as well as women and faith movements offer strong transforming theological and spiritual dynamics for contemporary churches. To discover this transformative potential, a new and different vocabulary for faith, spirituality and Church is needed. Clues for this different vocabulary may be found in the application of a typology of the characteristics of feminist religious imagination, derived from Bednarowsky (1999) and illustrated amongst others by the life and work of Sor Juana Inez de la Cruz; the various implications of the 'quotidian turn' (de Certeau) for theology; the 'ekklesiality' (sense of community) of feminist theology and the importance of the experiences of God's presence. Central for the transformative potential on all levels is the on-going, creative ambivalence that women and other marginalised people have about the status quo of both Church and society. These 'relative outsiders' have contradictory experiences combining simultaneously a deep sense of alienation and a deep sense of belonging and commitment. It is this inescapable ambivalence which maintains a dialogue both critical and committed with the Christian tradition; which offers a creative and transformative approach to traditional Church content, symbols and rituals; and which calls to imagine a community/ecclesiology in which plurality and differences may be considered 'mixed blessings'.

In diesem Beitrag wird die These vertreten, dass, im Gegensatz zu den Behauptungen der säkularen wie der nachchristlichen Feministinnen als auch der Anti-Gender-Ideologie mancher Kirchen, feministische Theologien genauso wie die Frauenbewegung und religiöse Gemeinschaften sehr wohl eine starke theologische und spirituelle Dynamik aufweisen. Um dieses transformative Potenzial zu entdecken, ist ein neues Vokabular für Glauben, Spiritualität und Kirche erforderlich. Ich sehe Ansätze dieses Vokabulars in a) der Anwendung der Typologie einer feministisch-religiösen Vorstellung nach Bednarowsky wie zum Beispiel im Leben und Werk von Sor Juana Inez de la Cruz; in b) den verschiedenen Implikationen des sogenannten *quotidian turn* in der Theologie und c) in dem, was ich die ‚Ekklesialität' der feministischen Theologie und die Bedeutung der Erfahrung der Gegenwart

Gottes nenne. Zentral für dieses transformative Potenzial auf allen Ebenen ist die fortlaufende kreative Ambivalenz von Frauen und anderen marginalisierten Menschen gegenüber dem Status quo in Kirche und Gesellschaft. Als vermeintliche relative Außenseiter haben wir widersprüchliche Erfahrungen von gleichzeitig einem tiefen Gefühl der Entfremdung und einem tiefen Gefühl der Zugehörigkeit und des Engagements. Es ist diese unausweichliche Ambivalenz, die sowohl den kritischen als auch den engagierten Dialog mit der christlichen Tradition vorantreibt. Dieser eröffnet einen Raum für einen kreativen und transformativen Umgang mit den traditionellen Lehren, Symbolen und Ritualen der Kirche und für eine Gemeinschaft, in der Pluralität und Unterschiede als ambivalente Segnungen gelten.

Introduction

For religious "outsiders" and secular intellectuals – among them many feminists – the combination of women and Church, synagogue or mosque seems hard to understand.[1] How can sensible women in our day and age still want to belong to or identify with "traditional", or better, "institutional" religion, given the fact that in general, these are not the most supportive places for women to be? How is it possible that women, who claim to be feminists, also call themselves Christian in these increasingly – at least in Europe – secular times, all the post-secular philosophy not withstanding?[2] But not only secular critics, feminist theologians like Mary Daly and Daphne Hampson also question this Church-engaged position of religious feminists.[3] Already in 1975,

---

[1] This article is a thoroughly revised and updated version of a text that was originally published as "A Sense of Belonging: The Challenging Complexity of Women and Church," in: *International Journal for the Study of the Christian Chuch* 4 (2004), 3, 249-261.

[2] On the post-secular see for instance Jürgen Habermas, "Notes on a Postsecular Society," in: *New Perspectives Quarterly* 25, 4 (2008), 17-19; Rosi Braidotti, "In Spite of the Times: The Postsecular Turn In Feminism," in: *Theory, Culture and Society* 25 (2008), 6, 1-24; Elaine Graham, *Between a Rock and a Hard Place: Public Theology in a Post-Secular Age* (SCM Press: London 2013); Rosi Braidotti, Bolette Blaagaard, Tobijn de Graauw and Eva Midden (eds.) *Transformation of Religion and the Public Sphere: Postsecular Publics* (Palgrave Macmillan: Basingstoke 2014). Note, however, that this "post-secular" and its "return" or "transformation" of religion is discussed by philosophers who claim to be not religious but who, notably after Nine-Eleven, came to see the public relevance of religion. Philosophers and social scientist seem to discover what religious feminists have known for years: the secular-religious divide does not work. See: Elaine Graham, "What's Missing? Gender, Reason and the Post-Secular," in: *Political Theology* 13.2 (2012), 233-245.

[3] Mary Daly, *Beyond God the Father Toward a Philosophy of Women Liberation* (Beacon Press: Boston 1985); Daphne Hampson, *After Christianity* (SCM Press: London 2002).

Daly wrote: "Christianity can 'include' feminism only in the sense that a cannibal includes his meal."[4] Contrary to many secular reflections on the relation between religion and women, feminist or not, none of these theologians would deny or reject the importance of spirituality, transcendence or "God". In fact, all feminist theologians, whether or not explicitly Christian or post-Christian, are convinced of the importance and the necessity of engaging in religion and spirituality, both in academic reflection and in religious or spiritual practice. The same would go for many contemporary women and men who left the various churches. They often consider themselves to be "spiritual but not religious", thus mostly indicating that they do not want to be identified with the Church.[5]

Though feminist theologians disagree about the reforming and transformational potential of the Church, it is strongly argued that feminist religious imagination and reflection, feminist theology and philosophy, as well as the praxis of many so called "women and faith movements" and other "counter or marginalised religious groups" have a lot to offer to institutional churches, since it is precisely their Christian faith that fuels their struggle for the transformation of society, Church, and theology. Therefore, one can wholeheartedly agree with Robert Schreitner, who in his book *The New Catholicity* describes Feminist Theology as one of the contemporary global flows that "point to the failures of global systems to live up to the value of equality and inclusion."[6] According to Schreiter, feminist theology, like theologies of liberation, ecology and human rights, can lay claim to being one of the new "universal" theologies.[7] While Schreiter emphasises the "universal" character of these theologies, I would like to stress the aspect of their being "new" and therefore

---

[4] Mary Daly, "A Short Essay on Hearing and the Qualitative Leap of Radical Feminism," in: *Horizons* 2 (1975), 121.

[5] Daly and Hampson in their times had to explain this position and explicitly "claim" a space for this non-Church religiosity or spirituality. The expression "spiritual but not religious" nowadays seems common speech. In that sense, it could be considered a sign of "secularisation". See for instance Nancy Ammerman, "Spiritual but not Religious? Beyond Binary Choices in the Study of Religion," in: *Journal for the Scientific Study of Religion* 52 (2013), 2, 258-278; Elaine Graham, "The Unquiet Frontier: Tracing the Boundaries of Philosophy and Public Theology," in: *Political Theology* 16, 1 (2015), 33-46; Linda A. Mercante, *Belief without Borders. Inside the Minds of the Spiritual but not Religious* (Oxford University Press: Oxford 2014).

[6] Robert J. Schreiter, *The New Catholicity. Theology between the Global and the Local* (Orbis Books: Maryknoll 1998) 18.

[7] Ibid., 21.

consider feminist theologies as important transforming movements and dynamics in contemporary churches.

But how to make sense of that which is for many people a contradictory phenomenon? And how to discover the transformative, critical, (theo)political, theological, and spiritual potential of the Christian tradition in its contemporary feminist theoretical and practical appropriation? Especially in a situation where, many Church leaders consider "gender" and gender informed theology to be one of the contemporary cultural and religious threats?[8] What is needed is a different perspective on both Church and transformation. What is also needed is a different "vocabulary" for theology, faith, spirituality, and Church. Reframing and renaming in order to be able to re-imagine are important methodological and epistemological tools for a gender specific theology.

The following contribution shall describe some of the elements in feminist theology that may contribute to the development of this different perspective and different theological vocabulary, and thus develop a different religious "cartography". First, a description of central characteristics of contemporary feminist theology shall be provided. Next, the meaning of the "quotidian turn" for theology and Church shall be considered. Lastly, a so-called "ekklesiality" of feminist theology and experiences of God's presence as central transformative dimensions shall be discussed.

Feminist theologians are developing many intelligent, scholarly, creative, evocative theologies, visions, rituals, and symbols, and many contemporary women are deeply engaged in the work in their parishes. This should however not conceal the highly complex and ambiguous relation between women and the Church. The mere description of the problem as a problem of "women and the Church" is an indication of this complexity. Why "women and Church"?

---

[8] See for instance the 2004 Vatican Letter to the Bishops of the Church: *On the Collaboration of Men and Women in the Church and in the World* (http://www.vatican.va/roman_curia/congregations/cfaith/documents/rc_con_cfaith_doc_20040731_collaboration_en.html, 8 February 2015). See also the more recent Vatican 2014 working document on the special synod on the family (http://www.vatican.va/roman_curia/synod/documents/rc_synod_doc_20140626_instrumentum-laboris-familia_en.html, 8 February 2015), or the discussion held by the Pontifical Council on Culture on the document titled *Women's Cultures: Equality and Differences* in February 2015 (see for instance http://www.associationofcatholicpriests.ie/2015/01/womens-cultures-equality-and-difference/, 16 March 2017). Both documents gave no rise to optimism. See Mary Hunt's critical comment on this last event (http://religiondispatches.org/vatican-council-on-women-would-be-funny-were-it-not-so-insulting/, 8 February 2015).

> *Reframing + renaming in order to be able to re-imagine and imp. methodological + epistemological tools for gender specific theology.*

Why not "men and Church"? Whose church? And who has the power to define what Church is?

In her study *The Religious Imagination of American Women*, Mary Farrell Bednarowksi describes the characteristics of US American women's religious thoughts at the end of the twentieth century.[9] Although she limits her findings to the US American context, it appears that her findings can also be applied in Europe and especially within a Christian context.

Bednarowsky's study is the first general description of the central themes and questions brought to the fore by women in religion, be it in academic studies or other religious writings. It offers an excellent starting point for further reflections. She distinguishes five key elements or themes in the religious writings of US American women:

> (1) an ongoing, creative and increasingly cultivated ambivalence toward their religious communities; (2) an emphasis on the immanence –that is, the indwelling of the sacred; (3) a regard for the ordinary as revelatory of the sacred; (4) a view of ultimate reality as relational; and (5) an interpretation of healing, both physical and spiritual, as a primary rather than a secondary function of religion.[10]

These are not just themes but rather characteristics of a broad and general interpretative framework that shapes both women's critical gender analyses in their churches and communities, and their approaches to theological and spiritual transformations of their traditions and communities. In fact, these themes shape our ways of doing theology. Bednarowsky is very convincing in claiming that these themes are not to be an exclusive – let alone "ontological" – religious mode for women. This theological preference has deep roots in the specific social and cultural history of women, and the same may be true of other "historical outsiders" – blacks, poor, LGBTQs, and colonised people – within Christianity. As such, all those different histories, experiences and memories have had their impact on both form and content of this "voicing of faith". Let us focus on some of these themes from a theological perspective and explore the possibilities of their transformational power for theology and the churches in the western context.

---

[9] Mary Farrell Bednarowski, *The Religious Imagination of American Women* (Indiana University Press: Bloomington 1999).
[10] Ibid., 1.

For a start, consider the following example in which some of these themes come to the fore. Of the few great women known to history, the Mexican nun Sor Juana Inés de la Cruz (1648-1695) is among the most famous. She is perhaps most celebrated for her outstanding Hispanic Baroque poetry, which made her into a great Spanish poet and one of the first "New World", Latin American colonial poets. Moreover, she was also an eminent scholar and a trained philosopher. There is only one well-known picture of her – by Miguel Cabrera the famous indigenous Zapotec painter of "New Spain", as Mexico was called in those colonial times. In this painting, Sor Juana is sitting at a table in a study or library, looking every bit the intellectual woman she is known to have been. She is portrayed as a woman who, alluding here to Virginia Woolf, occupies "a space of her own". Or the other way around, it is this concrete "space" that "constructs" her religious and scholarly identity, even though many theologians never heard of her.

As a self-conscious intellectual woman of her times, especially among the religious, Sor Juana had to deal with attacks by misogynists and betrayal by her spiritual, moral, and legal superiors, who apparently could not bear such creativity, intelligence, and wisdom in a woman. This resulted in a temporary prohibition of reading and her banishment to the simplest work done in her convent. There she discovered that her observations of daily life led her to important philosophical insights and experiential knowledge: "For although I did not study in books, I studied all the things that God created."[11] After describing all she learned working in the kitchen, she concludes with the famous quote, "Had Aristotle cooked, he would have written a great deal more."[12] A woman, who was considered a threat or a nuisance by influential men in her surroundings, valued the insights and knowledge gained from such everyday activities as cooking and gardening, the gaining of knowledge in so-called "women's places". It is therefore not surprising that feminist scholars, with good reason, and with all the reservations necessary for such a comparison, consider her a "proto-feminist", a title manifest primarily in her humorous awareness of marginalisation and oppression evidenced by gender in her writings.[13] After her description of what she learned while cooking, she

---

[11] Sor Juana Inés de la Cruz, *The Answer/La Respuesta: Including a Selection of Poems* (The Feminist Press at the City University of New York: New York 1994), 73.
[12] Ibid., 75.
[13] Michelle A. Gonzales, *Sor Juana: Beauty and Justice in the Americas* (Orbis Books: Maryknoll 2003), 113.

mockingly writes, "But in truth my Lady, what can we women know, save philosophies of the kitchen?" [14]

All this makes Sor Juana, her writings and the image we have of her an apt first example for the points to be made in this contribution.[15] It is here that one find parts of the historical conditions of women mentioned earlier. In Juana's case: banned to the kitchen and other "women's places" and forbidden to read. But more important here, Sor Juana also discovered that there are more and different ways of gaining knowledge – theological knowledge included – than by reading the works of the great philosophers and theologians. Daily life, even against Sor Juanna's own expectation, turned out to be a rich source of valuable knowledge and insight in the works of God. In the insights, knowledge and wisdom gained in the course of actual lives lived by those on the margins of Church and society, one finds the sources and conditions for the recent turn to the epistemological meaning of everyday life in cultural studies, philosophy and theology. And women scholars were among the first to emphasise its importance.[16] Translated into the more explicitly religious terms of Bednarowsky's analysis we can label this epistemological preference as "a regard for the *ordinary* as revelatory of the sacred."[17] Really honouring this knowledge would mean a shift in the epistemological power structures of both theology and Church.[18] Aside from the epistemological importance, one may point at another theological reason for this prevalence of everyday life in the works of so many feminist and liberation theologians.

---

[14] Ibid., 75.

[15] There is a great amount of scholarly literature on the life and works of Sor Juana. For a good theological introduction to her work, see Gonzales, *Sor Juana* above. For a feminist introduction, see Stephanie Merrim (ed.), *Feminist Perspectives on Sor Juana Ines de la Cruz* (Wayne State University Press: Detroit MI. 1999); Theresa A. Yugar, *Sor Juana Ines de la Cruz: Feminist Reconstruction of Biography and Text* (WIPF & STOCK: Eugene OR. 2014). Perhaps the most famous introduction to her life and work is Octavio Paz, *Sor Juana: Or, the Traps of Faith* (The Belknap Press: Cambridge MA 1990).

[16] See for instance Maaike de Haardt, "A Way of Being-in-the-World: Traces of Divinity in Everyday Life," in: Maaike de Haardt and Anne-Marie Korte (eds.), *Common Bodies. Everyday Practices, Religion and Gender* (LIT Verlag: Münster 2002), 11-27. For an overview of this approach, see also Maaike De Haardt, "A Momentary Sacred Space: Religion, Gender and the Sacred in Everyday Life," in: Angela Berlis, Kune Biezeveld and Anne-Marie Korte (eds.) *Everyday Life and the Sacred* (Brill: Leiden 2017).

[17] Bednarowski, *The Religious Imagination of American Women*, 1.

[18] Elaine Graham, "Power, Knowledge and Authority in Public Theology," in: *International Journal of Public Theology* 1 (2007), 42-46.

In everyday life – regardless of both its conceptual and actual messiness – one finds what Michel de Certeau calls the tactics of appropriation, that is, the dynamics of contest and struggle, of resistance and protest.[19] Even more important from a theological perspective is that in the messy actuality of daily life, *lo cotidiano*, one can find the hope, dreams, and longings for a better life.[20] This point shall be retaken later in the context of the experiences of God's presence.

The messiness of everyday life and the epistemological challenges everyday life offers lead to Bednarowsky's first point, the on-going, creative ambivalence of women and other marginalised people regarding the status quo of both Church and society.

Virtuous Ambivalence and Creative Appropriation

Many metaphors used to describe the relations between women and other marginalised persons and their religious traditions are spatial. Insider/outsider, margin and centre, and resident aliens are some of the most famous metaphors used in feminist, black and postcolonial studies. They question traditional centres and insiders; they criticise the power structures implied in these images and create room for new definitions. It is also clear that the "original insider", the "ecclesial centre" or the "non-alien resident" is the male/mainstream tradition of the churches. As such, these critical metaphors also reflect the deep sense of estrangement, exclusion, humiliation, and distrust that is one aspect of these "double space" expressions. It is important to keep in mind an awareness of this estrangement, this permanent "uneasiness" of women, blacks and other marginalised persons, for whom the relation to – and place within – Church (or society) is never completely obvious. The other facet of these metaphors emphasises the affirmative part of women's religious experiences: their/our acknowledgment of the formative, inspiring, sustaining, spiritual power of the Christian tradition, in spite of exclusion in any form. The contradictory experiences expressed by these metaphors mirror the fundamentally ambivalent nature of women's relation to their traditions: a deep sense of alienation and an equally deep sense of belonging, familiarity and commitment.[21]

---

[19] Michel de Certeau, *The Practice of Everyday Life* (University of California Press: Berkeley, Los Angeles and London 1984), translated by Steven Rendall.
[20] Ada Maria Isasi-Diaz, *En La Lucha / In the Struggle* (Fortress Press: Minneapolis 1993).
[21] Bednarowsky, *The Religious Imagination of American Women*, 19.

In what may be described as a "scientific post Enlightenment society" with its strong emphasis on rationality and non-contraction, ambivalence is not a highly-respected attitude, even among theologians. By contrast, Bednarowsky highly values this ambivalence and even speaks of it as "a new religious virtue". It is precisely this ambivalence that keeps women in dialogue with their tradition without losing their own religious balance and identity, and without expecting too much or too little from their churches or themselves, she says. Ambivalence is a virtue, because it maintains both a critical and a committed dialogue with tradition; it offers ways of dealing with tensions and contradictions as well as a creative approach to traditional content, symbols and rituals. Furthermore, as Bednarowsky notices, although women acknowledge the truth of other religions, they generally continue to speak the language of their "own" tradition. One may assert that this being able to deal with a plurality of truth claims also demonstrates insight in the fundamental ambiguity of the epistemological foundations of one's own tradition, as well as every other tradition. Even more so – and in following the British philosopher and theologian Ruth Page – since the world itself is ambiguous, ambiguity is our condition. Page herself, feminist cultural scientist Mieke Bal and postmodern thinkers such as Zygmunt Bauman all point at this ambiguity and ambivalence as our – whether or not "post" – modern condition.[22]

This ambivalence implies that in our religious expressions, theological research, and religiously motivated acts, women do not simply repeat the language, symbols, rites or acts of the Christian tradition but do so in their own voices and interpretations of Christianity. In doing so, they expand the meaning of the concepts, symbols or rituals of their own traditions. There is more to this than self-creation or establishing oneself as an autonomous religious subject. Following the earlier mentioned French theologian and cultural scientist Michel de Certeau, these acts may be considered as creative appropriations of the Christian tradition, in which the sustaining, subversive, emancipatory, liberating, and celebratory power of the tradition is presented in a new light.[23]

---

[22] Ruth Page, *Ambiguity and the Presence of God* (SCM Press: London 1985); Zygmunt Bauman, *Modernity and Ambivalence* (Polity Press: Oxford 1991); Mieke Bal, *Traveling Concepts in the Humanities. A Rough Guide* (University of Toronto Press: Toronto Buffalo London 2002).

[23] For the notion of appropriation and its transformative and subversive meanings, see Michel de Certeau, *The Mystic Fable. Volume One, Sixteenth and Seventeenth Centuries* (The University of Chicago Press: Chicago and London 1992), translated by Michael B. Smith; See also Michel de Certeau, *The Practice of Everyday Life*. Appropriation as a notion is also used by

In a way, these forms of appropriation are actual "transformations" of tradition by giving different meanings to a shared language, making visible the inherent ambiguity or even openness of the tradition. In finding God and God's works in the kitchen, Juana was able to appropriate her belief and theology, and by doing so, to transform this theology at the same time.

What is ignored in the dismissal of many feminist contributions to Church and theology is the ongoing "conserving", "continuing" as well as transforming character of many of such creative appropriations of tradition in feminist writings.

The "positive" side of this ambivalence, women's explicit commitment to their religious tradition in spite of all the opposition and exclusion, as well as their appropriation and affirmation of religious and spiritual attitudes, reflects a deep sense of belonging. It is this deep sense of belonging – actual belonging and a longing to belong – which ultimately fuels the continuing dialogue, on many different levels, with Church and tradition. This is where the ambivalence demonstrates its most virtuous, creative and strong communal power, where it ultimately finds its ground, spirit and motive. This sense of belonging and desire to belong is in the end an expression of the divine, "in which we live move and have our being" – as many feminists would translate Act. 17:28.

On Ekklesiality and the Presence of God

The spoken sense of belonging also indicates what may be one of the most striking characteristics of feminist theology, that is, their strong "ekklesiality". This notion can be understood primarily on the basis of feminists' overwhelming emphasis on community. It is no coincidence that the Wicca theologian Starhawk is often quoted on this subject by both Christian and other feminist theologians, when she states that "Earth-based spiritual traditions are rooted in community. They are not religions of individual salvation, but of communal celebration and collective change."[24] Or, as Roman Catholic theologian Rosemary Radford Ruether notes, "One important aspect of this emerging feminist

---

US womanists and black theologians to name the specific Biblical interpretations by black people and black theologians (female/male). See, among others, Delores S. Williams, *Sisters in the Wilderness. The Challenge of Womanist God-talk* (Orbis Books: Maryknoll 1993).

[24] Miriam Starhawk, *Truth or Dare. Encounters with Power, Authority and Mystery* (Harper San Francisco: San Francisco 1990), 23.

religion or spirituality is its recognition of the need for intentional communities of faith and worship."[25]

This feminist ekklesiality, this "community dimension" is not focused solely on the internal structures of, and changes to, contemporary institutional churches. In this sense, it is preferable not to speak of a feminist ecclesiology in the strict sense of the word,[26] even when this general ekklesiality, as an expression of this communal dimension or desire for community, has good ecclesiological credentials.[27] Hence, no strict ecclesiology is hereby maintained, despite the fact that the history of the Christian feminist movement has its origins in the churches, and despite the fact that the reformation of the churches has been, and for many still is, one of the movement's important goals. Gradually, the aim of the feminist movement in the churches became not only reforming or adapting the Church to the visible presence of women, but a more fundamental transformation. Women's "sense of belonging" does not have anything to do with the Greek *kyriakos* ("belonging to the Lord") in its traditional patriarchal and hierarchical meaning. If women belong to someone or something, then it is only in the sense of a far more indefinable belonging to a kind of "community of God". A sheer institutional belonging – regardless of how greatly the Church as institution is valued by many Christian feminists – would not cover this sense of belonging, nor answer the desire to belong.

"Belonging" has a different meaning here. It has to do with the manifold experiences of the relation with, and the presence of, the Divine in this world, with the meaning of this divine presence for women's daily lives and the need

---

[25] Rosemary Radford Ruether, *Women-Church. Theology and Practice* (Harper and Row: New York 1985), 3.

[26] As is the choice made by Rebecca Chopp for linguistic convenience and by way of claiming that feminist discourse on ekklesia continues classical ecclesiology. See Rebecca Chopp, *Saving Work. Feminist Practices of Theological Education* (Westminster John Knox Press: Louisville 1995). Elizabeth Schüssler Fiorenza speaks of ekklesia-logy as the discourse on the ekklesia of women; see Elizabeth Schüssler Fiorenza, *Discipleship of Equals. A Critical Feminist Ekklesia-logy of Liberation* (SCM Press: London 1993). In later publications, Schüssler speaks of the "ekklesia of wo/men" as a heterogeneous, multi-voiced open space or forum; see Elizabeth Schüssler Fiorenza, *Transforming Vision Explorations in Feminist Theology* (Fortress Press: Minneapolis 2011), 89-95.

[27] See Rebecca Chopp, *The Power to Speak. Feminism, Language, God* (Crossroad: New York 1991), 73. Chopp refers to Schleiermacher and Barth for their insistence on desire for community as the nature of Church.

for women to speak of these experiences.[28] Sor Juana, after her banishment, continued to speak. This explicit and unremitting talk of God's presence, despite the general Western cultural tendency to consider speaking of God a taboo, makes one think of feminist theology as well as the women-and-faith movement, as perhaps the least "secularised" theological approach in contemporary Western society.

Contrary to a large part of contemporary Western academic theology, the aim of this speaking of God is not to prove the coherence of God-talk, nor is it to speak of God's absence or of the hidden or absolute transcendent God, but rather to discuss the meaning of God and the experience of God in everyday life.[29] Without rejecting a definitive distinction between God and world, this feminist emphasis on the presence of the Divine – in Bednarowsky's terms the emphasis on immanence – is an attempt to overcome a dominant dualistic approach of God and world, to overcome a traditional preference for a distant transcendence, and to emphasise the revelatory power of creation, the materiality and embodiment of life. With this "immanent approach", feminist reflection wants to make explicit the well-rooted conviction that both the experience and speaking of God matter and that this becomes most evident in the theologically and spiritually neglected practices of everyday life.[30] In "regular academics", everyday life is mostly seen as trivial, since it is the domain of

---

[28] For a more empirical report on these experiences of Divine Presence and immanence, see Maaike de Haardt, "Feminist God-praxis in religion to Feminist Theology," and its South African counter text by Susan Rakoczy, "Feminist Reflections on God in South Africa: Presentation and Analysis of Feminist God-praxis in Relation to Feminist Theology," both in: Nico Schreurs and Thomas Plastow (eds.), *Juxtaposing Contexts. Doing contextual theology in South Africa and the Netherlands* (Cluster Publication: Pietermaritzburg 2003), 98-132 and 63-97, respectively. In this respect, it is a rather ironic coincidence that at the very moment marginalised people – theological outsiders – entered the field as self-conscious theological subjects, many philosophers and theologians spoke of the death of the subject, proclaimed the absence of God and prioritised God's transcendence and ultimate incomprehensibility.

[29] See for instance Elizabeth Johnson, *She Who Is. The Mystery of God in Feminist Theological Discourse* (Crossroad: New York, 1995); Laurel C. Schneider, *Re-Imagining the Divine* (Pilgrim Press: Cleveland 1998); Anne-Claire Mulder and Kune Biezeveld (eds.), *Towards a Different Transcendence: Feminist Findings on Subjectivity, Religion and Values* (Peter Lang Pub Inc: Oxford 2001); Elaine Graham (ed.), *Grace Jantzen: Redeeming the Present* (Ashgate: Farnam 2009); Catherine Keller, *On the Mystery. Discerning God in Process* (Fortress Press: Minneapolis 2008).

[30] See for instance Maaike de Haardt, "Vinde, comei de meu pao.... Consideratiocoes exemplares acerce do divino no cotidiano," in: Lieve Troch (org.) *Passos comPaixao, Uma teologia do dia-a-dia* (Nhanduti Editoria: Sao Bernardo do Campo 2007), 59-84; Maaike de Haardt and

women and other marginalised persons. At this point, one can see the inherent theological connection between Bednarowky's theme of immanence and the epistemological preference for the ordinary as revelatory. That, and the question of whether God matters at all, should therefore be the centre of theology and Church. In the end, speaking of the "matter of God" only matters in a perspective of life abundant for all; in a perspective of shared hope, solidarity, survival, joy, resistance, and celebration of the gift of life; or in the perspective of the full humanity of women and men, to name but a few of the images used to formulate the ultimate meaning of the "matter of God". In the end, it is this perspective that fuels the dreams and hopes and the power to survive.

It is in this vision and perspective of "life abundant" that one also finds both the centrality of the themes of relationship and the healing mentioned by Bednarowsky, in their specific Christian formulation. Thus, it is no coincidence that many feminist Christian theologians are engaged in a re-thinking and re-imagining of their sense of belonging, both in their re-thinking of "God" and in their re-thinking of Church. And in doing so, they are actively and effectively constructing images and practices of "ecclesia", or, as Elizabeth Schüssler Fiorenza prefers to put it, "ekklesia of wo/men", as this "different community" is named in order to distinguish this community from the Church as belonging to *kyriakos*.[31] This is not just an academic perspective. One finds the same approach not just in feminist theological reflection but also in accounts of religious experiences. To give just one example: a small research project in which a group of Dutch members of the "women-and-faith movement" was asked to state their personal creeds, similar results were found. Only a small number of respondents mentioned the institutional Church in a spiritually meaningful way, while the notion of community and the longing for community was strongly present in their creeds.[32]

Anne-Marie Korte (eds.), *Common Bodies. Everyday Practices, Gender and Religion* (Lit Verlag: Münster, 2002).

[31] It was Elizabeth Schüssler Fiorenza who first coined the term Ekklesia to name the specific form of women Church. See Schüssler Fiorenza, *Discipleship of Equals*. Rebecca Chopp, following the early Schüssler Fiorenza, speaks of the "practice of ecclesia" to describe not only the community focus of feminist theology, but also in order to name the ambivalent relation to the Church; see Chopp, *Saving Work*.

[32] This group consists of the participants in feminist theological seminars that were offered annually for a wider audience by the Catharina Halkes/Unie NKV Chair for Religion and Gender Chair at the Faculty of Theology at Nijmegen until 2015. The participants can be considered part of the "women and faith movement" in the Netherlands, which may be seen as the "natural

The importance of the notion of community, in its relational and healing dimensions, also opposes and criticises, as Starhawk claimed, a strong subjective, individualistic interpretation of salvation and reconciliation, in favour of a far more communal salvation and a communal responsibility for salvation and well-being for all. This characteristic also influences the interpretation of Christ. It is one of the reasons that classical Christological language and symbols in their highly individualistic interpretation of salvation have lost their adequacy and relevance for many Western contemporary women, as well as men. Therefore, the re-imagining of Christological concepts and symbols in a far more relational as well as communal perspective is also an important part of feminist theological reflection.[33] However, one should avoid calling this re-interpretation of central Christian doctrine a "de-Christianisation" of religion, or a simple rejection of these affirmations. Rather, it seems better to speak of an opening up of the continually changing interpretations of the meaning of Christ, a capacity the Church leaders seem to have lost over the last centuries. It is yet another demonstration of the fundamental ambiguity of concepts and dogmas and of the power of tradition to renew itself with the help of those who

---

base" of feminist theology. The Dutch "women and faith movement" can be described as a very loose movement with different levels of organisation, no central address or institution, and no affiliation to a specific denomination. Within this broader movement, all kinds of groups and organisations can be found, such as (parts of) the traditional confessional Women's Organisation, the Netwerk IFWT (a network of feminist theologians), The Dutch Women Synod, diocesan women-faith-society groups, and all kinds of other formal and informal groups. Some of these groups and organisations were established with a specific social-justice goal, such as the Religion and Incest group, the Sexual Violence in Pastoral Relations Foundation, or the Committee of Women Religious against the Trafficking of Women. There are also many individual women and men who consider themselves part of this movement, but who are not affiliated to a specific group and who participate in occasional events. Most of the women (and men) participating in this broad movement are (still?) members of one of the larger Christian churches. Some of them have left their church, without giving up their Christian or religious commitment and inspiration.

[33] See for instance Rita Nakashima Brock, *Journeys by Heart. A Christology of Erotic Power* (Crossroad: New York 1988); Mary Grey, *Redeeming the Dream. Feminism, Redemption and Christian Tradition* (SPCK Press: London 1989); Manuela Kalsky, *Christaphanien. Die Re-Vision der Christologie aus der Sicht von Frauen in unterschiedlichrn Kulturen* (Kaiser/Gütersloher Verlagshaus: Gütersloh 2000); Muriel Oreville-Montenegro, *The Jesus of Asian Women* (Orbis Books: Maryknoll 2006); Marion Grau, *Of Divine Economy* (T&TClark: New York London 2004); Wonhee Ann Joh, *Heart of the Cross. A Postcolonial Christology* (Westminster John Knox Press: Louisville 2006); Lisa Isherwood and Elaine Bellchambers, *Through Us, With Us, In Us. Relational Theologies ino the Twenty-First Century* (SCM Press: London 2010).

have the courage to reject one-dimensional or logical explanations and interpretations. Proposing a variation on Page's notion, the justification of these processes can be found in the effectiveness in which the attractiveness of this faith, the experience of the presence of God and the vision of an all-inclusive life abundance or well-being, is conveyed to contemporary culture.[34]

Difference and Plurality: Mixed Blessings

Whenever feminist 'ekklesiality' aimed at a homogeneous and harmonious community, the actual diversity of the feminist movements, religious and/or secular, soon put an end to this romantic and otherworldly image.[35] The proclaimed classic image of feminism as "sisterhood", based on assumed unity, reciprocity and equality, appeared to be exclusionary to many women. Differences of race, class, sexual orientation, and ethnicity were erased because of the vision of this new and different community. This ideal of community was soon to be exposed as white, Western and middle class.[36] This led to a rethinking of the meaning of community as well as diversity and differences within communities. Audre Lorde's insight is still provocative in this respect:

> Certainly there are very real differences between us of race, age, and sex. But it is not those differences between us that are separating us. It is rather our refusal to recognize those differences, and to examine the distortions which result from our misnaming them and their effects on human behavior and expectations.[37]

All this did not imply the loss of the notion of communities as places of hope, solidarity, joy, celebration, resistance, sustenance, and sharing – in other words, communities as places of divine revelation. But this notion was complemented by a new acknowledgment of other fundamental characteristics of community: a diversity of heterogeneity, of unwanted or unknown mechanisms of exclusion, of the balance of power within communities, of existing conflicts and privileges, contradictions and – one again – ambivalences and ambiguity.

---

[34] Ruth Page, *Ambiguity and the Presence of God*, 117.
[35] This is excellently documented in Elizabeth M. Bounds, *Coming Together/Coming Apart. Religion, Community and Modernity* (Routledge: New York 1997).
[36] In white Christian theology, one of the first reflections on challenges offered by the critics of black women's reflection can be found in Susan Thistlethwaite, *Sex, Race, and God. Christian Feminism in Black and White* (Crossroad: New York 1989). Many others followed.
[37] Audre Lorde, *Sister Outsider. Essays and Speeches* (The Crossing Press: Trumansburg 1984), 115.

In the words of Letty Russell: "trouble and beauty together."[38] The feminist ecclesiological and theological challenge is not to see these contradictions as threats that have to be eradicated as soon as possible, but to accept differences and diversity as contradictions and ambiguities one has to live with, both in the actual situatedness of concrete communities and on the theoretical level of reflection on these communities. In this perspective, one has to read Sharon Welch's remark that

> (...) to be a Christian is to belong to a community that extends beyond the individual, and to find meaning in participation in the affirmation of the struggle for humanity. The hope of resurrection is the hope for the power of solidarity to transform reality, a hope that human identity is found in relation to others, in participation in the formation of a community that transcends us now and after death.[39]

In her later work, Welch stresses repeatedly the importance of community, as well as the importance of an immanent transcendence.[40] One also finds in her work, as in that of many other feminist theologians, the emphasis on the here and now, on the inevitable vulnerability and particularity of this time and place and of finite, embodied, relational human existence, as the only place from which one can love the world. In a creative use of her ambivalence towards "traditional" theological language, Catherine Keller uses Moltmann's expression of "the spirit of life", to speak about the presence and power of God and the communion of the holy spirit that enables the members of the community to resist "the powers and principalities" and so, in a new way, to represent the body of Christ.[41] Keller not only succeeds in demonstrating the primacy of praxis, she also shows again and again that the community and God are the locus of hope and transformation.

However, a continuous self-criticism and self-reflection is needed in order to respect differences and plurality, actual distance and different locations, as

---

[38] Letty M. Russell, *Church in the Round. Feminist Interpretation of the Church* (Westminster John Knox: Louisville 1993), 196.
[39] Sharon D. Welch, *Communities of Resistance and Solidarity* (Orbis Books: Maryknoll 1985), 45.
[40] Sharon D. Welch, *A Feminist Ethic of Risk* (Fortress Press: Minneapolis 1990) is very explicit on these points.
[41] Catherine Keller, *Apocalypse Now and Then. A Feminist Guide to the End of the World* (Beacon Press: Boston 1996), 221. This is a recurring theme in Keller's work; see for instance her *On the Mystery, Discerning God in Process* (Fortress Press: Minneapolis 2008) and her *Cloud of the Impossible. Negative Theology and Planetary Entanglement* (Columbia University Press: New York 2015).

recent publications by post-colonial and queer theologians demonstrate.[42] For that reason, Mary McClintock Fulkerson prefers the notion of affinity instead of the much-used notion of solidarity with the other, as "Affinity acknowledges love's inability to know the other, to resist the domination of the other."[43] Although these different approaches do not necessarily exclude each other, McClintock Fulkerson's notion of affinity reminds one of the inalienable otherness of others and the risks posed by an all too easy inclusiveness. "The continued approbation of reality as God requires from us the capacity to see grace in the lives of those who speak of God's way under the adverse conditions we rarely or never live in."[44] Formulated as an appeal to feminist theologians, it seems equally important and challenging to all theologians and churches.

Concluding Remarks
What can be the meaning of all these reflections on the characteristics of "women's faith" for the future of the Church? If it is true that, since the Enlightenment, "religion joined women in the margins of modernity, in the realm of the private, in the so-called non-essential real, women's religiosity comes to look more and more intuitive of religion itself,"[45] this would imply that the characteristics and actual forms of "women's faith" as described here are shared by many women and men. Recent empirical research projects indeed confirm this development.[46] According to the view presented here, institutional churches need to integrate these characteristics of faith and community in their

---

[42] Catherine Keller, Michael Nausner and Mayra Rivera, *Postcolonial Theologies. Divinities and Empire* (Chalice Press: St. Louis 2004); Kwok Pui-Lan, *Postcolonial Imagination & Feminist Theology* (SCM Press: London 2004); Catherine Keller and Laurel C. Schneider, *Polydoxy. Theology of Multiplicity and Relation* (Routledge: London/New York 2011); Marcella Althaus Reid, *Indecent Theology* (Routledge: London/New York 2001); Marcella Althaus-Reid, *The Queer God* (Routledge: London/New York 2003); Lisa Isherwood and David Harris, *Radical Otherness. Sociological and Theological Approaches* (Acumen: Durham 2014); Stephen D. Moore and Mayar Rivera (eds.) *Planetary Loves. Spivak, Postcoloniality and Theology* (Fordham University Press: New York 2010).
[43] Mary McClintock Fulkerson, *Changing the Subject. Women's Discourses and Feminist Theology* (Fortress Press: Minneapolis 1994), 384.
[44] Ibid., 391.
[45] Chopp, *The Power to Speak*, 118.
[46] See for instance Hans Georg Ziebertz and Ulrich Riegel (eds.) *Europe: secular or post-secular* (LIT Verlag: Münster 2008); Linda Woodhead and Rebecca Catto (eds.) *Religion and Change in Modern Britain* (Routledge: London/New York 2012).

theology, rituals, concepts, images, and the structure and centre of their institutions. Otherwise, they risk alienating more and more people who still feel a belonging or want to belong. The plurality of images, models and structures, as developed in the "women and faith movement" and in feminist theology, offer alternative and constructive contributions for transformations. They exhibit a viability of faith that utilises hidden strands of tradition to empower itself. The question of whether institutional churches are willing to take up these challenges is up to them. In any case, since the "women and faith movement" is Church – as feminist theologians emphasise – these transformations have already started.

> **Maaike de Haardt** is professor of Religion and Gender at Radboud University, Nijmegen. She studies the interaction of religion, culture and gender in the broadest sense of the word. She investigates to what extent religious or spiritual motives, questions and dimensions can be recognised in human activities and forms of expression (from cooking to art), and if and how these practices can be related to central images and concepts in the Christian tradition. This theology of everyday life may be considered a form of public theology, in which the notions of post-colonialism, post-secularism and cosmopolitanism are important theoretical frames.

Marta María Zubia Guinea

Ecclesia semper reformanda. Hacia una Iglesia laica, al estilo del movimiento de Jesús

Este antiguo axioma Ecclesia semper reformanda, tan importante para las Iglesias de la Reforma, pasó a ser también fundamental para la Iglesia católica, con el espíritu reformador impulsado por el concilio Vaticano II, frente a las errores eclesiológicos adquiridos con el tiempo por la Iglesia. Pero las corrientes conservadora-tridentinas pronto frenaron este impulso, dando paso a nuevas desviaciones: volviendo la espalda al movimiento de Jesús y de las comunidades primitivas, reforzaron unas estructuras de poder que alimentan la Iglesia como monarquía absolutista, única garante de la fe, situada con los poderosos y que excluye a las mujeres; todo ello presentado como establecido por Dios, cuando, en realidad, no es sino una ideología patriarcal de poder, en clave religiosa.

Hoy, el papa Francisco, consciente de estas desviaciones, está tratando de impulsar importantes novedades eclesiológicas: "dejemos las estructuras caducas: ¡no sirven! No tengamos miedo de cambiar las cosas según la ley del Evangelio".

Si la Iglesia católica tiene realmente el coraje de "volver a las Fuentes" y adoptar el Reino, iniciado por Jesús, como marco referencial y principio hermenéutico de sus reflexiones eclesiológicas; si la Iglesia quiere ser al estilo del movimiento de Jesús, de las comunidades primitivas; si quiere llevar adelante la misión que Jesús nos dejó a cuantas personas formamos la Comunidad de sus seguidoras y seguidores de llevar su mensaje de salvación a las mujeres y varones de hoy, a fortiori, pasará a ser una Iglesia laica, derivada de la condición laica de Jesús y de su movimiento.

This ancient axiom – *Ecclesia semper reformanda* – so important for the Reformation Churches, became fundamental also for the Catholic Church thanks to the impulse of reform resulting from the Second Vatican Council. It enabled the Church to be aware of its ecclesiological errors over time. However, the conservative trends, still inspired by the Council of Trent, were able to curb this impulse. That led to new biases: they turned their back on the movement starting with Jesus and on the primitive communities, strengthening power structures that feed the Church as if it were an absolutist monarchy, the only guarantee of faith, near to the powerful people and excluding women. All these biases are presented as if they were established by God, when, in fact, they are a patriarchal ideology of power, with a religious expression.

Pope Francis is aware of these biases and is trying to give a new impulse to the Church: "let us leave the decrepit structures aside: they are of no worth anymore! Let us not be afraid of changing things in accordance with the gospel order".

If the Catholic Church really has the courage to "return to the sources" and to adopt the Kingdom initiated by Jesus as the frame and the hermeneutical principle of its ecclesiology; if the Church wants to follow in the steps of the movement starting with Jesus, the movement of primitive communities; if the Church wants to carry on the mission Jesus gave to all of us, who are the communities of his mission, a mission of salvation to women and men, *a fortiori*, it will transform itself into a lay church, following the lay condition of Jesus and of his movement.

El Vaticano II,[1] sin duda, uno de los mayores acontecimientos para la historia de la Iglesia, aportó grandes novedades eclesiológicas, pero también dejó importantes cuestiones de fondo sin resolver, como, por ejemplo, las estructuras de la Iglesia, lo que supone "uno de los legados más perjudiciales del Concilio".[2] Así, en sus documentos, se distinguen dos eclesiologías, que responden a dos modelos de Iglesia:[3]

- *una eclesiología conservadora*, con elementos del Vaticano I: planteamientos esencialistas fundamentados en la ley natural; estructura jerárquico-piramidal que pervierte la estructura carismática, característica y constitutiva de la comunidad eclesial;[4] potestad plena papal, ministerios masculinos entendidos como poder y privilegios, reducción de la comunión a la uniformidad y ahogo de todo vestigio de pluralismo, pues pone en peligro la unidad de la Iglesia y fomenta el secularismo, el relativismo[5] y la ideología de género. Todo ello presentado como establecido por Dios, cuando no es sino una *ideología patriarcal de poder, en clave religiosa;*
- *eclesiología reformadora:* que entiende la Iglesia como *Comunión* engendrada por el Espíritu; como *Pueblo peregrino del Dios* liberador, plural y vivo, que camina en la historia, comprometido a continuar con su obra, la

---

[1] *Documentos del Vaticano II* (BAC: Madrid 1967).
[2] Elisabeth Schüssler Fiorenza, "Ecclesia semper reformanda", en: *Concilium* 279 (1999), 101-109, aquí 104.
[3] Casiano Floristán, "Iglesia", en: Casiano Floristán Samanes, Juan José Tamayo-Acosta (eds.), *Conceptos fundamentales del Cristianismo* (Trotta: Madrid 1993), 588-602, aquí 600.
[4] Carmen Bernabé, "Mujeres en la Iglesia. ¿Corresponsabilidad o minoría de edad?", en: *Iglesia Viva* 266 (2016), 67-76, aquí 73.
[5] Juan Antonio Estrada, *Una eclesiología desde los laicos: laicado, comunidad y sacerdocio* (Instituto teológico de Vida religiosa: Vitoria 2008), 95.

construcción del Reino en el mundo; como *sacramento de salvación,* que busca una presencia profética, concientizadora, con constante necesidad de purificación y reforma, con un ministerio eclesial compartido y estructuras reformadas; que pasa del inadecuado binomio *jerarquía-laicado* al de *comunidad-carismas y ministerios,*[6] restituyendo la ontología de la gracia, en la que se arraiga su misión para el mundo, propia de todas las personas bautizadas, con una variedad de formas vinculadas a carismas personales.

El espíritu reformador del Concilio impulsó a la Iglesia a convertirse en una fuerza en pro de los derechos humanos, la justicia social, la democracia radical y la paz mundial; a superar un catolicismo eurocéntrico y romano imperialista.[7] Pero la corriente conservadora pronto frenó este impulso y dio paso a serias desviaciones. Así, por ejemplo, el Concilio habló de *volver a las Fuentes*: a Jesús, a las Comunidades primitivas, varones y mujeres que le acompañaron y se comprometieron en la construcción del Reino, como Buena Noticia para las personas marginadas y excluidas. Movimiento que continuó en comunidades cristianas corresponsables, con un especial protagonismo de las mujeres y cuya organización priorizaba las relaciones igualitarias. Habló también de *volver a la Tradición,* esa corriente viva que recoge la intuición de la novedad original y la actualiza, acogiendo los destellos que el Espíritu infunde en el Pueblo de Dios, por tanto, dinámica, histórica y plural.[8] Pero la eclesiología conservadora no llegó a los orígenes, como veremos, sino que, selectivamente, se paró cuando la Iglesia ya estaba institucionalizada o la redujo a la *Tradición tridentina,* que presenta como palabra de Dios.[9]

Desde ahí, fue desviándose hacia una Iglesia oficial aliada con el poder, clerical, piramidal y patriarcal, que invisibiliza a las pequeñas comunidades y grupos que tratan de vivir el ideal evangélico y a quienes considera *situaciones fuera de control,*[10] como veremos. Y se fue envolviendo en una maraña de contradicciones que distorsiona lo más nuclear del mensaje cristiano; por

---

[6] Bruno Forte, *La Iglesia, icono de la Trinidad* (Sígueme: Salamanca 2003), 41-53, aquí 58.
[7] Schüssler Fiorenza, "Ecclesía semper reformanda", 105; Bernabé, "Mujeres en la Iglesia", 72-74.
[8] Carmen Bernabé, "El canon: constitución y consecuencias", en: Juan Antonio Estrada (ed.), *Tiempo de disenso. Creer, esperar, crear* (Tirant Humanidades: Valencia 2013), 129-151, aquí 151.
[9] José María Vigil, "El paradigma pluralista: tareas para la teología. Hacia una relectura pluralista del cristianismo", en: *Concilium* 319 (2008), 39-49, aquí 43.
[10] Schüssler Fiorenza, "Ecclesía semper reformanda", 104.

ejemplo, si el anuncio de la Buena noticia, que es tal porque SALVA no sólo en la *eskhatía* como plenitud, sino también en nuestro *ya sí* como adelanto, ¿cómo se puede hablar a las personas marginadas de Buena noticia y salvación, en nombre de un Dios marginador y misógino, *de facto*?

Muchas veces el problema no está tanto en las declaraciones que se hacen, cuanto en sus claves hermenéuticas, como ocurre con la categoría *Comunión*,[11] cuando se cae en teorizaciones especulativas que matan la acción o en nominalismos declaracionistas.[12]

Historia de una perversión

La forma de ejercer la autoridad es clave en la Iglesia de hoy, pues urge una verdadera revolución eclesial, para transformar radicalmente las actuales relaciones de poder y adecuarlas al mandato evangélico.[13]

La raíz de todos los males que aquejan a la Iglesia está, a mi juicio, en el poder *en* y *de* la Iglesia, actualización del primer pecado bíblico "*seréis como dioses*" (Gn 3,5), porque seréis más que los demás, tendréis más privilegios, estaréis por encima y les dominaréis. De hecho, el papa Francisco lanza sus mayores diatribas contra una jerarquía y un clero que se agarran al poder y lo utilizan para someter al pueblo, les recuerda cómo Jesús reprochó *a los doctores de la ley* que atenazaran al pueblo con muchas pequeñas leyes, algo incompatible con el espíritu del Evangelio, y denuncia "el afán de poder y de tener que no conoce límites".[14]

La Iglesia, llamada a continuar el proyecto de Jesús, tiene que generar modelos de organización adecuados a las necesidades del momento y del lugar, para tratar de visibilizar el amor de Dios en este mundo, global, plural y democrático y, para saber cómo hacerlo, debe volver sus ojos a Jesús, a las primeras comunidades, pues debe fundamentarse en ellas y no, en la ley natural.

---

[11] Joseph Ratzinger, *Algunos aspectos de la Iglesia considerada como comunión.* (http://www.vatican.va/roman_curia/ congregations/cfaith/documents/rc_con_cfaith_doc_28051992_communionis-notio_sp.html, 30 septiembre 2016).

[12] Francisco, *Carta al Presidente para la Comisión de América latina.* (w2.vatican.va/content/francesco/es/letters/2016/documents/papa-francesco_20160319_pont-comm-america-latina.html, 25 septiembre 2016).

[13] Luis Pérez Aguirre, *La Iglesia increíble* (Triple: Uruguay 1993), 40.

[14] Francisco, *Evangelii gaudium* [EG], n. 56 (https://www.aciprensa.com/Docum/evangeliigaudium.pdf, 30 julio 2016).

El poder en los orígenes

En los evangelios no consta que Jesús tuviera conflicto con sus discípulos por motivos de dinero, pero sí, por motivos de poder y fue intransigente: desenmascaró la sutil búsqueda de poder personal y subvirtió su lógica, contraria a la lógica del Reino, reprendió con firmeza a quienes querían ocupar los primeros puestos para estar por encima de los demás, como hacen los poderosos, y dejó claro cómo han de entender la autoridad y el ejercicio del poder los suyos, "los últimos serán los primeros y los primeros serán los últimos" (Mt 20,27).

Ese mismo espíritu fue el que caracterizó al movimiento cristiano primitivo, al llevar adelante su proyecto. Cada comunidad se consideraba *ekklesia*, asamblea de ciudadanas y ciudadanos libres, que reconocían la presencia de Dios cuando estaban reunidas en su nombre y cuando decidían entre todos lo que afectaba a todos: "hemos decidido el Espíritu Santo y nosotros" (Hch 15, 28). *Ekklesia*, viviendo un *discipulado de iguales*,[15] en comunión, hermandad, mutualismo, equidad e interdependencia, sin organización ni estructura institucionalizadas, con un ejercicio del liderazgo tanto de mujeres[16] como de varones, basado en la autoridad carismática y en la elección, entre todos, de las personas idóneas para ejercer los diferentes ministerios y que, a pesar de las dificultades y las tensiones, se sentían *"un solo corazón y una sola alma"* (Hch 4,32).

De todo ello, podríamos concluir que, si este funcionamiento *democrático* es característico de la Iglesia del primer milenio, esa forma de ejercicio del poder es perfectamente compatible con los principios de la Iglesia y con la Tradición.[17] Sin embargo, la eclesiología conservadora defiende que el poder en la Iglesia es jerárquico[18] y no, democrático, pues viene de Dios y, por ende, no puede concederlo el pueblo. Confundiendo la forma con el fondo, identifica el origen del poder con la forma de ejercerlo y, así, deduce que la Iglesia ni es ni puede ser democrática, que todo el poder, su ejercicio y la autoridad en la Iglesia han de concentrarse en la jerarquía y que cualquier intento de democratizar la Iglesia es negar el origen divino del poder: "Solo la jerarquía tiene el derecho y la autoridad, la multitud no tiene otro derecho que el dejarse

---

[15] Elisabeth Schüssler Fiorenza, *Discipulado de iguais. Uma ekklesia-logia feminista crítica da liberação* (Vozes: Petropolis 1995), 120-131.
[16] Karen Jo Torjesen, *Cuando las mujeres eran sacerdotes. El liderazgo de las mujeres en la Iglesia primitiva y el escándalo de su subordinación con el auge del cristianismo* (El Almendro: Córdoba 1996), 23-90.
[17] José Mª Castillo, "Iglesia: la democracia anulada", en: *Frontera* 55 (2010), 37-58, aquí 47.
[18] Estrada, *Una eclesiología desde los laicos*, 95.

conducir y, como dócil rebaño, seguir a sus pastores".[19] La jerarquía, pues, marginando la acción del Espíritu en el conjunto de la Comunidad, usurpa un poder que no le corresponde.[20] Ahora bien, si el poder que se atribuye no tiene su origen en Cristo – no consta que Jesús diera un poder decisivo a personas determinadas – ¿con qué autoridad se lo apropia? Ciertamente, la Iglesia no es una democracia, pero mucho menos una monarquía absolutista.[21] Es Comunión y la comunión cristiana no es "menos"[22] democracia, es mucho más que una democracia; su norma suprema no es una constitución, sino el Evangelio. "La vida comunitaria que anuncia y promueve el Nuevo Testamento está indisolublemente amasada con los valores de participación, solidaridad y no dominio, que constituyen el alma más auténtica de toda democracia".[23]

Perversión del poder

El *proceso de cambio* se inició cuando las autoridades eclesiales se arrimaron al poder y asimilaron las estructuras del Imperio, sus órdenes. Olvidando el espíritu evangélico, dieron un giro copernicano y convirtieron la Iglesia en una institución de poder,[24] dividida en dos grupos a modo de castas: el *clero*, con el poder, honor y privilegios, considerado mediador entre Dios y los fieles y el *pueblo*, destinado a obedecer ciegamente al clero. De la mano del Pseudo-Dionisio (s.VI), esta concepción fue adquiriendo una base ideológica pseudo-teológica, según la cual, Cristo instituyó directamente la división entre clero y laicado, por lo tanto, es divina y nunca podrá ser modificada.

Esta perversión privó a la Comunidad de lo que sí es de derecho divino: "el poder para elegir a sus ministros, para quitarlos cuando son indignos y para que su decisión no la pueda cambiar ni siquiera el recurso a Roma";[25] el *quod omnes tangit, ab omnibus tractari et aprobari debet*,[26] principio fundamental

---

[19] Pío X, *Vehementer Nos*, n.3 (w2.vatican.va/content/piusx/en/encyclicals/documents/hf_p_enc_11021906_vehementer-nos.html, 2 septiembre 2016).
[20] Castillo, "Iglesia", 48.
[21] Willy Obrist, "La jerarquía eclesiástica, impedimento para la democratización de la Iglesia católica", en: *Concilium* 243 (1992), 45-59, aquí 45-47.
[22] Énfasis en el original.
[23] Andrés Torres Queiruga, *La democracia en la Iglesia* (Santa María: Madrid 1995), 15.
[24] Bernabé, "Mujeres en la Iglesia", 72-74; Elisabeth Schüssler Fiorenza, *En memoria de ella* (EDB: Bilbao 1989), 145-203, 343-377.
[25] Cipriano, "Epistola67" 3-4, en: *Corpus Scriptorum ecclesiasticorum latinorum* [CSEL] 738.
[26] Véase Yves Congar, "Quod omnes tangit, ab ómnibus tractari et aprobari debet", en: *Revue historique de Droit française et étranger* 36 (1958), 210-269.

de las primeras comunidades, y el reconocimiento de la relación dinámica entre el origen divino de la autoridad en la Iglesia y la soberanía de la *universitas fidelium*, declarada solemnemente por el concilio de Constanza.[27] Y, así, erigió una Iglesia de estructuras de poder, de centros de poder y saber y de periferias, de varones privilegiados y de mujeres postergadas.[28] A partir de entonces, la concepción y hermenéutica eclesiológica sería de arriba a abajo, cuando en los orígenes de la Iglesia era de abajo a arriba, respetando siempre la acción y convocatoria del Espíritu. Vivir en esta clave de poder ha llevado a la Iglesia oficial a las mayores contradicciones: por ejemplo, mientras numerosas investigaciones de cartas pontificias e inscripciones han demostrado que, durante los mil primeros años de la historia de la Iglesia, las mujeres ejercieron el sacerdocio,[29] ella declara delito castigado con excomunión *latae sententiae*[30] la ordenación de mujeres.

Quede claro, pues, que la división entre pueblo y clero, como clase superior y grupo de poder en la Iglesia, no proviene de Jesús, sino de los dirigentes clericales para convertirse en clase privilegiada, rompiendo claramente con el proyecto de Jesús y entrando en un proceso de degeneración de lo que fue aquella originalidad de la primera hora.[31]

Estructuras de poder
La actual estructura de la Iglesia es *jerárquico-piramidal-patriarcal*, fundamentada no en Jesús ni en el Reino ni en las primeras comunidades, sino el *iusnaturalismo*, considerado de origen divino, y en la *revelación* entendida como un conjunto de verdades sobrenaturales, absolutas, ahistóricas y definitivas, cuyo conocimiento e interpretación competen solo al Magisterio. Sin embargo, Jesús denunció las estructuras que oprimían y sometían a las personas y arremetió, especialmente, contra una religión pervertida y transformada en un instrumento de poder y dominio. Mantener, pues, inamovibles las estructuras

---

[27] Giuseppe Alberigo, *Chiesa conciliare. Identità y significato del conciliarismo* (Paideia: Brescia 1981) 187-240.
[28] Pérez, *La Iglesia increíble*, 35-37.
[29] Véanse Kevin Madigan y Caroline Osiek (eds), *Mujeres ordenadas en la Iglesia primitiva* (Verbo divino: Estella 2006); y Torjesen, *Cuando las mujeres eran sacerdotes*.
[30] Congregación para la Doctrina de la fe, *Decreto relativo al delito de atentada ordenación sagrada de una mujer*. (http://www.vatican.va/roman_curia/congregations/cfaith/documents/rc_con_cfaith_doc_20071219_attentata-ord-donna_sp.html, 25 agosto 2016)
[31] José María Castillo, "Los ministerios y el clero", en: *Revista Latinoamericana de Teología* 133 (1994). (http://www.servicioskoinonia.org/relat/133.html, 14 agosto 2016)

de la Iglesia choca frontalmente con la fe en la Humanización de Dios, con el dinamismo del Espíritu en la historia y con los signos de los tiempos. Así, bien podríamos aplicarles lo que Juan Pablo II llamaba *estructuras de pecado*,[32] porque son unas *estructuras de poder, dominadoras* y *opresoras,* especialmente para las mujeres[33] y que poco tienen que ver con el movimiento de Jesús. Así, Francisco reconoce la necesidad de cambios estructurales en la Iglesia:[34] "dejemos a un lado las estructuras caducas: ¡no sirven! ¡Son inútiles! Cojamos odres nuevos, los del Evangelio. Ésa es la novedad traída por Jesús. No tengáis miedo de cambiar las cosas según la ley del Evangelio".[35]

Usurpación del poder por parte del clero: clericalismo
Vaticano II recuperó el *sacerdocio universal* de todos los creyentes, pero subrayando que, entre éste y el sacerdocio ministerial, hay una diferencia *esencial,* no sólo gradual[36] y, así, el clero, hoy, continúa manteniendo sus prerrogativas y usurpando el *munus docendi, sanctificandi y regendi*, mientras el laicado queda condenado a una permanente minoría de edad, participando de la vida eclesial bajo su tutela y en la medida en que éstos les dejan,[37] como colaboradores o suplentes, cuando falta clero. Porque, dicen, "el oficio del clero, que recibe del Espíritu, tiene su legitimación en la participación de la misión de Cristo, pero el del laico, en la delegación de los pastores; no la recibe del Espíritu, sino de los pastores."[38] Ciertamente, característicos de la propia estructura de la Iglesia, desde las primeras comunidades, son la *sucesión apostólica* y los *ministerios,* pero eso no justifica que obispos y ministros eclesiales tengan que ser varones ordenados ni que pretendan poseer todos los

---

[32] Juan Pablo II, *Sollicitudo rei socialis, n.* 37. (https://www.aciprensa.com/Docum/srs.htm, 30 agosto 2016)
[33] Marta Zubía Guinea, *Para nuestra memoria histórica. Las mujeres en la voz de los papas* (Verbo Divino: Estella 2011), 274-279.
[34] Francisco, EG n. 27.
[35] Francisco, *Homilía en Santa Marta*. (http://www.revistaecclesia.com/misa-santa-marta-tener-miedo-los-cambios-en-la-iglesia-viernes-5-septiembre-2014, 10 junio 2016)
[36] Vaticano II, "Lumen Gentium" [LG] n.10, 32, en: *Documentos del Vaticano II*, 21-112, aquí 45, 73.
[37] Véase Rémi Parent, *Una Iglesia de bautizados: para una superación de la oposición clérigos-laicos* (Sal Terrae: Santander 1987).
[38] Instrucción interdicasterial, *Sobre algunos aspectos relacionados con la colaboración de los laicos en el sagrado ministerio de los pastores.* (www.franciscanos.org/docecle/colablaicos1.html, 27 septiembre 2016), y Juan Pablo II, *Christifidelis laici,* n. 23. (http://w2.vatican.va/content/john-paul-ii/es/apost_exhortations/documents/hf_jp-ii_exh_30121988_christifideles-laici.html, 25 agosto 2016)

carismas y funciones comunitarias: "El Espíritu y sus dones no son propiedad de la jerarquía eclesiástica".[39] Todos los ministerios deben ser laicales, es decir, ministerios del pueblo de Dios, porque, en el Nuevo Testamento, se habla mucho de *diakonía*, de ministerios y oficios eclesiales, que ejercían tanto varones como mujeres (también obispas),[40] pero no, de clero dirigente de las comunidades eclesiales. Así, la contraposición entre ministerios clericales y ministerios laicales, entre Iglesia docente e Iglesia discente, entre elementos activos y pasivos del Pueblo de Dios no tiene sentido eclesial; debe ser superada, pues todos, en virtud de la dignidad bautismal y según el carisma recibido del Espíritu, son, al mismo tiempo, Iglesia que enseña e Iglesia que aprende, Iglesia que recibe e Iglesia que da el Espíritu.

Por otro lado, el poder en la Iglesia siempre ha estado ligado a lo sagrado, a su control y dominio. Los *profesionales de lo sagrado*, por tener una consagración, una dedicación a lo sagrado, pretenden ser administradores de Dios o más tú de Dios que quienes se dedican a lo profano, pretensión inadmisible y anticristiana, mucho más, cuando se presenta en nombre de Dios. Para la fe cristiana, Dios se hace mundo, se hace *radicalmente profano*, en su *Humanización* en la persona Jesús de Nazareth, en la forma concreta de realizarse su existencia humana, que es la convicción central y específica del cristianismo. Jesús, el *Emmanuel*, el Dios-con-nosotros, santifica, pues, lo profano; Jesús, el Hijo de Dios, fue una persona divina, pero no, un personaje sagrado y rechazó una religión transformada en un sagrado mágico de la vida, muy ocupada de Dios y de su Ley, pero muy poco preocupada por las personas y por su mundo. Y los *responsables de lo sagrado* le acusaron de sacrílego y pervertidor.

Hoy, Francisco denuncia especialmente el *clericalismo*, "uno de los peores males de la Iglesia", por eso dice: "Señor, libera a tu pueblo del espíritu del clericalismo y ayúdale con el espíritu de profecía",[41] porque "olvida que la visibilidad y sacramentalidad de la Iglesia pertenece a todo el Pueblo de Dios

---

[39] Francisco, *Carta al Presidente de la Pontificia Comisión para a América Latina.* (w2.vatican.va/content/francesco/es/letters/2016/documents/papa-francesco_20160319_pont-comm-america-latina.html, 25 septiembre 2016)

[40] En la basílica de santa Práxedes, en Roma, puede verse un mosaico en que aparecen cuatro mujeres, una de ellas enmarcada en la leyenda *Theodora episcopa*.

[41] Francisco, *Homilía en Santa Marta.* (http://www.periodistadigital.com/religion/vaticano/2013/12/16/francisco-senor-libera-a-tu-pueblo-del-clericalismo-iglesia-religion-dios-jesus-papa-vaticano.shtml, 25 agosto 2016)

y no solo a unos pocos elegidos; disminuye y desvaloriza la gracia que el Espíritu puso en el corazón de cada creyente; coarta las iniciativas y osadías necesarias para poder llevar la Buena Nueva del Evangelio a todos los ámbitos del quehacer social y político y va apagando el fuego profético que la Iglesia entera está llamada a testimoniar en medio de los pueblos".[42]

En definitiva, que mientras se mantenga la división clero-pueblo, se podrá hablar de castas, de desigualdades en la *Comunidad de la comunión de iguales* y, con Francisco, se podrá afirmar que "en una comunidad cristiana, la división es uno de los pecados más graves, porque lo convierte en signo no de la obra de Dios, sino de la obra del diablo, que es por definición quien separa, quien arruina las relaciones".[43]

El poder papal

Francisco reprende a la jerarquía por su afán de poder[44] y ha reconocido que "el papado y las estructuras centrales de la Iglesia necesitan una conversión" (*Evangelii Gaudium* 32; 98), pero no hace referencia alguna a lo que le afecta a él personalmente: su *poder absoluto,* cuando, precisamente, urge acometer a fondo su transformación, pues su tabú ha bloqueado tácitamente, desde el Vaticano II, todas las reformas que hubieran requerido revisar posiciones dogmáticas anteriores.[45]

Con la reforma gregoriana en el siglo XI, se inaugura la *ideología del poder absoluto del papado,* cuyo soporte ya no es Jesucristo pobre, humilde y débil, sino el Dios omnipotente del cosmos y fuente única del Poder. *De facto,* se establece el principio de que obedecer a Dios es obedecer a la Iglesia y obedecer a la Iglesia es obedecer al papa y, en consecuencia, obedecer al papa es

---

[42] Francisco, *Carta al Presidente para la CAL.* (w2.vatican.va/content/francesco/es/letters/2016/documents/papa-francesco_20160319_pont-comm-america-latina.html, 29 septiembre 2016)

[43] Francisco, *Audiencia general.* (w2.vatican.va/content/francesco/es/audiences/2014/documents/papa-francesco_20140827_udienza-generale.html, 30 septiembre 2016)

[44] Francisco, *Discurso ante el Comité coordinador del CELAM* (w2.vatican.va/content/francesco/es/speeches/2013/july/documents/papa-francesco_20130728_gmg-celam-rio.html, 30 septiembre 2016); *Homilía en la Apertura del Sínodo sobre la familia.* (w2.vatican.va/content/francesco/es/homilies/2014/documents/papa-francesco_20141005_omelia-apertura-sinodo-vescovi.pdf, 30 septiembre 2016); *Encuentro con los obispos de Méjico.* (w2.vatican.va/content/francesco/es/speeches/2016/february/documents/papa-francesco_20160213_messico-vescovi.html, 30 septiembre 2016)

[45] Hans Küng, "Llamamiento al papa Francisco", en: *Diario El País,* 9 marzo 2016. (http://elpais.com/elpais/2016/02/26/opinion/1456503103_530587.html, 20 de septiembre 2016)

obedecer a Dios. Y Vaticano I[46] (*Pastor Aeternus* 1870) elevó a dogma de fe y Juan Pablo II ratificó con el Nuevo Código de Derecho Canónico:

- el *poder absoluto y arbitrario*, obviando que la *potestas* (suprema, plena, universal e inmediata) de la Iglesia es el amor de Dios en Cristo, que reciben y comparten los creyentes, en apertura a todos los seres humanos, de manera que ese mismo amor es el primado de la Iglesia.[47] Se le atribuye el poder sobre todos y cada uno de los fieles, *ex sese, sine consensu ecclesiae*; se le considera el representante de Dios, la cabeza visible de Cristo que, a su vez, es la cabeza invisible de la Iglesia, por lo que nadie puede juzgar al papa e, incluso, puede *cerrar o abrir las puertas del cielo*. A él, una criatura humana, se le atribuyen, pues, atributos que sólo competen a Dios;
- la *infalibilidad*, considerada como privilegio personal,[48] obviando que inexorablemente va ligada al *principio de recepción*, pues es propia de toda la Comunidad, en quien habita el Espíritu haciéndole partícipe en la revelación. "Por el don del Espíritu Santo, todos los miembros de la Iglesia poseen el sentido de la fe",[49] es una especie de "instinto espiritual",[50] que permite *sentire cum Ecclesia* y discernir lo que es conforme a la fe apostólica y al espíritu del Evangelio. Es sentir, pensar y querer dentro de la Iglesia.[51] "Es el *sensus fidei* del santo pueblo fiel de Dios, que, en su unidad, nunca, nunca se equivoca."[52]

Todo ello ha llevado a que el papa y la jerarquía se identifiquen con la Iglesia, de la que se creen únicos responsables, de manera que la discrepancia con sus normas se considera rechazo a la fe y a la Iglesia. Urge, pues, que la Iglesia, no el Magisterio, afronte el serio problema teológico de ver qué es más acorde

---

[46] Bernard Sesboüé, *Le magistrère à l'épreuve* (Desclée de Brouwer: París 2001), 42.
[47] Ignacio de Antioquia, cit. en Xavier Pikaza, "Causas y consecuencias del clericalismo", en: *Iglesia Viva* 266 (2016) 23-43, aquí, 33.
[48] Hans Küng, *Verdad controvertida. Memorias* (Trotta: Madrid 2009), 195-246; Bernard Sesboüé, *La infalibilidad de la Iglesia. Historia y teología* (Sal Terrae: Santander 2014), 289-324, y Sesboüé, *Le magistrère à l'épreuve*, 173-180.
[49] Sesboüé, *Le magistrère à l'épreuve*, 96-103.
[50] Énfasis en el original.
[51] Francisco, *Discurso a la Comisión teológica internacional*. (w2.vatican.va/content/francesco/es/speeches/2013/ december/documents/papa-francesco_20131206_commissione-teologica. html, 20 septiembre 2016)
[52] Francisco, *Homilía 1 enero 2014*. (w2.vatican.va/content/francesco/es/homilies/2014/documents/papa-francesco_20140101_omelia-giornata-mondiale-pace.html, 15 agosto 2016)

con el Evangelio: que el ejercicio del poder en la Iglesia tenga una estructura monárquico-absolutista o una estructura democrática. Y, si es la segunda, se podría concluir que ejercer el poder según una monarquía absolutista es un abuso de poder que carece de fundamentación teológica. Obviamente, no se trata de destruir la Iglesia, sino de edificarla, porque *Ecclesia semper reformanda*; ni se trata de un relativismo trivial, que socava los cimientos éticos de la Iglesia y de la sociedad, pero tampoco de un inmisericorde dogmatismo que mata el espíritu empecinándose en la letra, que impide una renovación a fondo de la vida y la enseñanza de la Iglesia y que bloquea cualquier avance serio en el terreno del ecumenismo. No hay que temer.[53]

Francisco, escuchando la invitación evangélica: "*No sea así entre vosotros*" (Mt 20,26), podría aprovechar su poder para derogar los dogmas del poder absoluto del papa y de la infalibilidad, porque la administración eclesiástica como poder choca con el espíritu evangélico.

Exclusión de las mujeres en nombre de Dios = profanación del nombre de Dios

Si en algún ámbito se explicita la usurpación clerical del poder, es en de las mujeres; con una pseudo-fundamentación teológica, se pretende justificar como voluntad de Dios lo que es *ideología patriarcal del poder, en clave religiosa* y, por ende, anti-evangélica. La exclusión de las mujeres en nombre de Dios es la mayor profanación de su nombre, porque resulta blasfemo usarlo para justificar el dominio patriarcal, peca contra el Espíritu, distorsiona al Dios de Jesús, destroza su proyecto pues encarna el anti-proyecto del Reino y resta toda credibilidad a la Iglesia y su mensaje. Es hora de que la Iglesia despierte, vuelva sus ojos al vivir y al hacer de Jesús y se abra al impulso del Espíritu dinamizador de la Historia; es hora de que desaparezca la misógina obsesión vaticana por la *ideología de género*,[54] que califica de abominable por ser contraria a la ley natural y pilar del relativismo moral: "la última rebelión de la creatura contra su condición de creatura", según Benedicto XVI.[55]

---

[53] Bernard Sesboüé, *¡No tengáis miedo! Los ministerios en la Iglesia hoy* (Sal Terrae: Santander 1998), 64, y Marta Zubía Guinea, "No temáis, varones de poca fe", en: *Iglesia Viva* 239 (2009), 49-66.
[54] Zubía, *Para nuestra memoria histórica,* 153-175.
[55] Benedicto XVI, "Ad romanam Curiam", en: *Acta apostolicae sedis* 101, 48-56, aquí 53.

Hoy, Francisco ha denunciado el *machismo* y la *ideología machista* en la Iglesia, ha reclamado su *presencia* donde se toman las decisiones importantes,[56] incluso, donde se ejercita la autoridad y ha aludido levemente a la formación de una comisión para el estudio del diaconado de las mujeres. Pero, al mismo tiempo, mantiene la *ideología patriarcal de poder, en clave religiosa*, como, por ejemplo, en lo referente a la ordenación de las mujeres ha respondido tajantemente en línea con sus antecesores: "la Iglesia ha hablado y ha dicho NO. Lo dijo Juan Pablo II con una formulación definitiva. Esa puerta está cerrada".[57] Pues bien, Francisco yerra, al menos, en dos cosas: la Iglesia no ha hablado; quien habló fue el papa, pero él no es la Iglesia y, además, Juan Pablo II no cerró la causa ni la declaró definitiva, porque no podía hacerlo; ciertamente, ésa era su voluntad, pero, para ser una definición o una causa cerrada, el papa tiene que hablar *ex cathedra*, con el *sensus fidelium* y proclamarlo adecuadamente. Francisco, pues, sigue manteniendo que la Iglesia no está autorizada a admitir a las mujeres a los ministerios ordenados porque Cristo fue varón y, sin condicionamientos socio-culturales, libremente, no eligió a ninguna de las mujeres, ni siquiera a su Madre, para formar parte de los Doce y, lo que se considera la causa fundamental (aunque sea una perversión teológica), la mujer no es *imago Dei* ni *imago Christi*. Desde una reflexión teológica seria, ninguno de los tres argumentos es admisible.[58]

Evidentemente, no se trata de que las mujeres accedan al ministerio ordenado para igualarse a los varones, sino de acceder, como sujetos iguales, a todas las instancias eclesiales y asumir ministerios eclesiales, para ejercer la responsabilidad y la misión recibidas como seguidoras y seguidores de Jesús. Si la Iglesia oficial volviera a las fuentes, al comportamiento de Jesús con las mujeres y al protagonismo de éstas en las primeras comunidades y se dejara afectar, tendrían que reconocer que su comportamiento patriarcal no puede basarse ni justificarse en Jesús ni en su movimiento, sino que es fruto de un contexto social dado y de la *ideología patriarcal de poder, en clave religiosa*.

---

[56] Francisco, EG 103, y Antonio Spadaro, "Entrevista al Papa Francisco", en: *Razón y Fe* (2013, número exclusivo) 1-27.
[57] Francisco, EG 104, y Darío Menor, "Entrevista de los periodistas al papa Francisco a la vuelta de las Jornadas mundiales de la juventud, en el avión", en: *Vida Nueva* 2.859 (2013).
[58] Véase Zubía, *Para nuestra memoria histórica*, 193-210, 255-264.

Hacia una Iglesia LAICA, al estilo del movimiento de Jesús

El marco referencial y el principio hermenéutico de las reflexiones eclesiológicas ha de ser el Reino iniciado por Jesús de Nazareth, la Sofía de Dios humanizada. Jesús, igual en todo a nosotros, excepto en el pecado (Rm 8,3), no fue sacerdote ni profesional de lo religioso[59] ni una persona sagrada, sino profana; un laico que antepuso lo laico a lo religioso y que, con su palabra y con su hacer, puso en entredicho todo un complejo religioso idolátrico: movido por el Espíritu, puso a la persona por encima de lo oficialmente sagrado y la arrancó de toda servidumbre, en especial, de la más escandalosa, la impuesta en nombre de Dios. Jesús de Nazareth, la imagen viva de Dios, no fue excluyente ni creador de desigualdades y privilegios.

Como buen judío, Jesús fue un cumplidor religioso que asistía al templo, pero vivió y enseñó que a Dios se le encuentra no solo en el templo y en lo sagrado, sino también, en lo profano; de hecho, vivió su experiencia espiritual, fundamentalmente, fuera de los marcos cultuales, en los ámbitos profanos, en la sencillez de la vida cotidiana. Su proyecto no fue un proyecto religioso, sino laico. No suprimió lo sagrado, sino que lo desplazó de lo religioso a lo humano, porque el lugar privilegiado de encuentro con Dios, desde su Humanización, es el ser humano en su historia concreta. Esto fue lo verdaderamente sagrado para Jesús. Por eso, desde él, la identidad cristiana es fundamentalmente profana, laica y, para quienes pretenden seguirle, lo profano, lo laico ha de ser el lugar privilegiado para encontrar a Dios. Lo que Jesús legó no es un marco institucional dado, sino un estilo de vida y unos valores que sirvan de guía; de hecho, los primeros cristianos no consideraban su seguimiento como una religión, sino como un proyecto de vida, un modo de vivir.

Así, pues, si Jesús fue laico, si su grupo era de mujeres y varones laicos, si las comunidades de los primeros siglos fueron laicas y si, de la condición laical de Jesús, no se deriva el sacerdocio clerical de unos pocos, sino la llamada a la Comunidad a llevar adelante su proyecto, solo podemos concluir, a mi juicio, que, si la *Iglesia* quiere ser *al estilo del movimiento de Jesús*, ha de ser una Iglesia laica. Ha de superar el error teológico de la teología tradicional, que considera que solo el sacerdote actúa *in persona Christi*, cuando esto es una dimensión de toda persona cristiana, pues la auténtica y única consagración es la del Bautismo, que nos hace miembros del pueblo de Dios. Todos los miembros de la Iglesia somos hijos e hijas de Dios, en igualdad, laicos, y a todos nos ha sido confiada la misión de anunciar la Buena nueva y la salvación.

---

[59] Pikaza, "Causas y consecuencias del clericalismo", 25-27; Bernabé "Mujeres en la Iglesia", 75.

Precisamente, su laicidad es lo que marca la originalidad del cristianismo respecto de las demás religiones: el romper con el dualismo tradicional de lo sagrado y lo profano, lo sacerdotal y lo laical, la religión y la vida cotidiana. Por eso, debe superarse la división entre clero-laicos; en la Iglesia de Jesús solo debe haber laicos, cada uno con su carisma y su ministerio al servicio de la comunidad,[60] pues, mientras exista el *orden*, estaremos hablando de castas, de desigualdades y no podremos hablar de la *Comunidad de la comunión de iguales*, al estilo del movimiento de Jesús. Ése es el contexto teológico y eclesial en que, a mi juicio, ha de enmarcarse la vida total de la Comunidad y los ministerios que en ella se reconozcan.

La *Comunidad de la comunión de iguales*[61] debe recuperar, pues, estas funciones que le fueron usurpadas por el clero. Solo desde ahí, podrá ser fiel al proyecto de Jesús y afrontar los signos de los tiempos, como los derechos humanos y la sociedad democrática, que claman por cambiar las estructuras de poder por las estructuras de comunión, la monarquía jerárquico-piramidal por la democratización de la Iglesia, la pre-cristiana dureza disciplinar eclesiástica por el pleno derecho a la libertad de los hijos e hijas de Dios y la ideología patriarcal en clave religiosa por el reconocimiento, teórico y *de facto*, de las mujeres como sujetos de pleno derecho de la Comunidad. *Comunidad de comunidades* que viven un discipulado laical de iguales, que cambian las relaciones de poder por las democráticas, co-responsables para pensar, discernir, decidir, gobernar, organizar, buscar, acompañar, celebrar, transmitir el mensaje y la fe y asumir la responsabilidad de los ministerios, según la comunidad vaya reconociendo los carismas derramados por el Espíritu para su servicio. Unos miembros serán liberados y otros no, en función de las necesidades de la comunidad y de la misión; pero, en ningún caso, los liberados podrán considerarse con un poder especial o superiores a los no liberados, pues todos son co-responsables de la misma misión que Jesús ha encomendado a quienes le quieran seguir.

Además, si la Iglesia quiere anunciar, hoy, lo que Jesús anunció, si quiere ofrecer a las mujeres y varones de hoy la liberación y la curación que Jesús les ofreció, debe cambiar su paradigma, su lenguaje religioso, las ideas e imágenes que utiliza y que, cada vez, resultan más incomprensibles en el siglo XXI. Porque, aunque su fin es meta-histórico, el Reino es algo histórico, que solo puede ocurrir en nuestra historia; no es solo utopía y futuro, sino presente y

---

[60] Estrada, *Una eclesiología de laicos*, 67, 97, 134.
[61] Recuérdese la obra de Schüssler Fiorenza, *Discipulado de iguais*.

realización histórica llevada a cabo por mujeres y varones concretos co-operando con el Espíritu. Lo que exige una *Ecclesia semper reformanda*.

Conclusión

En definitiva, si la Iglesia católica tiene realmente el coraje de *volver a las Fuentes* y adoptar el Reino iniciado por Jesús como marco referencial y principio hermenéutico de su eclesiología; si la Iglesia quiere ser al estilo del movimiento de Jesús y de las comunidades primitivas; si quiere llevar adelante la misión de Jesús de llevar su mensaje de salvación a las mujeres y varones, *a fortiori*, pasará a ser una *Iglesia laica*, derivada de la condición laica de Jesús y de su movimiento, en fidelidad al proyecto de Jesús y a toda la riqueza de la Tradición, preservando la unidad en la comunión, reimplantada en el marco de un proyecto laico y democrático en este mundo global, democrático y plural y ecuménico y, firmemente, comprometida con las demás confesiones eclesiales para acabar con el escándalo de sus enfrentamientos, apelando al mismo Cristo.

Marta María Zubia Guinea Doctora en Teología Sistemática; Lda. en Filosofía y Letras, en Ciencias Eclesiásticas y en Teología y Mtr. en Pedagogía. Miembro de Asociación teólogas españolas y de ESWTR. Profesora de Derechos humanos y cristianismo, en la Univ. de Deusto, y de Filosofía, en Bachillerato. Autora de Para nuestra memoria histórica: las mujeres en la voz de los papas, Derechos humanos y cristianismo: inseparables para la fe, conflictivos en la vida y Mujeres y ciudadanas: artesanas invisibilizadas de Derechos humanos, entre otros, así como de diversos artículos. Líneas de investigación: Derechos humanos. Eclesiología; ambas en perspectiva de género.

Gotlind Ulshöfer

Aus der Reformation lernen? Impulse im Zeitalter der Digitalisierung

Von der Reformation kann nicht gesprochen werden kann, ohne das Geschehen als ein multilokales zu sehen und als ein Prozess der vielseitigen, nicht nur theologischen Veränderungen zu verstehen. In diesem Beitrag wird gefragt, welche Impulse für einen interreligiösen Dialog im digitalen Zeitalter von diesem Geschehen ausgehen können. Dabei wird als eines der Kennzeichen der Reformation die Neu-Interpretation einer Religion herausgegriffen und damit auf die Bedeutung der Selbstinterpretation einer Religion verwiesen. Die Bedeutung der Selbstinterpretation und ihrer Kriterien, wirft Fragen nach der Autorität und den Machtinnehabenden auf. Gerade im digitalen Zeitalter zeigen Untersuchungen zur „digital religion", dass sich hinsichtlich der Autoritäten über die Selbstinterpretation einer Religion ein Pluralismus entwickelt hat, der zentralisierte Autoritäten unterlaufen kann. Die dem Artikel zugrundeliegende These ist, dass Selbstinterpretationen von Religionen in Auseinandersetzung mit ihrem Umfeld und anderen Religionen und Weltanschauungen geschehen und dass dies theologisch zur Frage führt, wie Kriterien für diese Selbstinterpretation entwickelt werden können. Dabei ergibt sich aus der zunehmenden Digitalisierung und Horizontalisierung gerade auch im Hinblick auf die Vermittlung religiöser Inhalte und Selbstverständnisse die grundlegende Frage, ob und inwiefern eine Verständigung über Kriterien auch Teil eines interreligiösen Dialogs werden kann.

In the research field of "religion and media", gender issues are often neglected. This is also the case for research dealing with religious authority in the internet. The article analyses how the notion and structure of religious authority has changed due to digitalisation and what can be learned from the Reformation concerning the questions of religious authority, also seen from a gender perspective.

En el campo de la investigación de la "religión y los medios de comunicación" las cuestiones de género frecuentemente se omiten, como así también sucede respecto a las investigaciones sobre la autoridad religiosa en los medios de comunicación electrónicos. Abordar los cambios en la noción y estructura de la autoridad religiosa gracias a la digitalización, cómo se continua o descontinúa en torno al legado de la Reforma respecto al poder religioso desde la perspectiva de género es el análisis de este artículo.

Gotlind Ulshöfer
Aus der Reformation lernen? Impulse im Zeitalter der Digitalisierung

Hinführung: Forschung zu Religion und Digitalisierung unter Gendergesichtspunkten

Die folgenden Überlegungen zur Bedeutung der Reformation für gegenwärtige Analysen von Religion und Digitalisierung werden unter dem Blickwinkel einer gender-sensiblen, protestantischen, deutschsprachigen Theologie entwickelt. Es werden Bezugspunkte zur aktuellen Forschung hinsichtlich Gender-Religion-Digitalisierung aufgezeigt.

Im deutschsprachigen theologischen Kontext sind es insbesondere die Praktische Theologie und die Systematische Theologie, die sich mit Fragen von Religion und Digitalisierung – verstanden im weitesten Sinne – beschäftigen. Dabei werden religionspädagogische Themen genauso reflektiert, wie die Frage nach Entwicklung einer "Theologie der sozialen Medien".[1] Betrachtet man den aktuellen Forschungsstand, so fällt auf, dass die sozialen Medien des Web 2.0 im Zentrum stehen. "Hauptmerkmal des Web 2.0 ist die gemeinsame Erstellung von Daten, die von vielen Nutzern gleichzeitig produziert, bearbeitet, gesammelt, verknüpft und konsumiert werden. Die Nutzer sind längst nicht mehr nur Konsumenten oder nur Produzenten von Informationen, sondern beides zugleich und werden daher als 'Prosumer' bezeichnet."[2] Wissenschaftliche Untersuchungen dazu geschehen jedoch selten unter Gendergesichtspunkten. Der nicht-inklusive Sprachgebrauch des eben präsentierten Zitats zeigt das exemplarisch. Oft wird auf Genderunterschiede nur implizit oder formal Bezug genommen. Schulbezogene Darstellungen unterscheiden beispielsweise nur rein schematisch zwischen Schülerinnen und Schülern. Eine Genderstudie zum Thema Religion

---

[1] Siehe in Auswahl: Ilona Nord / Swantje Luthe (Hg.), *Social Media, christliche Religiosität und Kirche. Studien zur Praktischen Theologie mit religionspädagogischem Schwerpunkt* (Edition Treskeia: Jena 2014); Rudolf Englert et al. (Hg.), *Gott googeln? Multimedia und Religion* (Neukirchner Theologie: Neukirchen-Vluyn 2012) Jahrbuch der Religionspädagogik (JRP) Bd. 28; Christina Costanza und Christina Ernst (Hg.), *Personen im Web 2.0. Kommunikationswissenschaftliche, ethische und anthropologische Zugänge zu einer Theologie der Social Media* (Edition Ruprecht: Göttingen 2012); Christina Ernst, *Mein Gesicht zeige ich nicht auf Facebook. Social Media als Herausforderung theologischer Anthropologie* (Edition Ruprecht: Göttingen 2015); Anne-Kathrin Lück, *Der gläserne Mensch im Internet. Ethische Reflexionen zur Sichtbarkeit, Leiblichkeit und Personalität in der Online-Kommunikation* (Kohlhammer: Stuttgart 2013); Johanna Haberer, *Digitale Theologie. Gott und die Medienrevolution der Gegenwart* (Kösel: München 2015).

[2] Christina Costanza / Christian Ernst, "Interdisziplinäre Zugänge zu einer Theologie der Social Media," in: Christina Costanza / Christina Ernst (Hg.), *Personen im Web 2.0. Kommunikationswissenschaftliche, ethische und anthropologische Zugänge zu einer Theologie der Social Media* (Edition Ruprecht: Göttingen 2012), 7-15, hier 9.

und Digitalisierung liegt im Bereich der deutschsprachigen Theologie noch nicht vor. Dieses Defizit in der modernen Genderforschung zeigt sich auch in benachbarten Wissenschaftsgebieten. Die Religionssoziologin Mia Lövheim fragt in Bezug auf das Forschungsgebiet *Media, Religion and Culture* "Why, then, is research that focuses on the experiences of women or analyzes the interplay between media, religion and contemporary cultures from a gender perspective so invisible in the field?"[3] Die ausgeführten Argumente, zeigen, dass das hier zur Diskussion stehende, relativ neue Forschungsgebiet zwar den Bezug zwischen Religion (in seiner institutionalisierten Form und als praktizierte Religiosität) und Medien herstellt, dass es dabei aber Genderfragen eher am Rand behandelt Auch Machtfragen werden vernachlässigt.

With the longstanding concern for the experiences of women and other marginalized groups, feminist and gender perspectives can contribute to open our eyes for a critical analysis of the distribution of power and resources as well as forms of resistance in the production and use of mediated religious and cultural values.[4]

Im Kontext der Analyse, wie aus der Reformation gelernt wurde und wird, ist eine Begriffsklärung nötig. Zwischen der Bezeichnung Reformation als Chiffre eines historischen Geschehens und der Verwendung des Begriffes zur Bezeichnung der Rezeption seiner theologischen Inhalte ist zu unterscheiden. Unter Gendergesichtspunkten wird im Folgenden nach der Relevanz der Bezugnahme auf die Reformation im Diskurs der Digitalisierung und nach der Konstruktion von *religious authority* im Internet zu fragen sein.

Methodische Überlegungen: Der Bezug auf ein historisches Ereignis zur Interpretation der Gegenwart oder: Was heißt, aus der Reformation lernen?

Das Gedenken an die Reformation ist insbesondere seit dem Beginn des Reformationsjahrs am 31. Oktober 2016 zumindest im deutschsprachigen Kontext nicht nur in einer evangelisch-kirchlichen Öffentlichkeit präsent gemacht, sondern medial auch für ein größeres Publikum aufbereitet worden. Dabei wird die Veröffentlichung von Martin Luthers 95 Thesen als das Datum verstanden, das symbolisch für den Beginn der Reformation stehen soll. Genderaspekte finden

---

[3] Mia Lövheim, "Introduction. Gender – A Blind Spot in Media, Religion and Culture?" in: Dies. (Hg.), *Media, Religion and Gender. Key Issues and New Challenges* (Routledge: London and New York 2013), 1-13, hier 2.
[4] Lövheim, "Introduction," hier 6.

in diesem Gedenken hauptsächlich auf einer historischen Ebene Eingang, indem beispielsweise der Frauen gedacht wird, welche die Reformation vorantrieben. Abgesehen davon ist zu fragen, ob überhaupt von *der* Reformation gesprochen werden kann, oder ob das Geschehen als ein multilokales und prozessuales zu verstehen ist, das zu vielseitigen, nicht nur theologischen Veränderungen geführt hat. Dieser Sichtweise ist eher in den Hintergrund getreten.[5]

Im vorliegenden Beitrag wird die Reformation als plurales Ereignis verstanden, wobei als ein Kennzeichen der Reformation die Neu-Interpretation einer Religion herausgegriffen und damit auf die Bedeutung der Selbstinterpretation einer Religion verwiesen wird.[6] Die Bedeutung der Selbstinterpretation und ihrer Kriterien, die in der Reformation mit *solus christus, sola gratia, sola scriptura* und *sola fide* beantwortet wurde, wirft Fragen nach der religiösen Autorität und den Machthabenden im Blick auf die Selbstinterpretation auf. Machtfragen, die den Zugang und die Verteilung von Macht umfassen, sind Fragen nach Gendergerechtigkeit. Dieser Aspekt des Reformationsgeschehens ist mit dem Freiheitsverständnis lutherischer Schriften in Beziehung zu bringen. So wird ersichtlich was diese für eine feministisch-theologische Perspektive austragen.

In einem kritischen Sinne ist zu, welche Impulse hinsichtlich der Selbstinterpretation und dem damit verbundenen Aspekt der religiösen Autorität von der Reformation ausgehen können – angesichts von sozialen Medien und interreligiösen Dialogen. Diese Fragestellung mag verwundern, da im 16. Jahrhundert weder ein interreligiöser Dialog in der Form, wie er heute üblich und möglich ist, existierte, noch etwas von Digitalisierung zu erkennen war. Dies zeigt sich deutlich, wenn Texte aus reformatorischer Zeit – wie zum Beispiel Luthers Schrift von 1543 "Von den Juden und ihren Lügen"[7] – massiv zur Abgrenzung und Diskriminierung gegenüber Juden und der Vernichtung von Synagogen sowie der Lebensgrundlage von Juden beziehungsweise deren Vertreibung – aufgerufen hat.

Das Reformationsgeschehen als Lernmöglichkeit zu verstehen bedeutet, Gegenwart verständlich zu machen und kritisch zu hinterfragen. Das geschieht,

---

[5] Vgl. Ulrich H.J. Körtner, *Reformatorische Theologie im 21. Jahrhundert* (TVZ: Zürich 2010) Theologische Studien N.F. 1, 13 und auch Hans-Jürgen Goertz, "Die Reformation – immer noch eine Baustelle. Zur Vorbereitung des Jubiläums 1517 bis 2017," in: *Ökumenische Rundschau* [ÖR] 64, 3 (2015), 398-404.

[6] Friedrich Schweitzer, *Interreligiöse Bildung. Religiöse Vielfalt als religionspädagogische Herausforderung und Chance* (Gütersloher Verlagshaus: Gütersloh 2014), 70.

[7] Martin Luther, *Von den Juden und ihren Lügen*. Neu bearbeitet von Matthias Morgenstern (Berlin University Press: Wiesbaden 2016).

indem historische Ereignisse und ihre politischen, ideologischen und in diesem Fall theologischen Grundlegungen aufgezeigt werden und auch hinsichtlich Inhalte kritisch analysiert und diese auch verurteilt werden.[8] Außerdem geht es auch darum zu zeigen, welchen Beitrag das historische Ereignis zur Identitätsstiftung der jeweiligen Gruppierung, die sich das Ereignis beziehen, wie bei der Reformation vor allen Dingen die Evangelische Kirche – aber auch darüber hinaus für andere Gruppierungen – geleistet hat.[9] Und dazuhin kann nach Neu-Interpretationen und Weiterentwicklungen angesichts gesellschaftlicher Veränderungen gefragt werden.

Die These ist, dass aus der Reformation insbesondere bezüglich ihres Freiheitsverständnisses eine kritische Verhältnisbestimmung zur Gegenwart gelernt werden kann – hinsichtlich der Frage nach dem religiösen Selbstverständnis und der Frage nach der Formierung religiöser Autorität im Internet. Aus Genderperspektive ist dazuhin besonders ein Kennzeichen des reformatorischen Denkens für eine plurale, digitale Welt von Interesse: das Denken in Paradoxien. Damit dies für die Gegenwart fruchtbar gemacht werden kann, bedarf es auch ethischer Überlegungen.

Rechtfertigung, Freiheit und die Bedeutung von Paradoxien – Kennzeichen der Reformation und deren Rezeption

Es zeigt sich, "dass das, was wir heute unter Reformation verstehen ..., überhaupt nur über einen 500jährigen Entwicklungsprozess greifbar ist."[10]

---

[8] Wie dies beispielsweise die Synode der Evangelischen Kirche in Deutschland mit ihrem Beschluss "Martin Luther und die Juden – Notwendige Erinnerung zum Reformationsjubiläum" vorgenommen hat. Evangelische Kirche in Deutschland, *Beschlüsse - Kundgebung "Martin Luther und die Juden – Notwendige Erinnerung zum Reformationsjubiläum"* (https://www.ekd.de/synode2015_bremen/beschluesse/s15_04_iv_7_kundgebung_martin_luther_und_die_juden.html, 1 September 2016) und zur Diskussion und weiteren Interpretation: Dorothea Wendebourg, "Ein Lehrer der Unterscheidung verlangt. Martin Luthers Haltung zu den Juden in Zusammenhang mit seiner Theologie," in: *Theologische Literaturzeitung* [ThLZ] 140, 10 (2015), 1034-1058.

[9] Im Hintergrund steht dabei die Vorstellung von "kollektiven Identitäten". Diese werden verstanden als "Diskursformationen; sie stehen und fallen mit den Symbolsystemen, über die sich die Träger einer Kultur als zugehörig definieren und identifizieren." Aleida Assmann, "Zum Problem der Identität aus kulturwissenschaftlicher Sicht," in: *Leviathan* 21, 2 (1993), 238-253, hier 240.

[10] Harry Oelke, "Reformationsjubiläen gestern und heute. Geschichtspolitische Einflussnahme und die reformatorische Säkularfeier 2017," in: *Pastoraltheologie* 15 (2016), 21-43, hier 42.

Gotlind Ulshöfer
Aus der Reformation lernen? Impulse im Zeitalter der Digitalisierung

Die reformatorischen Anfänge: Die Betonung der Freiheit und Paradoxien[11]
Ein wesentlicher Gedanke, der die Reformation und deren Rezeption geprägt haben, ist eine Konzentration auf ein am Individuum orientiertes Freiheitsverständnis. Luthers Schrift "Von der Freiheit eines Christenmenschen"[12] weist auf die mehrfache Ausrichtung eines christlichen Freiheitsverständnisses hin. Aus protestantischer Perspektive gründet die Freiheit des Menschen in Christus, und das Handeln des Menschen soll auf den Nächsten hin in Liebe orientiert sein. Die Paradoxie von Gebundenheit und Freiheit kennzeichnet dieses qualifizierte Verständnis von Freiheit. Freiheit ist also nicht als absolut zu verstehen, sondern relational. In der umsonst empfangenen Gnade ist der Mensch frei und kann frei handeln in dieser Welt bei gleichzeitigem Bewusstsein der Voraussetzung des Geschenks der Gnade von Gott. Luther geht von einem Verständnis des Priestertums aller aus. Das heißt, dass auch religiöse Autorität für Luther zunächst jeder und jede Gläubige selbst hat, denn die Gnade Gottes ist ihr und ihm geschenkt, wobei die politische Obrigkeit durchaus zu respektieren sei. Auch wenn die Macht bei Gott liegt und nur Gott Autorität gebührt, so ergibt sich für die gläubigen Menschen, dass diese mit religiöser Autorität – das heißt, was geglaubt und wie der Glaube gelebt werden soll – zunächst beschenkt werden, ihr religiöses Leben als Aufgabe zu verstehen und Verantwortung im Blick auf den Umgang mit den Nächsten zu übernehmen. Dass dieses Verständnis von religiöser Autorität auch Auswirkungen auf das Selbstverständnis von Frauen hatte, lässt sich an Beispielen wie Argula von Grumbach aufzeigen, die mit selbstverfassten Flugschriften, die auch weite Verbreitung fanden, die Reformation unterstützte und so religiöse Autorität zeigte.[13] Das heißt, dass aus reformatorischer Perspektive religiöse Autorität immer auch aus der Perspektive der Rechtfertigungslehre und deren anti-hierarchischen Impetus verstanden werden sollte, denn: "Diese Botschaft von der Rechtfertigung, die Luther in der Auslegung des

---

[11] Zu den Paradoxien vgl. DeAne Lagerquist / Caryn D. Riswold, "Historical and Theological Legacies of Feminism and Lutheranism," in: Mary J. Streufert (Hg.), *Transformative Lutheran Theologies. Feminist, Womanist, and Mujerista Perspectives* (Fortress Press: Minneapolis 2010), 15-29.
[12] Martin Luther, *Von der Freiheit eines Christenmenschen*, herausgegeben und kommentiert von Dietrich Korsch, (Evangelische Verlagsanstalt: Leipzig 2016) Große Texte der Christenheit 1.
[13] Katharina Kunter, *500 Jahre Protestantismus. Eine Reise von den Anfängen bis in die Gegenwart* (Bundeszentrale für Politische Bildung: Bonn 2013), 46-47.

Römerbriefs neu entdeckt hatte, ist für die lutherischen Kirchen die Summe des Evangeliums und Maßstab seiner Auslegung."[14]

Das Verständnis der Reformation als Kriterium für die Gegenwart – Akzentverschiebungen im 20. Jahrhundert
Stehen Freiheit und das Wissen um die damit verbundene Verantwortung des freien Handelns auch im Gedenken an die Reformation immer wieder im Mittelpunkt,[15] so vollzieht Karl Barth in seinem Vortrag "Reformation als Entscheidung"[16] 1933 eine Akzentverschiebung. Auch er betont die Freiheit der an Christus Glaubenden, die sich aus der geschenkten Gnade ergibt. Barth stellt sie in engen Bezug zu einer Ausrichtung auf Gott, die das ganze christliche Leben bestimmen soll. Bezüglich des Reformationsgeschehens stellt Barth dann die Entscheidung in den Mittelpunkt, so dass er sagen kann: "Evangelische Kirche im Sinne der Reformation ist da und ist nur da, wo es um die reine *Lehre* der christlichen *Wahrheiten* geht."[17] Barth nimmt in seinem Gedenken an die Reformation als Entscheidungsgeschehen eine doppelte Perspektive ein: auf einer inhaltlichen Ebene hebt er hervor, dass christliche Freiheit nicht bedeutet, den Menschen in den Mittelpunkt zu stellen, sondern Gott und indem er das historische Geschehen der Reformation als Entscheidungsgeschehen darstellt, andererseits verknüpft er es mit der historisch politischen Situation von 1933 in Deutschland und Europa.

Paul Tillich, der Deutschland aufgrund der Nazi-Herrschaft verlassen musste, hat sich immer wieder mit der Frage auseinandergesetzt, was für eine Gegenwartsbedeutung der Protestantismus hat. So geht er in seinem Aufsatz "The End of Protestant Era?"[18] auch dieser Frage nach, wobei er dezidiert vom Protestantismus spricht, und die Reformation als Geschehen bei ihm eher in den Hintergrund rückt. Ihm geht es, wie Barth, um die Frage nach der Entscheidung. Allerdings in einem anderen Sinne. Tillich fragt wie die Wirklichkeit zu betrachten ist, und was dazu aus protestantischer Perspektive gesagt

---

[14] Konrad Raiser, *500 Jahre Reformation weltweit* (Luther: Bielefeld 2016), Studienreihe Luther 7, 75.
[15] Oelke, "Reformationsjubiläen".
[16] Karl Barth, "Reformation als Entscheidung," in: Walther Fürst (Hg.), *"Dialektische Theologie" in Scheidung und Bewährung 1933-1936. Aufsätze, Gutachten und Erklärungen* (Chr. Kaiser: München 1966), 103-121.
[17] Barth, "Reformation", 106 (Hervorh. i. Org.).
[18] Paul Tillich, "The End of the Protestant Era?", in: Ders., *The Protestant Era* (Chicago University: Chicago 1948), 222-233.

werden kann. Er fasst dazuhin das Verständnis von protestantisch sehr weit und kann sagen, dass der Beitrag des Protestantismus die der prophetischen Kritik ist: "the principle of prophetic protest against every power which claims divine character for itself."[19] Auch hier wird im Blick auf das Selbstverhältnis des Menschen und seiner Beziehung zu Gott geschlussfolgert, dass eine protestantische Perspektive den Blick vom Egoismus und der Selbstgefälligkeit des Menschen weg und auf Gott hin lenkt. Dabei ist es Tillich jedoch wichtig zu betonen, dass er dies als protestantisches Prinzip verstanden wissen will. Das wiederum kann durchaus auch von Nicht-Protestantinnen und -Protestanten vertreten werden kann, denn es geht um "resistance against the distortion of humanity and divinity."[20] Die Reformation steht für Tillich daher nicht so sehr als historisches Geschehen im Zentrum, sondern sie evoziert eine Geisteshaltung, die ein kritisches Verhältnis gegenüber den Autoritäten und Mächten ermöglicht, deren Vorgehen gegen die Humanitas des Menschen gerichtet ist. Dabei bezieht auch Tillich das Protestantische Prinzip aus dem lutherischen Verständnis der Rechtfertigung allein aus Gnaden.[21]

Es ergibt sich aus dem kurzen Blick in die Rezeptionsgeschichte der Reformation, dass – ausgehend von der Betonung der Rechtfertigungslehre – die christliche Freiheit sowie die Anerkennung von Paradoxien im Zentrum stehen. Sowohl Barth als auch Tillich machen deutlich, beim Reformationsgeschehen sind es die Inhalte, die prägend für die Beurteilung der Gegenwart sind.

Das 20. und 21. Jahrhundert: Feministisch-theologische Perspektiven auf die Reformation
Lernen aus der Reformation war gerade unter feministisch-theologischen Gesichtspunkten im 20. Jahrhundert auch geprägt von einem Lernen durch Abgrenzung und Neuinterpretation. Die Diskussionen um die Deutung der Rechtfertigungslehre und deren Voraussetzungen und theologischen, zum Beispiel hamartiologischen, Bezugspunkten zeigen diese Vorgehensweise auf.[22] Im Zentrum der Kritik an der Rechtfertigungslehre und auch ihrer Neuinterpretation

---

[19] Tillich, "The End", 230.
[20] Tillich, "The End", 233.
[21] Raiser, *500 Jahre*, 66.
[22] Exemplarisch: Gotlind Ulshöfer, "Frauen und Rechtfertigung – Charakteristika feministisch-theologischer Kritik an der Rechtfertigungslehre," in: Hans-Martin Dober / Dagmar Mensink (Hg.), *Die Lehre von der Rechtfertigung des Gottlosen im kulturellen Kontext der Gegenwart. Beiträge im Horizont des christlich-jüdischen Gesprächs* (Akademie der Diözese Rottenburg-Stuttgart: Stuttgart 2002) Hohenheimer Protokolle Bd. 57, 156-166.

stehen die Erfahrungen von Frauen, die den Ausgangspunkt der Überlegungen darstellen und dazu führen, dass kritisch hinterfragt wird, was in Bezug auf den Kontext der Gerechtigkeit Gottes bzw. der Gnade bedeuten kann. Auch ein aktueller Sammelband zur feministisch, womanistisch und mujerista-Perspektiven auf lutherische Theologie, den Mary J. Streufert herausgegeben hat,[23] greift unter den vier Topoi, die lutherische Theologie kennzeichnen und deren Bedeutung für die Gegenwart relevant sind, in dem Kapitel von DeAne Lagerquist und Cary D. Riswold,[24] die Themen Gnade (*grace*), Beruf (*vocation*), Autorität beziehungsweise Kompetenz (*authority*) und Paradox (*paradox*) auf. Für die folgenden Überlegungen stelle ich die beiden Aspekte von *authority* und *paradox* heraus. Ausgehend von der Vorstellung des Priestertums aller Gläubigen zeigen sich hinsichtlich des Verständnisses von *authority* bei Luther eine Einschränkung und eine Ausweitung: Autorität ergibt sich für Luther nicht aus menschlichem Handeln, sondern zeigt sich in der Betonung der Gnade, die sich in Jesus Christus manifestiert. Autorität ist also – so Lagerquist und Riswold – aus lutherischer Perspektive nicht gottgegebene Herrschaft der einen über andere, sondern gehört Gott alleine. Gleichzeitig ergibt sich aus dem damit ermöglichten emanzipatorischen Denken das Hinterfragen von Autoritätsstrukturen. Dabei weist gerade die Freiheitsschrift Luthers, in welcher der Mensch als dienstbarer Knecht und als freier Mensch bezeichnet wird, auf die Bedeutung des Denkens in Paradoxien bei Luther hin. Das zeigt sich auch in der Vorstellung vom verborgenen und offenbaren Gott. Das Denken in Paradoxien hilft bei der kritischen Analyse von Wirklichkeit.

Feminism in the twenty-first century works with an intersectional methodology, taking seriously the fact that human life is lived at the intersection of identities. These identities emerge from the socially constructed meanings of race, gender, social class, age, ethnicity, sexuality, and many other things. Living in the tensions that often emerge when one is, for example, simultaneously oppressed and oppressor on the basis of different axes of identity (gender and race, perhaps) is what feminists, womanists, and mujeristas work to make sense of today. The Lutheran theological idea of one person as both saved and sinning can ground exploration of privilege and oppression in a new way.[25]

---

[23] Streufert, *Transformative Lutheran Theologies*.
[24] Lagerquist / Riswold, "Historical and Theological Legacies of Feminism and Lutheranism".
[25] Lagerquist / Riswold, "Historical and Theological Legacies of Feminism and Lutheranism", 28.

Gotlind Ulshöfer
Aus der Reformation lernen? Impulse im Zeitalter der Digitalisierung

Digitalisierung und die Frage nach religiöser Autorität im Netz - Wege zur Selbstkonstituierung von Religion

Die Gegenwart kann digitales Zeitalter genannt werden, weil sie geprägt ist von Computerisierung und der damit verbundenen Digitalisierung. Eine Trennung von *online-* und *offline-*Welt ist heute kaum mehr nachzuvollziehen. In dieser *infosphere*,[26] wie sie der Philosoph Luciano Floridi nennt, hat über die sozialen Medien jeder und jede Zugang zu einer weltweiten Öffentlichkeit. Als das Internet Verbreitung fand, verfasste John Perry Barlow 1996 die "Unabhängigkeitserklärung des Cyberspace"[27] als große Freiheitsverheißung, wie es für die frühen Internetaktivisten paradigmatisch ist: Das Internet wird als ein Frei-Raum dargestellt, in dem der Staat keine Macht haben sollte, sondern das Netz sich selbst organisieren soll. Barlow schreibt: "We are creating a world where anyone, anywhere may express his or her beliefs, no matter how singular, without fear or being coerced into silence or conformity."[28] Dass zwanzig Jahre später die Ambivalenzen der Freiheit, insbesondere im Blick auf die Redefreiheit, angesichts von *Hate-speeches* und Cybermobbing etc., in erschreckender Weise aufgetreten sind, erinnert aus theologischer Perspektive an die Charakterisierung des Menschen als *homo iustus et peccator*.

Gleichzeitig ist aber die Einschätzung von Barlow, dass das Netz ganz neue Freiräume für alle, die dazu Zugang haben, ermögliche, erhalten geblieben. Dies lässt sich insbesondere auch bei der Frage nach dem Selbstverständnis von Religionen und damit auch religiösen Autoritäten aufzeigen. Soziale Medien, die durch die aktive Partizipation ihrer Nutzerinnen und Nutzer gekennzeichnet sind, bieten für religiöse Kommunikation[29] und auch für die Entwicklung von kollektiven Identitäten der Nutzerinnen und Nutzer im Blick auf eine Religion Freiräume.[30] Im digitalen Zeitalter, das durch die Ubiquität

---

[26] Luciano Floridi, *The Fourth Revolution. How the infosphere is reshaping human reality* (Oxford University Press: Oxford 2014).
[27] John Perry Barlow, "A Declaration of the Independence of Cyberspace 1996" (https://w2.eff. org/Censorship/Internet_censorship_bills/barlow_0296.declaration, 1 Oktober 2016).
[28] Barlow, "A Declaration".
[29] Dazu: Christoph Seibert, "Religiöse Kommunikation unter den Bedingungen der Social Media", in: Ilona Nord / Swantje Luthe (Hg.), *Social Media, christliche Religiosität und Kirche. Studien zur Praktischen Theologie mit religionspädagogischem Schwerpunkt* (Garamond: Jena 2014), Reihe Populäre Kultur und Theologie 14, 77-100.
[30] Dabei kann die Situation als "medienreligiöse Marktsituation" gekennzeichnet werden, so Wilhelm Gräb, "Multimedia – epochemachende Herausforderung für Religion und Theologie", in:

von Medien und deren technischen Voraussetzungen geprägt ist, stellt sich daher in einem ganz neuen Sinne die Frage, wie die Selbstkonstituierung von Religion vonstattengehen kann. Neben den Texten von Bibel, Koran, etc. und deren Auslegung durch theologisch Gebildete und Gläubige, sowie neben den selbstauferlegten kirchlichen Strukturen und Gesetzen, den Vorschriften, wie eine Religion als Institution aufgebaut ist, tritt heute die Möglichkeit und das Ansinnen, online, über die sozialen Medien wie Facebook, Twitter etc. eigene religiöse Ansichten verbreiten und *follower/innen* zu finden. Die Bloggerin Antje Schrupp weist dazuhin darauf hin: "Eine der größten Veränderungen, die das Internet mit sich bringt, ist die, dass nicht mehr die Sender und Senderinnen von Informationen entscheiden, was relevant ist und was nicht, sondern die Empfängerinnen und Empfänger."[31] Die damit verbundenen neuen Formen von Öffentlichkeit führen auch dazu, wie Schrupp weiter ausführt, dass die Unterscheidungen zwischen Laien und Laiinnen, die als Gläubige aktiv in der Kirche oder ihrer Religionsgemeinschaft sind und dies über soziale Medien öffentlich machen und gegebenenfalls auch kommentieren oder entsprechend bloggen, und den Pfarrerinnen und Pfarrern sich relativiert.[32] Gleichzeitig ist es auch wichtig darauf hinzuweisen, dass gerade die sozialen Medien und ihre Strukturen nicht neutral sind, sondern über bestimmte Algorithmen etc. Meinungsbildung beeinflussen können und dass hierbei auch ökonomische Interessen eine wichtige Rolle spielen.

Wie kirchlicherseits auf die neuen Medien und die Reformation Bezug genommen wird, und welches Medienverständnis von Religionsvertreterinnen und -vertretern dabei zugrunde liegt, wird deutlich, wenn im protestantischen Bereich immer wieder auf die Bedeutung der damals neuen Medien, wie der

---

Rudolf Englert et al. (Hg.), *Gott googeln? Multimedia und Religion* (Neukirchner: Neukirchen-Vluyn 2012), Jahrbuch Religionspädagogik [JRP] 28,19-22, hier 20.

[31] Antje Schrupp, "Inside – aus der Perspektive einer Bloggerin und evangelischen Publizistin. Erfahrungen, Analysen, Konzepte für die Zukunft", in: Ilona Nord / Swantje Luthe (Hg.), *Social Media, christliche Religiosität und Kirche. Studien zur Praktischen Theologie mit religionspädagogischem Schwerpunkt* (Garamond: Jena 2014), Reihe Populäre Kultur und Theologie 14, 431-440, hier 433.

[32] Vgl. dazu auch: Christina Ernst, "Bekenntnisformen im Social Web. Kommunikationen des Glaubens in neuen Formaten, die Tradition haben", in: Ilona Nord / Swantje Luthe (Hg.), *Social Media, christliche Religiosität und Kirche. Studien zur Praktischen Theologie mit religionspädagogischem Schwerpunkt* (Garamond: Jena 2014), Reihe Populäre Kultur und Theologie 14, 143-162, hier 150-155.

Gutenberg-Presse, für die Ausbreitung der Reformation verwiesen wird.[33] Daraus kann abgeleitet werden, dass die evangelische Kirche zur Verbreitung ihrer Botschaft die neuen Medien nutzen kann und sollte. Inhaltlich wird dabei auf das Selbstverständnis der Bedeutung des Priestertums aller Gläubigen verwiesen. Dieses relativ anti-hierarchische Denken bezüglich der Strukturierung von Autorität im religiösen Kontext wird dann genutzt, um wiederum Parallelen zu den sozialen Medien zu ziehen. In den Dokumenten der EKD-Synode "Kundgebung: Kommunikation des Evangeliums" vom 9.-12.11.2014, heißt es: "Die Reformation hat dem Priestertum aller Getauften und dem partizipativen Charakter des Evangeliums besonderen Ausdruck verliehen. Heute bietet das Kommunikationsmodell des Netzwerkes hierfür eine neue Realisierungsmöglichkeit."[34] Das kann durchaus als exemplarisch für die Argumentationslinien in der protestantischen Kirche gesehen werden. Es zeigt sich, dass das Reformationsgeschehen als Chiffre genutzt wird, zur Ausprägung der eigenen Identität, die wiederum dann zur Interpretation gegenwärtiger Geschehnisse dient. Die sozialen Medien werden in diesem Papier vor allen Dingen als Kommunikationsräume aufgefasst, in denen auch die Kommunikation des Evangeliums stattfinden kann und soll, wobei durchaus darauf hingewiesen wird, dass dies in einem neuen Sinne ein partizipativer Prozess aller Beteiligten ist. Offen bleibt, wie genau diese neue Kommunikation beschrieben werden kann, und wie diese wiederum Auswirkungen auf das Selbstverständnis und religiöse Identitäten hat.

Blickt man auf empirische Befunde zur Beschreibung des Phänomens der *digital religion*, gemeint sind hier dezidiert religiösen Äußerungen, Webseiten und Online-Beiträgen, die von Seiten soziologischer beziehungsweise religions- und kommunikationswissenschaftlicher Analysen in dem Bereich der *Religion and Media Studies* vorgenommen wurden, werden als Veränderungen, die religiöse Identitäten durch das Netz erfahren, vor allem genannt: *authority, authenticity, agency*.[35]

---

[33] Exemplarisch: Richard Janus, "Vom Apophtegma zum Tweet. Minimalisierung als emergente Identitäts- und Weltkonstruktion", in: Ilona Nord / Swantje Luthe (Hg.), *Social Media, christliche Religiosität und Kirche. Studien zur Praktischen Theologie mit religionspädagogischem Schwerpunkt* (Garamond: Jena 2014), Reihe Populäre Kultur und Theologie 14, 195-207, hier 195.

[34] Evangelische Kirche in Deutschland, *Kundgebung der 11. Synode der Ev. Kirche in Deutschland auf ihrer 7. Tagung zur Kommunikation des Evangeliums in der digitalen Gesellschaft. Wahrnehmungen und Folgerungen.* (https://www.ekd.de/download/s14_iv_4_kundgebung_ schwerpunktthema(1).pdf, 2 Oktober 2016)

[35] Mary E. Hess, "Digital storytelling. Empowering feminist and womanist faith formation with young women," in: Mia Lövheim (Hg.), *Media, Religion and Gender. Key issues and new challenges* (Routledge: London 2013) 169-182, hier 170.

Man betont, dass religiöse Identität nicht mehr allein in und mit Hilfe von religiösen Institutionen wie Kirchen, Synagogen oder Moscheen gestiftet wird, sondern dass das Netz bezüglich religiöser Identitätsausbildung auch Unterstützung beziehungsweise Orientierung bietet. Das Phänomen, dass religiöse Aussagen und Aktivitäten, sowohl von Laien und Laiinen als auch vom Klerus zur Inspiration dienen und zu religiöser Identitätsbildung führen, wird in den genannten Untersuchungen unter dem Stichwort *religious authority* bearbeitet.[36] Mit Stewart Hoover ist darauf hinzuweisen, dass es jenseits von Max Webers Analyse von Autorität, der diese erstens im rechtlichen System verankert sieht, zweitens in der Tradition beziehungsweise traditionellen Institutionen und drittens im Charisma einer Person, um Konsensfragen geht. "In modern times, a dimension of Weber's theory that he touches on but does not emphasize now deserves more attention: the role of consent in the establishment and maintenance of systems of authority."[37] Hinsichtlich der Beantwortung der Frage nach der Schaffung von religiöser Autorität im Netz, werden drei parallele Entwicklungen gesehen: Erstens zeigt sich mit der Kritik an Autoritäten und dem Versuch, neue religiöse Autoritäten online zu entwickeln eine disruptive Entwicklung, die die bestehenden Autoritäten unterlaufen kann oder will.[38] Zweitens hat sich bezüglich traditioneller religiöser Institutionen und Amtsträger und Amtsträgerinnen gezeigt, dass diese Soziale Medien zur Unterstützung ihrer religiösen Autorität nutzen. Dies kann als komplementäre Entwicklung bezeichnet werden, die Synergien fördert.[39] Drittens kann von einer neuen Form von religiöser Autorität gesprochen werden, die sich zwar einerseits im religiösen Traditionsgut verankert, dieses jedoch in persönlicher Weise neu für sich interpretiert und für eine breitere Öffentlichkeit zugänglich macht und ihre Autorität nicht aus der Institution der Religionsgemeinschaft ableitet, sondern aufgrund der Kompetenzen und auch der Authentizität, die

---

[36] Zum Beispiel in: Stewart M. Hoover (Hg.), *The Media and Religious Authority* (Penn State University: University Park 2016), und Heidi A. Campbell (Hg.), *Digital Religion. Understanding religious practice in new media worlds* (Routledge: New York 2013), und Heidi A. Campbell, *When Religion meets New Media* (Routledge: New York 2010).
[37] Stewart M. Hoover, "Religious Authority in the Media Age," in: Ders. (Hg.), *The Media and Religious Authority* (Penn State University: University Park 2016) 15-36, hier 21.
[38] Pauline Hope Cheong, "Authority", in: Heidi A. Campbell (Hg.), *Digital Religion. Understanding Religious Practice in New Media Worlds*, (Routledge: London and New York 2013), 72-87.
[39] Pauline Hope Cheong, "Tweet the Message? Religious Authority and Social Media Innovation", in: *Journal of Religion, Media and Digital Culture* 3, 3 (2014), 1-19 (http://jrmdc.com/papers-archive/volume-3-issue-3-december-2014/, 1 Oktober 2016), hier 4.

den jeweiligen Personen zugerechnet werden. Dass die Trennlinien zwischen diesen drei Entwicklungen nicht scharf zu ziehen sind, zeigt sich darin, dass teilweise in den jeweiligen religiösen Traditionen entsprechende kommunikative Strukturen schon vorliegen können.[40] Dabei ist diese Beschreibung noch nicht unter ethischen Gesichtspunkten geschehen, denn so kann es über den Aufbau von religiöser Autorität auch zu missbräuchlichen Abhängigkeitsbeziehungen bzw. zum Aufruf von Gewalttaten kommen.[41]

Betrachtet man insbesondere die soziologischen Untersuchungen, die selbst auch empirische Studien aus verschiedenen Religionen umfassen, so lässt sich zusammenfassend konstatieren, dass religiöse Autorität viel stärker als in vergangenen Zeiten Interaktionscharakter hat. Mit Stewart Hoover kann religiöse Autorität beschrieben werden als "fluid and elastic."[42] Gerade unter Gendergesichtspunkten ist diese fließende Situation von Interesse, weil sie überkommene Strukturen aufweichen kann. Betrachtet man *digital religion* unter Gendergesichtspunkten so zeigen Untersuchungen, dass Frauen neue Medien gerne nutzen, um darin ihren Ansichten und Meinungen Ausdruck zu geben, insbesondere, wenn der Zugang zu traditionellen Medien für sie eher schwer beziehungsweise verwehrt ist.[43]

Herausforderungen angesichts der reformatorischen Erkenntnisse im Zeitalter der Digitalisierung – oder was aus der Reformation gelernt werden kann
Dass "das Reformatorische eine dynamische Größe"[44] ist, wird auch im Gedenken an das Reformationsgeschehen und die durch die Jahrhunderte

---

[40] Lynn Schofield Clark, "Afterword: The Media and Religious Authority," in: Stewart M. Hoover (Hg.), *The Media and Religious Authority*, (Penn State University: University Park 2016), 253-268, hier 262.
[41] Beispielsweise weist Abdel Bari Atwan auf die Bedeutung der Digitalisierung und der Sozialen Medien für den Aufbau des Islamischen Staates und eines "Jihad-Netzwerkes" hin, vgl.: "In the past, the leadership would produce and release material; now, every jihadist is his or her own media outlet, reporting live from the frontline in tweets, offering enticing visions of domestic bliss via short films..., posting links to the group's propaganda materials... All of this output is systematically retweeted and, by clever use of hashtags, generates a huge audience." Abdel Bari Atwan, *Islamic State. The Digital Caliphate* (Saqi Books: Chatham 2015), 3.
[42] Hoover, "Religious Authority in the Media Age," 32.
[43] Mia Lövheim, "Media, religion and gender. Key insights and future challenges," in: Dies. (Hg.), *Media, Religion and Gender. Key issues and new challenges* (Routledge: New York 2013), 183-195, hier 185.
[44] Körtner, *Reformatorische Theologie*, 79.

verschiedenen Interpretationen deutlich. Dies hat Auswirkungen auf die Beantwortung der Frage hat, wie Religion vermittelt wird und wie sich religiöse Selbstverständnisse entwickeln. Aus einer protestantischen Perspektive ergeben sich drei Potenziale dessen, was diesbezüglich aus der Reformation gelernt werden kann, und wo neue Lernprozesse initiiert werden sollten.

Freiheit, Religiöse Autoritäten und Gender angesichts multipler Öffentlichkeiten – das emanzipatorische Potenzial
Digitalisierung birgt die Möglichkeit, dass sich religiöse Autorität auch jenseits institutionalisierter Formen von Religion – wie Kirche, Moscheen, Synagogen oder Dachverbänden von Religionen – entwickelt. Dabei zeigt sich, dass diese nicht einen Angriff auf traditionelle religiöse Institutionen darstellen müssen, sondern komplementär gedacht und partizipativ gestaltet werden können. Es kann zurzeit nicht genau gesagt werden, welchen Anteil Frauen oder Männer im Aufbau religiöser Autorität beitragen und wie die entsprechenden Frauen- und Männerbilder im Kontext von *religious authority* gestaltet werden. Hier besteht noch Forschungsbedarf. Ausgehend von den Untersuchungen zur Veränderung des Öffentlichkeitsverständnisses zeigt sich jedoch, dass sich im Netz Genderstereotype reproduzieren und dass verschärft gegen Genderthemen vorgegangen wird. Andererseits werden gerade für neue Bilder und Rollenverständnisse von männlich und weiblich und darüber hinaus Freiräume geboten. Die mit dem Internet verbundene Relativierung der Sphären von Öffentlichkeit und Privatheit trägt auch zu "neuen Konfigurationen im Geschlechterverhältnis"[45] bei. Ambivalenzen hinsichtlich des Umgangs mit Frauen- und Männerrollen werden sichtbar, was auch seinen Niederschlag bei religiösen Autoritäten findet.[46]

Es ergibt sich ein Freiheitsverständnis, dass Freiheit nicht mit einem *anything goes* gleichsetzt, sondern relational zu verstehen ist. Freiheit ist aus theologischer Perspektive immer eine gebundene Freiheit: "Freiheit resultiert aus der Wahrheit, welche die christliche Religion zu behaupten beansprucht. Sie ist

---

[45] Brigitte Aulenbacher / Michael Meuser / Birgit Riegraf, "Hegemonie und Subversion. Zur Pluralisierung hegemonialer Verhältnisse im Verhältnis zu Öffentlichkeit und Privatheit," in: Birgit Riegraf et al. (Hg.), *Geschlechterverhältnisse und neue Öffentlichkeiten. Feministische Perspektiven* (Westfälisches Dampfboot: Münster 2013), 18-36, hier 23.
[46] Vgl. die Analyse zum Männlichkeitsideal US-amerikanischer Evangelikaler und dessen politischer Dimension in: Kristin du Mez, "Donald Trump and Militant Evangelical Masculinity," in: *Religion and Politics*, 17th Jan 2017 (http://religionandpolitics.org/2017/01/17/donald-trump-and-militant-evangelical-masculinity/, 1 Februar 2017).

deshalb das Ziel, um das es im Gebrauch von Macht in erster Linie gehen soll und insofern auch das Kriterium, an dem sich jeder Gebrauch von Macht kritisch prüfen lassen muss."[47] Das emanzipatorische Potenzial dieses qualitativen Freiheitsbegriffs liegt gerade darin, dass Freiheit zu einem verantwortlichen Umgang mit den Möglichkeiten, die das Netz bietet, führen sollte. Hinsichtlich der Pluralität der Meinungen, ergibt sich aus dem emanzipatorischen Potenzial reformatorischen Denkens ein kritisches Hinterfragen der Meinungsbildungen im Netz sowie des Phänomens der *religious authority*. Dabei gilt es nicht nur die Autorität, die sich aus der Anzahl der *follower*, der Aufrufe, den *likes* oder auch dem Weiterleiten der Informationen und den *re-tweets* ableitet, kritisch zu betrachten. Es gilt auch die mit dieser Autorität verknüpften Inhalte zu analysieren sowie den damit verbundenen Machtanspruch. Mit Tillich und seinem protestantischen Prinzip ist es unverzichtbar, religiösen Autoritäten im Netz gegenüber kritisch zu sein, indem diese auf ihre Ausrichtung, ihre Orientierung am Nächsten, ihren Wahrheitsgehalt und ihre Gerechtigkeitsvorstellungen hin befragt werden. Jenseits der soziologischen Untersuchungen hinterfragt eine theologisch-protestantische Perspektive nicht nur das inhaltliche Verständnis von religiöser Autorität. Es steht in Zweifel, ob sich *religious authority* überhaupt diese Autorität anmaßen sollte – oder ob nicht besser von einem religiösen Selbstverständnis, das sich in kommunikativer Freiheit entwickelt und öffentlich auswirkt, ausgegangen werden sollte.

Freiheit als Aufgabe – das gestalterische Potenzial angesichts technischer und ökonomischer Herausforderungen
Das reformatorische Denken in Paradoxien erweitert die Perspektive, wie Wirklichkeit wahrgenommen werden kann. Digitalisierung kann eine plurale Weltsicht unterstützen. Gleichzeitig kann Digitalisierung aber auch dazu führen, dass aufgrund von einer "Filterbubble"[48] nur noch eine eingeschränkte Perspektive einer bestimmten Weltsicht das Verständnis prägt. Öffentlichkeit verliert ihren den pluralen Charakter. Sie wird eine eingeschränkte Öffentlichkeit.

---

[47] Hans-Peter Großhans, "Die Wahrheit wird euch frei machen. Zum Verhältnis von Religion, Wahrheit und Macht," in: *Zeitschrift für Theologie und Kirche* [ZThK] 104 (2007), 336-356, hier 349.
[48] Eli Pariser, *Filter Bubble. Wie wir im Internet entmündigt werden* (Carl Hanser Verlag: München 2012).

Digitalisierung fordert dazu heraus, mit Paradoxien gestaltend umgehen zu können. Im Gegensatz zur Freiheitsvorstellung der ersten Internetaktivisten wie Barlow, die von einem gesetzesfreien und sich selbst regulierenden Internet ausgegangen sind, braucht auch die Digitalisierung gestalterische Maßnahmen. Aus reformatorischer Perspektive weist Luther mit seiner Vorstellung des Menschen als sündig und gerechtfertigt zugleich auf die Bedeutung von Gestaltung hin, nicht nur im individuellen, sondern auch im politischen Bereich – um des Nächsten Willen. In den Blick zu nehmen sind dabei jedoch nicht allein gesetzliche Vorgaben oder auch Verhaltensorientierungen, sondern auch die technischen Dimensionen des Internets.

Neue Medien stellen tatsächlich neue Kommunikationsräume für Religion dar. Spezifisch christlich gedacht, sei auf die neuen Möglichkeiten der Verkündigung des Evangeliums verwiesen. Darüberhinausgehend gilt es jedoch die sozialen Medien auch als neue Lebensräume zu verstehen, da sich jenseits der reinen Kommunikation Leben und Handeln der Menschen nicht mehr von den digitalen Technologien trennen lässt. Dies führt dazu, dass die Strukturierungen, die Technik vorgibt, bei der Frage, wie sich kollektive Identitäten gestalten und was dies für religiöse Autorität bedeutet, mit zu bedenken sind. Diese implizite Normativität, die sich in der Art und Weise zeigt, wie beispielsweise Internetplattformen gestaltet oder Algorithmen entsprechend programmiert sind, gilt es bei den Analysen von dem Verhältnis von Religion und neuen Medien zu bedenken.

I believe we need to understand much more about the intertwined relations of algorithmic and commercial authority with other societal forms of authority. Otherwise, it is possible that all religious authority will be rendered either useful and usable by, or largely irrelevant to, larger systems of governance and power.[49]

Das heißt, dass Technik nicht als neutrales Instrumentarium verstanden werden sollte, sondern auf seine Machtmöglichkeiten hin untersucht werden muss. Hier kann noch einmal auf Tillichs Verständnis des protestantischen Prinzips Bezug genommen werden, das gerade hinsichtlich Machtstrukturen kritisches Hinterfragen nach deren Wert für das menschliche Miteinander einfordert. Dies ist auch unter Gendergesichtspunkten zu vollziehen, um so ungerechte Differenzen und gruppenspezifische Diskriminierungen aufdecken zu können

---

[49] Clark, "Afterword", 265.

und gestalterisch auf entsprechend gendergerechte technische Strukturierungen und Programmierungen einzuwirken.

Plurale und interreligiöse Kontexte – und das transgressive Potenzial
Über das Reformationsgeschehen hinausgehend hat sich in den Überlegungen zu Digitalisierung und *religious authority* gezeigt, dass sich die verschiedenen Phänomene religiöser Autorität und die damit verbundenen Selbstinterpretationen einer Religion in einem religiös pluralen Umfeld vollziehen. Hierbei gilt es, die reformatorischem Denkimpulse über ihren eigentlichen christlichen Kontext hinaus, weiter zu denken. Unter dem Stichwort transgressives Potenzial kann beschrieben werden, was jenseits von reformatorischen Kontexten ein protestantisches Prinzip im Tillich'schen Sinne einfordert. Jenseits der Unterschiede in den Religionen kann es strukturelle Gemeinsamkeiten geben, die sich darin zeigen, wie sich religiöse Autorität gestaltet und entwickelt. Vor dem Hintergrund dieser Gemeinsamkeiten kann es zu einer interreligiösen Analyse kommen, die Kriterien für eine Selbstinterpretation im interreligiösen Kontext[50] entwickelt. Ein solches Vorgehen ist anzuregen, weil damit versucht werden kann, religiöse Glaubenshorizonte und theologische Analysen in ein kritisches Gespräch zu bringen, um die Chancen und Grenzen einer gemeinsamen Kriteriologie auszuloten, die dann eventuell auch für Fragen nach säkularen Autoritäten im Internet interessant sein könnte. Um hierbei interreligiös weiter voranschreiten zu können, bedarf es unter anderem der Berücksichtigung zweier Aspekte:

> Neben der Frage, wie die christlich orientierten religiösen Autoritäten im Internet in Beziehung zu setzen sind zur verfassten Kirche und ob überhaupt von protestantischer Perspektive aus von religiöser Autorität gesprochen werden kann, ergibt sich eine erste ekklesiologische Fragestellung, die das "Fremde im Vertrauten"[51] theologisch verankert sein lässt beziehungsweise interreligiös kompatibel ist und noch darüber hinausgeht.

Zweitens geht es um die theologischen und methodologischen Fragen, wie es zu Kriterien der Selbstinterpretation, dem Ausweis religiöser Identität und damit der Wirkung religiöser Autorität kommen kann und wie diese unter

---

[50] Christian Danz, *Einführung in die Theologie der Religionen* (LIT: Wien 2005), Lehr- und Studienbücher zur Theologie 1.
[51] Thomas Wabel, *Die nahe ferne Kirche. Studien zu einer protestantischen Ekklesiologie in kulturhermeneutischer Perspektive* (Mohr Siebeck: Tübingen 2010).

Gendergesichtspunkten aussehen sollten. Zur Vertiefung dieses Aspekts sei methodologisch auf Vorgehensweisen der *comparative religious ethics* verwiesen.[52] Es wird von der Vorstellung ausgegangen, dass ein *shared moral space* vorliegt, der unterschiedliche Weltanschauungen und religiöse Perspektiven umfasst. Ein interreligiöses Vergleichen und die Verständigung angesichts einer theologisch-ethischen Fragestellung, wie hier die Bedeutung von religiöser Autorität in Bezug auf Freiheit und Paradoxien, verhilft dann dazu, "'analogical insight in translation'"[53] zu gewinnen und so zu gemeinsamen Erkenntnissen im Blick auf Unterschiede und Gemeinsamkeiten zu kommen.

Aus der Reformation zu lernen ist vielseitiger Prozess, der in Aufnahme von Vorstellungen wie der bedingten Freiheit und dem Denken in Paradoxien auch für die Frage nach Möglichkeiten und Grenzen von *religious authority* im Internet von Interesse ist. Unter Gendergesichtspunkten zeigt sich, dass die Potenziale reformatorischen Denkens insbesondere hinsichtlich des emanzipatorisch-kritischen Faktors hilfreich sind, weil sie Abhängigkeiten und Machtstrukturen aufdecken helfen. Gleichzeitig zeigt sich bei Themen von Religion, Gender und Digitalisierung ein Forschungsbedarf.[54]

Gotlind Ulshöfer seit Februar 2016 DFG-Heisenberg-Stipendiatin; 2013 Habilitation, Ev.-theol. Fakultät der Universität Tübingen; 2012/2013 Vertretung des Lehrstuhls für Systematische Theologie, Universität Bamberg. 2009 Bonhoeffer-Gastdozentin, Union Theological Seminary, New York (USA). 2001- Januar 2016 Studienleiterin, Evangelische Akademie Frankfurt. Studium der ev. Theologie und Volkswirtschaftslehre an den Universitäten Tübingen, Heidelberg, Princeton Theological Seminary und der Hebräischen Universität Jerusalem.

---

[52] Zur Einführung: Elizabeth M. Bucar / Aaron Stalnaker, "Introduction. The third wave of comparative religious ethics," in: Dies. (Hg.), *Religious Ethics in a Time of Globalism. Shaping a Third Wave of Comparative Analysis* (Palgrave Macmillan: New York 2012).

[53] Michael Jon Kessler, «Differences, Resemblance, Dialogue. Some Goals for Comparative Political Theology in a Plural Age," in: Ders. (Hg.), *Political Theology for a Plural Age* (Oxford University Press online: Oxford 2013) 1-37. (Published to Oxford Scholarship Online: September 2013 DOI: 10.1093/acprof:oso/9780199769285.001.0001, 5 September 2016), hier 18, William Schweiker zitierend.

[54] Der Aufsatz ist im Rahmen der DFG-Heisenberg-Förderung (UL 191/4-1) entstanden. Der Dank geht an die Herausgeberinnen für Hinweise zur Überarbeitung.

Ninna Edgardh

Embracing the Future: The Church of Sweden in Continuous Reformation

The whole world followed the events in Lund, Sweden, on October 31, 2016, when for the first time a joint ecumenical commemoration of the Reformation took place between the Lutheran World Federation (LWF) and the Roman-Catholic Church. A photo distributed worldwide shows Pope Francis and the Archbishop of the Church of Sweden, Antje Jackelén, embracing each other. The photo contains both hope and tension. The Church of Sweden tries to balance the tension between its heritage as ecumenical bridge-builder, launched already by Archbishop Nathan Söderblom a hundred years ago, and its pioneering role with regard to issues of gender and sexuality. These seemingly contradictory roles are hereby set into the wider context of the journey Sweden has made from the time of the Lutheran reformation up to the present. A uniform society characterised by one people and one Christian faith, has gradually transformed into a society where faith is a voluntary option. The former state church faces new demands in handling religious as well as cultural diversities. Leadership is increasingly equally shared between women and men. The Church of Sweden holds all these tensions together through the approach launched on the official website of a church in constant need of reform.

Por primera vez la Federación Luterana Mundial y la Iglesia Católica Romana celebraron conjuntamente una conmemoración ecuménica de la Reforma un hecho que ocurrió en Lund, Suecia, el 31 de octubre de 2016 y que fue ampliamente difundido por el mundo, a través de una fotografía distribuida globalmente donde aparecen abrazándose el Papa Francisco de la Iglesia Católica y la arzobispa Antje Jackelén de la iglesia de Suecia, reflejando esperanza y tensión a la vez. La iglesia de Suecia intenta encontrar un equilibrio entre una tradición ecuménica de diálogo – inaugurada hace un siglo por el arzobispo Nathan Söderblom – y su papel pionero en cuestiones de género y sexualidad. En el artículo se desprende que estos roles, aparentemente contradictorios, están presentes en el contexto más amplio de la transformación que ha hecho Suecia desde la Reforma hasta hoy. Cómo cambia la sociedad sueca, desde ser una sociedad uniforme, con una población homogénea en una sola fe cristiana hasta convertirse en una cuestión de opción voluntaria el ser creyente. Esta situación plantea nuevas exigencias a quien fue anteriormente la religión oficial del estado, ya que debe adaptarse tanto a la diversidad religiosa

Ninna Edgardh
Embracing the Future: The Church of Sweden in Continuous Reformation

como cultural. Respecto a las construcciones en las relaciones de género, el liderazgo es compartido entre hombres y mujeres. Para visibilizar los avances en estos temas sociales es que en su sitio web la iglesia de Suecia presenta un enfoque de estar continuamente en Reforma.

Auf der ganzen Welt hat man die Ereignisse am 31. Oktober 2016 im schwedischen Lund verfolgt, als zum ersten Mal in ökumenischer Gemeinschaft an die Reformation erinnert in einer Veranstaltung worden ist, die vom Lutherischen Weltbund und der römisch-katholischen Kirche getragen wurde. Das Foto, auf dem sich Papst Franziskus und die Erzbischöfin der Kirche von Schweden, Antje Jackelén, umarmen, ist um die ganze Welt gegangen. Es zeigt sowohl Hoffnung als auch Spannung. Die Kirche von Schweden versucht, eine Balance zu finden zwischen ihrer Herkunft als ökumenische Brückenbauerin – eine Rolle, die schon Erzbischof Nathan Söderblom vor 100 Jahren für seine Kirche gesehen hat, und ihrer Vorreiterrolle im Blick auf Fragen von Gender und Sexualität. In dem Artikel werden die scheinbar gegensätzlichen Pole in einen größeren Zusammenhang gestellt, der den Weg beschreibt, den die Kirche von Schweden von der lutherischen Reformation bis in die Gegenwart gegangen ist. Eine einstmals einheitliche Gesellschaft, charakterisiert durch ein Volk und einen christlichen Glauben, hat sich sukzessive zu einer Gesellschaft hin entwickelt, in der Glaube eine freiwillige Option darstellt. Die ehemalige Staatskirche ist mit neuen Herausforderungen konfrontiert sowohl im Blick auf religiöse als auch auf kulturelle Diversitäten. Leitung wird mehr und mehr zu gleichen Teilen von Frauen und Männern geteilt. Die Kirche von Schweden hält diese unterschiedlichen Spannungen zusammen durch den Ansatz, der auf für das Selbstverständnis der Kirche grundlegend ist: Kirche zu sein, die ständig Reform braucht.

The whole world followed the events in Lund, Sweden, on October 31, 2016, when for the first time a joint ecumenical commemoration of the Reformation took place between the Lutheran World Federation (LWF) and the Roman-Catholic Church. The chair of the LWF, the Palestinian bishop Munib Yunan, the LWF General Secretary, Martin Junge, and the head of the Roman-Catholic Church, Pope Francis led the service together. The aim was to highlight the ecumenical developments between Catholics and Lutherans during the last 50 years, including the joint declaration on the doctrine of justification from 1999.[1]

This starting point for this article is one of the photos taken at the liturgy and distributed worldwide, showing Pope Francis and the Archbishop of the Church of Sweden, Antje Jackelén, embracing each other. Jackelén was the local host for the event together with the Roman-Catholic bishop for Sweden,

---

[1] https://www.lutheranworld.org/lund2016, 5 November 2016.

Anders Arborelius. Antje Jackelén visited Pope Francis in Rome already in May 2015, less than a year after she was installed as Archbishop. Being of German origin, and the first woman in her office, her encounter with Jorge Bergoglio, the first Jesuit pope and the first to come from the Southern hemisphere, raised a lot of attention and had a deep ecumenical significance, which in a way was fulfilled by the meeting in Lund 2016.

The ecumenical role of the Church of Sweden is multifaceted. A photo of a male Roman-Catholic Pope and a female Lutheran Archbishop embracing each other contains many levels of both tensions and promises. Can the two church leaders be actually seen as embracing the future together?

The aim of the current article is to sketch a background to the event from a Swedish Lutheran perspective, with a special focus on how the Church of Sweden handles the tension between its ecumenical commitment and its radical attitude with regard to gender and sexuality.

Bridge-builder
The Church of Sweden has led a tradition of ecumenical bridge-building during the 20th century.[2] The role dates back to a meeting in Stockholm 1925, initiated by Archbishop Nathan Söderblom. The meeting became the starting point for the Life and Work movement, which came to be an important part of the creation of the World Council of Churches (WCC) in 1948. At the time of the Stockholm meeting, ecumenism was embryonic and the meeting had been a unique effort to build bridges across divides of previous condemnations and bans. One important actor was missing though. In an often-quoted sermon given at the end of the meeting, Archbishop Söderblom addressed the absence of the Roman Catholic Church at the gathering, talking about the apostle Peter being late and of Christianity thus still being sundered, against the will of Christ.[3]

In Lund 2016, the belated Petrine ministry "was" present, with Pope Francis talking respectfully about Martin Luther and the Reformation in a joint act of commemoration with the Lutheran World Federation. The embrace between the Pope and the Archbishop was thus a longed-for symbol, surely wholehearted and filled with joy from both sides. Still, the divisions were far from finally bridged. Rome does still not welcome Lutherans to the Eucharistic table, and does not formally accept the ministry of Lutheran priests, male or

---
[2] Björn Ryman, *Brobyggarkyrkan: Svenska kyrkans engagemang i utrikesfrågor* [Bridge-builder: Church of Sweden's Engagement in Foreign Affairs] (Artos: Skellefteå 2010).
[3] Jonas Jonson, *Nathan Söderblom: Called to Serve* (Eerdmans: Grand Rapids, MI 2016), 373.

female. The embrace in Lund was probably as far as Pope Francis was able to reach. He was highly praised in media before and after the event. At the same time, the Roman-Catholic Church has also suffered severe critique concerning the exclusion of women from the ordained ministry, its hostility towards same-sex relations, and its failure to deal properly with sexual assaults committed by clergy.

The Church of Sweden has today an equal share of male and female priests. It has an officially adopted policy on gender equality.[4] The directives for a revision of the worship manual from 1986 include instructions for using inclusive language.[5] In 2009, The Church decided to adapt to the new civil law on gender neutral marriages and use the same wedding ritual for all, irrespective of gender.[6] At the time of writing this article, the Church's official website illustrates its general information about wedding ceremonies with a photo of two women getting married, and the text welcomes "all" to have their wedding in the church.[7]

All of these steps place the Church of Sweden in a pioneering and controversial role with regard to gender and sexuality. The largest church in the LWF, the Ethiopian Mekane Yesus Church, decided in 2013 to break its ties with both the Evangelical Lutheran Church in America (ELCA) and the Church of Sweden, because of their positive attitudes towards same-sex relations.[8] The Russian Orthodox Church had demonstrated its dislike of the blessing of same-sex relations in the Church of Sweden already in 2005.[9]

---

[4] Anders Bäckström, Ninna Edgardh and Per Pettersson, *Religious Change in Northern Europe: The Case of Sweden. From State Church to Free Folk Church. Final Report* (Verbum: Stockholm 2004), 150.

[5] "Fortsatt arbete med översyn av Den svenska kyrkohandboken. Direktiv beslutade av Kyrkostyrelsen den 19 april 2006". (https://www.svenskakyrkan.se/kyrkohandbboken/dokumenten, 6 November 2016).

[6] The new gender neutral wedding liturgy is part of a proposed new worship manual, but is already in effect with the help of an amendment to the manual from 1986, still in use. See www.svenskakyrkan.se/handboken, 5 November 2016. For a more comprehensive information with translations into several languages, see https://www.svenskakyrkan.se/samkonade-aktenskap, 5 November 2016.

[7] https://www.svenskakyrkan.se/vigsel, 4 November 2016.

[8] https://www1.svenskakyrkan.se/983098, 5 November 2016; Katherine Weber, "Ethiopian Church Severs Ties with Lutherans over Homosexuality," in: The Christian Post, 8 February 2013. (http://www.christianpost.com/news/ethiopian-church-severs-ties-with-lutherans-over-homosexuality-89745, 5 November 2016)

[9] http://www.ortodoxkristendom.se/#moskva, 5 November 2016.

Bridges are built, but new cracks appear. Below, the ambiguities in the present ecumenical role of the Church of Sweden shall be set into context, with the help of an overview built on quite a huge amount of research which has been produced in Sweden recently, on Luther, the Reformation, and Lutheran theology. The literature reflects the journey Sweden has made from the time of the Lutheran reformation up to the present, from a society characterised as "one people and one faith" to a society where a variety of faiths are seen as voluntary options.

A Lutheran Church for a Secularised People

Sweden has a double reputation as the most secularised and the most women-friendly country in the world, although both – and the possible relationship between them – may well be contested. The Church of Sweden is the third largest Lutheran Church in the world, with more than 6 million members, representing about 64 percent of the population.[10] However, most of them do not regard themselves as Christians and rarely attend worship.[11]

Up until some fifty years ago, being a Swede was tantamount to being a member of the national church. The Church of Sweden has been separated from the state since the year 2000. However, people tend to stay on as members, even though they do not go to church very often. Swedes are even said to believe in their belonging to the church, rather than in Christian faith.[12] They tend to share the values of the Church, and respect Jesus as a role model, but shy away from the designation "religious" or "Christian". Most Swedes

---

[10] https://www.lutheranworld.org/news/more-74-million-members-lwfs-145-churches, 5 November 2016. A little less than two thirds (63.2 percent) of the Swedish population belong to the Church of Sweden. Nearly half (45.5 percent) of all new-born are baptised. A third (27.8 percent) of the young reaching maturity are confirmed. A third (33.5 percent) of the weddings and three quarters (76.5 percent) of all burials are performed in the Church. Data as of 31 December 2015, at: www.svenskakyrkan.se/statistik, 5 November 2016.

[11] For a thorough discussion of "the Swedish paradox" of a high degree of belonging to the Church vs. low participation in Sunday worship, see Bäckström, Edgardh and Pettersson, *Religious Change*, and Anders Bäckström and Anders Wejryd (eds.), *Sedd men Osedd: Om folkkyrkans paradoxala närvaro inför 2020-talet* (Verbum: Stockholm 2016).

[12] Anders Bäckström, "Believing in belonging: The Swedish way of being religious," in: Riikka and Esko Ryökäs (eds.), *Urban Faith 2000* (University of Helsinki: Helsinki 1993), Publications of Church Sociology, A/8, 31-42. The idea was taken up by the British sociologist of religion, Grace Davie, and integrated in her wider idea on the vicarious role of religion. See Grace Davie, *Religion in Modern Europe. A Memory Mutates* (Oxford University Press: Oxford 2000).

prefer choosing their own blend of Christianity, sometimes with some self-interpreted element of Buddhism attached.[13]

Individual autonomy and self-expression are commonly shared Swedish values.[14] Swedish mentality has even been characterised as a kind of "statist individualism", as the ideal of personal autonomy is combined with a high degree of trust in other people as well as in the public authorities guaranteeing the welfare of citizens in need.[15]

The Church of Sweden still holds a privileged position, but in many respects, it has to compete with other faith communities in attracting the interest of people. Popular faith has been characterised as "light" rather than "hard".[16] It has a great deal to do with belonging not only to the Church, but to the community called Sweden, where Christmas and Easter are celebrated but not necessarily in church, and where the Bible is part of culture but not a book opened very often. The relation of the Swedish people to the Lutheran tradition is deeply enmeshed with these basic traits of late-modern Swedish mentality.

After its separation from the state, the role of the Church of Sweden is still regulated by Swedish law, in which the Church is designated as an Evangelic Lutheran faith community.[17] This is also confirmed in the Church's own constitution.[18] How this confessional character should be interpreted is less clear. In fact, the designation "Lutheran" was not much used until Sweden's confessional unity was beginning to dissolve in the 19th century.[19]

---

[13] David Thurfjell, *Det gudlösa folket. De postkristna svenskarna och religionen* (Molin & Sorgenfrei Akademiska: Stockholm 2015).

[14] Swedish attitudes towards individual autonomy and self-realisation as basic values are clearly shown by the World Values Survey and illustrated in the Cultural map of the world, based on the WVS-data. (http://www.worldvaluessurvey.org/WVSContents.jsp, 5 November 2016)

[15] Henrik Berggren and Lars Trägårdh, *Är svensken människa: Gemenskap och oberoende i det moderna Sverige* (Norstedts: Stockholm 2015), 2nd exp. Ed.

[16] Bäckström and Anders (eds.), *Sedd men Osedd*, 32.

[17] The Church of Sweden Act. § 1. SFS 1998:1591. (http://www.riksdagen.se/sv/dokument-lagar/dokument/svensk-forfattningssamling/lag-19981591-om-svenska-kyrkan_sfs-1998-1591, 5 November 2016)

[18] *Kyrkoordning för Svenska kyrkan*, introduction to the first section. (https://www.svenskakyrkan.se/kyrkoordningen, 5 November 2016)

[19] Lars Eckerdal, "Om Svenska kyrkan som trossamfund. Svenska kyrkans beteckning, bestämning och benämning i svensk lagstiftning," in: *Svensk kyrkohistorisk årsskrift* (1988), 87-106. [English summary: "The 'Church of Sweden' – its designation and definition in Swedish legislation," 99-101]

Ninna Edgardh
Embracing the Future: The Church of Sweden in Continuous Reformation

The systematic-theologian, Professor Thomas Ekstrand, emphasises that there is no common theological understanding of the legal paragraphs dealing with the confessional identity of the Church. Based on a study of contemporary confessional material from the Church, he argues that the meaning of "Evangelic Lutheran" ranges from quite narrow confessional statements to much wider cultural interpretations.[20] Today, the statement that the Church is Lutheran might simply mean that it has a Lutheran heritage. Another cultural interpretation is that the Lutheran tradition serves as the basis for a society that respects the religious maturity of people. Common interpretations of a more confessional kind are that the Church adheres to the idea of justification by faith alone, or that the Lutheran confessions are normative for the interpretation of the gospel. In-between the confessional and the cultural, one finds the idea that "Evangelic Lutheran" primarily means that the Church is constantly in need of reform, according to the principle *"ecclesia semper reformanda"*. This attitude, it shall be argued, dominates the commemoration of Reformation, both at the national level of the Church and as presented on its official website.

The attitude described above is also commonly used to support reforms related to gender and sexuality. The introduction of a gender-neutral wedding liturgy has been less internally controversial in the Church of Sweden than in many other churches, probably because research-based conversations on attitudes towards homosexuality in the Bible and the Christian tradition have been ongoing since the 1970s. Several bishops have taken a radical stance in the discussions, one of them being the bishop of Stockholm, Caroline Krook. In 2004, she was even invited to inaugurate the popular Pride Festival in Stockholm. In one of the major daily newspapers, *Dagens Nyheter*, she had motivated this role with reference to the 16th century Swedish reformer, Olaus Petri, who had served as a preacher himself in the Cathedral in Stockholm. Olaus Petri had been a deacon (at that time, a temporary office before becoming a priest), and as such forbidden to marry. He revolted against what he perceived to be the hypocrisy of celibacy, in light of the common knowledge of the many unrecognised children fathered by priests. When he was wedded to Kristina in 1525 in the Cathedral of Stockholm, he was threatened with excommunication. Bishop Krook sees Olaus Petri as a role model in defending

---

[20] Thomas Ekstrand, "The Construction of Lutheran Identity in Church of Sweden," in: Anne-Louise Eriksson, Göran Gunner and Niclas Blåder (eds.), *Exploring a Heritage: Evangelical Lutheran Churches in the North* (Pickwick: Eugene, Oregon 2012), 249-264, here 262. Church of Sweden Research Series 11.

what he thought was right and the will of God. She ends her article: "You cannot always wait for theological consensus. Then Olaus Petri would never have married, women would never have been pastors, I would not have been a bishop and homosexuals would have to wait forever outside the entrance of the church."[21]

The bishop's phrasing is persuasive and illustrates well how the reformation heritage may be used as an argument for continued reform and readiness to move ahead of other churches in ecumenical terms. This should not be seen as contempt towards ecumenism. Rather, it belongs to the Church's present understanding of itself as prophet and pioneer with regard to gender issues. This role builds on the image of Sweden as a forerunner with regard to gender equality and of the Church as a church of the people. As such, it is influenced not only by theological traditions, but also by values shared by the population at large.

Lutheranism as Obligation

This usage of the Reformation is, however, of quite recent date. A longer Swedish tradition ties Reformation with the creation of Sweden as a nation. Luther's nailing of his theses in Wittenberg in 1517 was not even celebrated in Sweden in 1617. Unlike the rest of Europe, Sweden instead chose to celebrate the centennial of Gustav Vasa's election as "hövitsman" of Dalarna 1621, the starting point for the reforming king in his project of uniting the Swedish nation and defending the country against the Danish king.[22]

Another year for which a centennial could be celebrated would have been 1527, when Gustav Vasa gathered a council in Västerås which gave him the right to confiscate Church property. The Swedish province of the Catholic Church, with Uppsala as its centre, was through this process taken over by the king and the relation to Rome had been broken.

The Uppsala Synod in 1593 confirmed and consolidated the reforms. The Augsburg Confession had been officially adopted, and Lutheran faith had become the only accepted form of faith in the country. Lutheranism became an obligation and Sweden celebrated Gustav Vasa, rather than Luther, as the great reformer, even though his interest in the Church had to do with its properties rather than its faith.

---

[21] Caroline Krook, "Respektfulla samtal krävs om homovigslar," in: DN Debatt, *Dagens Nyheter*, 28 July 2004, 4 (translated into English by the author).

[22] Carl Axel Aurelius, *Luther i Sverige: Den svenska Lutherbilden under fyra sekler* (Artos Norma bokförlag: Skellefteå 2015), 2nd ext. Ed., 22. Forskning för kyrkan 30.

The Religious Utilisation of Luther's ideas

This narrative has given rise to the idea that Luther was never important in Sweden. The argument is however refuted by the Luther researcher, bishop emeritus, Professor Carl Axel Aurelius.[23] Aurelius studied Luther's image and the utilisation of his ideas in Sweden from the 17th to the 20th century, and concluded that Luther's influence has been immense. His works were not read and used in their entire breadth, but the books that were used became highly influential, in various ways in various epochs.

Aurelius specifically mentions three strands of influence. The "table of duties" in the Small Catechism played an immense role in shaping cultural unity during the first centuries of Lutheran confession. Reading and learning the Catechism was obligatory according to the 1686 Church law. The emancipating feature of this part of the Lutheran heritage has to do with the role played by Catechism in teaching the gospel, and thereby teaching both men and women to read. Other parts of Luther's works were influential in the hands of the pietists, in a period when the cultural unity created by reformation was beginning to break up. For the pietists, the focus had been Luther's words concerning personal faith. Finally, Luther's works were highly utilised by revival movements in the 19th century. With the feudal agrarian society dissolved, the "table of duties" had become outdated and Luther had been quoted in advocacy for the freedom of religion against the monopoly of the state Church.[24]

As shown by the late historian Inger Hammar, Swedish feminists in the 19th century used Lutheran theological arguments in favour of the emancipation of women. In opposition to male clergy who argued for a traditional Lutheran-Christian interpretation of the relationship between the sexes, female pioneers had asserted that God had not destined women to subordination.[25]

Luther's ideas have thus been used in Sweden for different purposes in different times, and the image of the reformer has changed accordingly.[26] Today, it may be argued, Luther inspires the Church of Sweden to defend the rights of women and LGBTQ-people against what is perceived as outdated ecclesial traditions based on false biblical interpretations.

---

[23] Ibid.
[24] Ibid., 171.
[25] Inger Hammar, *Emancipation och religion: Den svenska kvinnorörelsens pionjärer i debatt om kvinnans kallelse ca 1860-1900* [Emancipation and religion: the pioneers of the Swedish movement and the debate over a woman's calling c. 1860-1900] (Carlsson: Stockholm 1999).
[26] Aurelius, *Luther i Sverige*, 230.

Luther and the Swedes

Despite all that was said above, Luther is far from being a popular figure among the Swedish population at large. This may be due to the long and close alliance between Church and state, associating Luther with the discipline set by the rulers. "Having Luther on one's shoulder" is an expression still quite frequently used in Sweden to describe an overly strong sense of duty, especially with regard to work.[27] As has been shown by Birgit Stolt, professor emerita of German language, this image of Luther has very little to do with his life or his writings. Stolt, a German immigrant to the country, wrote her thesis on Martin Luther's Table Talks in the 1960s, and found in the texts nothing of the heavy and boring image of Luther she encountered for the first time in Sweden. Quite to the contrary, she found Luther sensitive, tolerant and gentle, points she exemplified by his metaphorical description of God as "changing [our] diapers" in forgiving our sins, and wanting us to "jump and laugh with joy" in response.[28]

Trends in Reformation Research

The books by Aurelius, Hammar and Stolt are only a few examples of a rather impressive amount of research carried out on Luther and the reformation during the last decade, and to a considerable extent, written by women. The body of research mirrors the ongoing change in Swedish society, from Lutheranism as a uniform costume, obligatorily worn by each and every one, to reformation theology acting as a potentially – but not self-evidently – liberating resource that may be interpreted in diverse ways. While earlier research had a confessional character and was primarily built on official textual sources, recent research has widened scope and aim, sources and perspectives, as the following examples shall illustrate.

A project involving a number of researchers from various disciplines highlighted the liberating potentials of Lutheran theology and ethics in a Post-Christian society.[29] Of special interest from a gender perspective is Cecilia

---

[27] Ekstrand, "The Construction of Lutheran Identity," 253.

[28] Birgit Stolt, *Luther själv: Hjärtats och glädjens teologi* (Artos: Skellefteå 2004); Birgit Stolt, *Martin Luther: Människohjärtat och Bibeln* (Artos: Skellefteå 2016).

[29] The project involved researchers from various theological disciplines and resulted in several books: Elisabeth Gerle (ed.), *Luther som utmaning; Om frihet och ansvar* (Verbum: Stockholm: 2008). Forskning för kyrkan 7; Eva-Lotta Grantén, *Utanför paradiset: Arvsyndsläran i nutida luthersk teologi och etik* (Verbum: Stockholm 2013). Forskning för kyrkan 20; Carl-Henric Grenholm, *Tro, moral och uddlös politik: Om luthersk etik* (Verbum: Stockholm 2014). Forskning för

Nahnfeldt's gender sensitive discussion of the Lutheran theology of calling, which she relates to the daily struggle of especially women in contemporary Sweden to put "the puzzle of daily life" together.[30]
Elisabeth Gerle contributes an innovative discussion of Martin Luther's texts in relation to historic and contemporary cultural attitudes towards the body and the senses. She argues that Luther introduced a new anthropology that saw the human being as a unity, in contrast to the mystical medieval tradition. Whereas these practices spiritualised the erotic, Luther reintroduced a positive view of real sexual relations between human beings. Senses and sexuality were not any longer seen as a competition to the love of God. Gerle argues that these resources can be used constructively today, both in relation to ascetic ideals of health and fitness and as a commitment to stand in solidarity with our neighbours.[31]

A large project run by Uppsala University shows the role of Lutheranism in furthering social welfare in Sweden and other Nordic countries. Case studies in eight European countries show the role of the historic churches in the organisation of welfare in Europe. In the final report, Thomas Ekstrand shows how theological factors interact with social and other factors in shaping the sharing of responsibility between Church and state in the Nordic countries. Ninna Edgardh addresses the issues of gender raised in the material and observes surprising similarities across national and confessional borders with regard to the specific role attributed to women concerning care and well-being.[32]

The Church of Sweden research unit has produced a number of volumes on the reformation heritage, both in its international and in its Swedish series.[33]

---

kyrkan 25; Elisabeth Gerle, *Passionate Embrace: Luther on Love, Body and Sensual Presence* (Wipf and Stock: Eugene, Oregon forthcoming) - originally published as *Sinnlighetens närvaro: Luther mellan kroppskult och kroppsförakt* (Verbum: Stockholm 2015). Forskning för kyrkan 28; Karin Johannesson, *Helgelsens filosofi: Om andlig träning i luthersk tradition* (Verbum: Stockholm 2014). Forskning för kyrkan 23; Cecilia,Nahnfeldt, *Luthersk kallelse: Handlingskraft och barmhärtighet* (Verbum: Stockholm 2016). Forskning för kyrkan 31.

[30] Nahnfeldt, *Luthersk kallelse*.
[31] Gerle, *Passionate Embrace*.
[32] Anders Bäckström, Grace Davie, Ninna Edgardh and Per Pettersson (eds.), *Welfare and Religion in 21st Century Europe: Vol 2 Gendered, Religious and Social Change* (Ashgate: Farnham 2011).
[33] Anne-Louise Eriksson, Göran Gunner and Niclas Blåder (eds.), *Exploring a Heritage: Evangelical Lutheran Churches in the North* (Pickwick: Eugene, Oregon 2012). Church of Sweden Research Series 5. This volume, taking a specific interest in the situation of women, depicts how the Lutheran Churches in Denmark, Iceland, Norway, and Sweden have shaped their identity as Lutheran.

In October 2013, it organised an international conference with the aim to constructively contribute to "a Lutheran theology that can be regarded as reasonable in a multicultural society."[34]

Several new books widen the scope from dogmatics to issues of Lutheran spirituality, Lutheran hymns and Lutheran preaching.[35] A recent Nordic project examines the relations between Lutheran traditions and the development of secular law in the Nordic region during the last 500 years.[36]

A book carrying the witty title, *Vid hans sida: Svenska prästfruar under 250 år* [*At His Side: 250 years of Swedish Pastors' Wives*], illustrates the advantages of widening the scope of sources used in research.[37] The abandonment of celibacy in Sweden in 1536 resulted in a completely new role in the parishes, namely that of the pastor's wife. These women often became "mothers" for the parishioners, involved in pastoral as well as health care. With regard to gender, the pastor's wife could be a role model for the parishioners, but she could never formally overtake the role of her husband, due to ecclesial law. Her role was limited and seldom recognised in public.

A type of research which had not been thinkable in a uniform Lutheran era is reformation history, written, as expressed in one of the titles, "from the perspective of the losers."[38] Here, the focus is far from seeking "liberating strands" in Lutheran theology, as in the aforementioned projects, but

---

[34] The conference resulted in two anthologies: Carl-Henric Grenholm and Göran Gunner (eds.), *Lutheran Identity and Political Theology* (Pickwick: Eugene, Oregon 2014), 3. Church of Sweden Research Series 9; Carl-Henric Grenholm and Göran Gunner (eds.), *Justification in a Post-Christian Society* (Pickwick: Eugene, Oregon 2014).

[35] Bengt Hoffman, *Hjärtats teologi: Mystikens plats hos Martin Luther* (Åsak: Delsbo 1989); Margareta Brandby-Cöster, *Att uppfatta allt mänskligt: Underströmmar av luthersk livsförståelse i Selma Lagerlöfs författarskap* (Karlstad University Studies: Karlstad 2001) 23; Henry Cöster, *Livsmodets språk: Förkunnelse och sakrament i en luthersk teologi* (Arcus: Lund 2009); Sven-Åke Selander, "Hjärtats tillit: Trosförmedling i luthersk tradition," in: *Årsbok för Svenskt gudstjänstliv*, 82 (Artos & Norma: Skellefteå 2007); Sven-Åke Selander and Karl-Johan Hansson (eds.), *Martin Luthers psalmer i de nordiska folkens liv* (Arcus: Lund 2008); Tomas Appelqvist, *Bönen i den helige Andes tempel: Människosyn och kyrkosyn i Martin Luthers böneteologi* (Artos: Skellefteå 2009).

[36] The project, titled "Protestant Legacies in Nordic Law: Uses of the Past in the Construction of the Secularity of Law" (ProNoLa) is financed by HERA (Humanities in the European Research Area), and described at http://heranet.info/pronola/index, 5 November 2016.

[37] Ulrika Lagerlöf Nilsson and Birgitta Meurling, *Vid hans sida: Svenska prästfruar under 250 år – ideal och verklighet* (Artos & Norma bokförlag: Skellefteå 2015).

[38] Magnus Nyman, *Förlorarnas historia: Katolskt liv I Sverige från Gustav Vasa till drottning Kristina* (Veritas förlag: Stockholm 2002), 2nd slightly rev. ed.

quite the contrary. In this new strand of research, primarily produced by Roman-Catholic scholars, popular resistance against the 16th century reforms is uncovered and attention is given to what was lost, rather than gained, by the reforms.[39]

The Reformation Year 2017
The Church of Sweden's ambition to combine ecumenical bridge-building on a national level with a pioneering role with regard to issues of gender and sexuality is manifested in various more or less successful ways. On the archbishop's official website, Antje Jackelén is presented as the 70th archbishop in a long line originating from 1164, when the first Church province was established in Sweden with Stefan av Alvastra as its bishop.[40]

A possible interpretation is that the church wishes to underline continuity rather than break, quite in line with the document *From Conflict to Communion*, which laid the basis for the event in Lund.[41] Roman-Catholic scholars in Sweden have however reacted strongly against this historical narrative and accused the Church of Sweden of unjustly claiming continuity with the Catholic tradition in Sweden. Not only had the reformation been a severe break with the Catholic past, according to their view, they also see it as a brutal reform imposed from above against the will of the people.[42]

From the perspective of this article, it seems clear that the Church of Sweden aims to stress continuity, not only with its reformation heritage, but also with a longer tradition of the presence of the Christian Church in what is now called Sweden. This continuity helps to authorise the simultaneous ambition of ecumenical bridge-building and playing a pioneering role with regard to a number of ecumenically sensitive issues. From this perspective, it is quite logical that the Church presents 2017 as "The Reformation Year 2017". The Church does not, according to its website, "celebrate", or even "commemorate" the Reformation,

---

[39] Fredrik Heiding SJ and Magnus Nyman (eds.), *Doften av rykande vekar: Reformationen ur folkets perspektiv* (Artos förlag: Skellefteå 2016).

[40] Antje Jackelén was elected on 15 October 2013 and installed in office on 15 June 2014. (https://www.svenskakyrkan.se/om-arkebiskop-antje-jackelen, 6 November 2016)

[41] *From Conflict to Communion - Including Common Prayer. Lutheran-Catholic Common Commemoration of the Reformation in 2017. Report of the Lutheran-Roman Catholic Commission on Unity* (Evangelische Verlagsanstalt and Paderborn: Bonifatius GmbH Druck – Buch – Verlag: Leipzig 2013).

[42] Anders Piltz and ten other Roman-Catholic scholars, in: *Dagen*, 10 September 2014. (http://www.dagen.se/debatt/svenska-kyrkan-forsoker-ta-monopol-pa-historien-1.92453, 5 November 2016)

but presents it as an ongoing event, which has been in process for 500 years and will continue still. The Church declares it will put extra energy in the course of 2017 into the weaving together of past, present and future.[43]

In a document published on the Church's official website, Professor Cristina Grenholm, in charge of theology and ecumenics at the national Church office, writes that the Christian confession starts not with letters, but with life. A living confession is a prerequisite for a tradition that will not be forgotten, but rather remain important.[44]

That the Church is in need of continuous reform — *semper reformanda* — thus seems to be the dominant paradigm of the Reformation year 2017, at least at the national level of the Church of Sweden. It might fit well with the expectations of those people who "believe in belonging". Parish journeys to Wittenberg in order to walk "in the footsteps of Luther" are popular nowadays.[45] But what "walking in his footsteps" really means is open for interpretation. The photo of Pope Francis and the Archbishop of the Church of Sweden embracing each other may be a sign of a new era of reformed walking together. Roman-Catholics and Lutherans in Sweden might need a longer process of truth and reconciliation in preparation for the walk, negotiating many and contradictory images of short-term and long-term winners and losers, not only with regard to spirituality, but also to gender, sexuality and human dignity.

> **Ninna Edgardh** is professor of ecclesiology, especially diaconal studies, at the Faculty of Theology, Uppsala University. She has published extensively in both Swedish and English in the fields of liturgy, Christian social practice, ecclesiology, and gender. Among her latest publications in English is an article on feminist ecclesiology in Sune Fahlgren and Jonas Ideström (eds.), *Ecclesiology in the Trenches: Theory and Method under Construction* (Pickwick: Eugene, Oregon 2015). She is the chair of The International Society for the Research and Study of Diaconia and Christian Social Practice, and co-editor and co-author of the two volumes of *Welfare and Religion in 21st Century Europe* (Ashgate: Farnham 2010, 2011).

---

[43] https://www.svenskakyrkan.se/reformationsaret2017, November 5 2016 (translated into English by the author)

[44] Cristina Grenholm, "Bekännelsen börjar i livet." (https://www.svenskakyrkan.se/bekannelsen-borjar-i-livet, 6 November 2016)

[45] Göran Agrell and Peter Strömmer, *I Luthers fotspår: En resebiografi* (Cordia: Stockholm 2010).

Thalia Gur-Klein

21st Century Anti-Judaism in Feminist Theology

Dealing with anti-Judaism in feminist theology of the 21st century, this paper rebounds with Katherina von Kellenbach and Fokkelien van Dijk-Hemmes, who had claimed, already 20 years ago, that certain 20th century Feminist theologians show propensities towards anti-Judaism. The rise of feminist and neo-goddess theologies has revolutionised our time. However, these movements have also developed tendencies to identify themselves by foiling on Judaism, the Hebrew God and the Hebrew Bible as the anti-thesis of the neo-pagan goddess and feminism. It is argued that such postulations regress into Anti-Judaism; and that such premises show selective and distorting representations of the Hebrew God, Bible and Judaism. Accordingly, the methodology used relies on an understanding of biblical Hebrew, Jewish sources, warranted biblical research, and emic reading of the original texts.

Untersucht werden anti-jüdische Tendenzen und Auslegungen bei Feministinnen und so genannten Göttinnen-Theologien im 21. Jahrhundert. Katherina von Kellenbach und Fokkelien van Dijk-Hemmes, die schon vor 20 Jahren behauptet hatten, dass gewisse feministische Theologinnen des 20. Jahrhunderts Neigungen zum Anti-Judaismus aufweisen, muss dabei weitgehend zugestimmt werden. Die Zunahme der neofeministischen und so genannten Göttin-Theologien hat unsere Zeit revolutioniert. Dabei entwickelten diese modernen Ansätze jedoch ihre eigene Identität in einem dezidierten Gegensatz zum Judentum. Sie bemühen sich, den hebräischen Gott und die hebräische Bibel als die Anti-These auszulegen. Ich behaupte, dass solche Postulierungen in den altbekannten Anti-Judaismus zurückfallen, und dass solche Prämissen selektive und verzerrende Darstellungen des hebräischen Gottes, der Bibel und des Judentums sind. Dementsprechend wird hier methodologisch dem Verständnis der biblischen hebräischen und jüdischen Quellen, der biblischen Forschung und der Lektüre der ursprünglichen Texte nachgegangen.

Foreword

In the early 1990s, Katherina von Kellenbach published her book-length research on anti-Judaic writings lurking in 20th century Christian and neo-goddess feminism. Her book reverberated with the late Fokkelien van Dijk-Hemmes' article discussing the same issue.[1]

Van Dijk-Hemmes left us with the legacy of her research on women's voices, feminised texts and women's actant roles in the Hebrew Bible. In a later book co-authored with Athalya Brenner, they ventured to deconstruct Hebrew Bible texts from female perspectives, conjecturing female authorship.[2] These texts reverberate with confluent researches like those of Phyllis Trible, Ilana Pardes or Nehama Aschkenasy.[3] While neither evading academic critical reading nor idealising the Hebrew Bible, van Dijk-Hemmes' writings refute claims that the Hebrew Bible, Hebrew deity and Judaism' silence negate or derogate women.

Von Kellenbach exposes propensities of Christian and goddess feminists to foil on the Hebrew Bible, Judaism and Hebrew deity by an antithetic theology that shows insufficient knowledge of Judaism and Hebrew texts, distorting and stereotyping them. Highlighting anti-Judaic feminism, von Kellenbach shows such trends to universalise patriarchy and blame it on the Hebrew Bible and its religion. The wrongs wrought upon Christian women by Christian androcentric politics are thus claimed to have sprouted in biblical patriarchy. Concomitantly, von Kellenbach shows neo-paganism to nurture confluent antithetic postulations to blame the Hebrew Bible and Judaism for oppressing and eliminating the primordial goddess, a libel equivalent to the *deicide* of Christ brought against the Jews. As a corollary, this movement accuses Judaism of robbing women of their innate matriarchal idyllic freedom and inherent empowerment that had unreservedly nurtured them during the golden days of the atavist goddess' sole reign.[4] Such postulations have been based on idealising matriarchy of primordial times, proven unwarranted

---

[1] Katharina von Kellenbach, *Anti-Judaism in Feminist Religious Writings* (Scholars Press: Atlanta 1994); Fokkelien van Dijk-Hemmes, "Feminist Theology and Anti-Judaism in the Netherlands," in: *Journal of Feminist Studies in Religion* 7 (1991), 117-123.

[2] Fokkelien van Dijk-Hemmes and Athalya Brenner, *On Gendering Texts: Female and Male Voices in the Hebrew Bible* (Brill: Leiden 1993).

[3] Phyllis Trible, *God and the Rhetoric of Sexuality* 2 (Fortress Press: Minneapolis 1978); Ilana Pardes, *Countertraditions in the Bible: A Feminist Approach* (Harvard University Press: Boston, Mass. 1993); Nehama Aschkenasy, *Feminine Images in Hebraic Literary Tradition* (Wayne State University Press: Detroit 1986).

[4] Von Kellenach, *Anti-Judaism*, 107-122.

by archaeology and historiography;[5] as are the movement's anti-Jewish libels, by extrapolation.

Katherina von Kellenbach analogises anti-Jewish trends in the writings of Christian and neo-pagan goddess feminism with the Church's historical anti-Judaism. According to von Kellenbach, antithetic feminism has reiterated Christian anti-Semitism by employing a derogative theology of hate and contempt, devaluing, appropriating, defaming, and foiling on the Hebrew Bible, the Hebrew God and Judaism. Such Christian and neo-pagan feminists have validated their theologies as a revolution of, liberation from, and substitution for the old, inferior and corrupt Judaism, all justifying its purge. Systematically analysing and refuting anti-Jewish claims, von Kellenbach associates antithetic feminism with "the teaching of contempt" of Christianity towards Jews and Judaism. The term had been epitomised by Jules Isaac, a Holocaust sole survivor of his family, who positioned the anti-Semitic politics of the Church as the breeding ground that had eventually led to the Holocaust.[6] Analogically, von Kellenbach calls upon Christian and neo-pagan feminists to turn away from a theology of contempt to the teaching of respect towards the Hebrew Bible and Judaism. In her call, she aspires to counterbalance anti-Judaic tendencies demonstrated by 20th century feminism and facilitate an inter-religious dialogue.[7]

Through the Antithetic Mirror from 20th to 21[St] Century

20th century, antithetic Christian and neo-pagan feminisms have re-constructed the biblical God as alienated to and devoid of the feminine divine, and Judaism as the eradicator of the ancient goddess. They claim that Judaism and the Hebrew Bible have converted divinity into a one-dimensional, non-relational, androcentric deity. Such claims have been made notwithstanding compelling scholarly literature that has verified ubiquitous figurations of the feminine divine in the Hebrew Bible and Judaism, evolving into multifaceted representations and images supported by the gendered nature of the Hebrew language.[8]

---

[5] Cynthia Eller, *Gentlemen and Amazons: The Myth of Matriarchal Prehistory, 1861–1900* (University of California Press: Oakland, CA 2011).
[6] Jules Isaac, *The teaching of contempt: Christian Roots of Anti-Semitism* (Holt, Rinehart and Winston: New York 1964).
[7] Von Kellenach, *Anti-Judaism*, 133-140.
[8] Gershom Scholem, *Elements of the Kabbala and its Symbolism*. Translated by Josef ben Shlomo (Bialik: Jerusalem 1976), 216-218; 260-262, 289 [Hebrew title: פרקי יסוד בהבנת הקבלה וסמליה].

Ironically, in appropriating Judaism as an antithetic foil, Christian and neo-pagan feminism turns self-defeating, since such policy contradicts the feminist call for a liberated, self-defined and autonomous identity, and for religious equality. Foiling on the Other induces mutual dependence instead of mutual dialogue between equals; and defining oneself by means of antithetic policy requires an antipode to reify one's identity. In Kristeva's conception, such relations precipitate a subject's dependence on an abject for its identity.[9]

What has changed in Christian and neo-pagan feminism? In the wake of the 21st century, the young radical feminists who had argued these issues grew older, became professors, teachers and chairwomen of recognised organisations and schools. If feminist anti-Judaism had previously been circulating in internal discussions, the issue is now in the hands of women who hold eminent positions at universities, teach new generations of young students, and have access to, and sometimes control of, media that ramify their ideas and propensities. Detecting anti-Judaism in 21st-century feminist religious writings is as disturbing, its teaching of contempt as poignant and threatening, and the call for teaching of respect towards Judaism as urgent as they had all been 20 years ago, especially as more women nowadays hold responsible positions. As the Talmud says: "Scholars, be careful with your words... The disciples who come after you, may drink of these evil waters (your words) and be poisoned, and the Name of Heaven will be desecrated" (Babylonian Talmud, *Avot* 1:11).

Two Religions Separated by One Book, God and Messiah
Von Kellenbach offers several criteria for detecting anti-Judaism in religious writings: foiling on Judaism as an antithesis, distortion, stereotyping, selective reading of the Hebrew Bible, reductionism, ignorance of Jewish sources, mimetic repetitions, and lacunae of warranting, emic understanding and knowledge of Jewish sources.[10] By extrapolation, these criteria are inter-dependent. Repetitions gloss over tautological conceptualisations, turning into self-evident truths. Distortion, selective and unwarranted readings, ignorance and lack of emic insight mutually lead to misrepresentations of the Hebrew Bible Hebrew deity and Judaism; while galvanising contextual particularities eventually precipitates stereotypisation, de-humanisation and objectification. Along these lines, I shall discuss several showcases of anti-Judaism in 21st feminist theology.

---

[9] Julia Kristeva, *Powers of Horror: An Essay on Abjection.* Translated by Leon S. Roudiez (Columbia University Press: New York 1982), 1-31.
[10] Von Kellenbach, *Anti-Judaism,* 1-13.

The Hebrew God and Abusive Patriarchy

One of the issues critiqued by von Kellenbach as unwarranted and tendentious is 20th-century feminism's representation of Judaism, the Hebrew God and the Hebrew Bible as the evil root of androcentric patriarchy. Antithetic Christian and neo-pagan feminists have reconstructed the biblical deity as a single father, one-dimensional male, disembodied, cruel, mono-generative, absolutist tyrant, who poses a danger to human relations, to human relationality, and to women. Such a deity concomitantly has generated an androcentric, ruthless, immoral, masculinised society alienated from femininity, whether divine or terrestrial.[11]

Showcasing Genesis 22, de Haardt's 21st century article reiterates anti-Jewish claims of 20th century feminism that associate biblical texts and the Hebrews with abusive patriarchal paternity, both on earth and in Heaven.[12] The story of Abraham and God in Genesis 22 has been in particular appropriated by such feminism to vilify the Hebrew deity and Abraham as earthly and divine prototypes of ruthless patriarchy.[13] Like her predecessors, de Haardt attributes tyrannical and abusive paternity to the Hebrews and their deity, conceiving a contingent ramification from the Hebrew Bible through the New Testament to our time. As corroboration, she juxtaposes three showcases: the biblical story of Abraham's intention to sacrifice his son, the sacrificial death of the Son of God Jesus, and a contemporary criminal case of the Austrian Fritzl, who had imprisoned his daughter in his inbuilt cellar for 20 years, raped her, and impregnated her with incestuous offspring.

De Haardt's essay adapts the antithetic representation of the Hebrew God as a single mono-generative male, and interlinks Him with androcentric fathers who, after their deity, demand absolute obedience of their subordinated wards so as to exert unchallenged rule for life and death over them. Such patriarchal contingency is showcased in God commanding Abraham to sacrifice his son; Abraham obeying God; by conjecture, Isaac obeying his father (Genesis 22); and the Christian God sacrificing his Son Jesus and demanding unequivocal obedience (Hebrews 11:17-19); eventually de Haardt juxtaposes both stories with the Fritzl case of sexual abuse of his daughter. Conjecturing *imitatie dei,* such a deity poses a model of an absolute tyrant, who poses danger to human

---

[11] Ibid., 92-101.
[12] Maaike de Haardt, "Monotheism as a Threat to Relationality?" in: Lisa Isherwood and Elaine Bellchambers (eds.), *Through Us, With Us, In Us: Relational Theology in the Twenty-First Century* (SCM Press: London 2010), 181-196;.
[13] Von Kellenbach, *Anti-Judaism,* 101-102, 105-106, 107-122.

-divine relations and to human-human relationality. By extrapolation, since biblical times to our own, androcentric patriarchy has encouraged offspring to rectify their fathers' power by blindly obeying them, and fathers to commit sexual abuse and infanticide.

Juxtaposing these three cases opens up a discussion of analogy and discrepancies. The problems at hand are, firstly, interrelating the three cases to one another, and, secondly, their relation to Judaism. At heart, the three cases fall under different categories of theology and genres, which thwarts their correlations.

As regards genres, the two biblical texts allude to stories of horror, while the Fritzl case belongs to factual events of atrocity and crime that call for the intervention of law. The former cases embody mimetic representations of atrocity conveyed by media of literature or art, meant as a caveat against acting out atrocities. Literature of horror repudiates acts of atrocity. In Aristotelian terms, it purports to arouse cathartic fear and pity, to precipitate the readers' empathy towards the suffering of a dramatic character and enlighten them as to the tragic consequences of atrocities.[14] Texts of horror are not meant to induce the reader to imitate crimes but to hinder them. By analogy, the story of Oedipus falls under literature of horror, serving as a caveat against violence and incest in the family, not as encouragement to act out on primal drives. In this line, the two biblical texts construe literature of horror aiming at arousing empathy for the victim through cathartic pity and fear and are meant to prevent – not to precipitate – crime and abuse like Fritzl's. The leitmotif of sacrificing a son thematises a victim's suffering: neither promulgating nor elevating suffering, but rather highlighting the sacrality of life and arousing cathartic pity and fear as a forewarning against victimisation.

On the theological stratum, de Haardt depicts the Hebrew Bible and New Testament texts as one coherent epiphany that promulgates human sacrifice as an ultimate ideal that ramifies into condonation and precipitation of violence and rape in the family. However, temporal and theological discrepancies divide the two biblical texts. Some 1000 years separate the Hebrew story and the New Testament; and the latter, moreover, being a Christian exegesis appropriating the former for its ends. Intertwining the New Testament text and the Hebrew one thus glosses over theological gaps, leading to incompatible messages. The theological gaps are accentuated by structural differences. The New Testament

---

[14] Aristotle, "On the Art of Poetry," in: Betty Radice (ed.), *Aristotle Horace Longinus: Classical Literary Criticism*. Translated by T.S. Dorseb (Penguin: Reading 1981), 29-76, here 48.

promulgates one unmodified divine order commanding a father to sacrifice a son, to occur. The Hebrew text revolves around two commands. The story opens with a divine request to sacrifice one's son and culminates in forbidding a father from harming him. In appropriating the Hebrew text, the New Testament magnifies the first commandment while obliterating the second. Turning reductionist and selective, the New Testament represents God's ordering a father to sacrifice his son as an unequivocal edict. Analogising a relation between earthly father and son, it is transcended into one between a heavenly father and a divinised son. The Hebrew story of Genesis. 22, however, does not divinise either father or son. Eventually, the gaps between the Hebrew narrative and the New Testament text represent worlds wide apart. Re-adapting the Hebrew story, the New Testament text relates a sacrifice eventually acted out under divine commandment. Thereby, the New Testament offers a reconstruction of the Hebrew story, in which human sacrifice is prevented by divine intervention. De Haardt's essay turns anti-Judaic by antithetically juxtaposing the Hebrew deity with ruthless patriarchy guided by a mono-generative and non-relational deity. Resonating with 20th-century antithetical feminist theology, de Haardt evokes Gerda Lerner at face value, unaware of von Kellenbach's criticism.[15] The Hebrew text is not a narrative about murderous patriarchy, but about demarcating its boundaries. Juxtaposing the Hebrew story with the Christian God the Father who sacrifices Jesus the divinised Son, rebounds Judaism with the *deicide* charge, with a twist of criticising patriarchy. Intersecting the Hebrew Bible and its deity with Christ's *crucifixion* and with Fritzl's paternal abuse and incestuous rape is incompatible. A sacrifice conjectures free will; obedience should entail a sense of duty mutually agreed upon between a legitimate authority and subject, based on moral conscience on both sides; while rape implies the lacuna of both, and is based on sexual coercion.

Emic Reading: Jewish Perspectives

What is the meaning of the Hebrew story in Jewish perspectives, and what is its emic relations to Hebrew moral conceptions of both God and Hebrew law?

Read every Jewish New Year in synagogues, the audience is shaken to hear God's first command, and finds a cathartic relief as God commands Abraham to withhold his hand from harming his son, with a ram eventually substituting for Isaac as the offering. The Hebrew story thus functions as a classical literature

---

[15] Gerda Lerner, *The Creation of Patriarchy* 1 (Oxford Paperbacks: Oxford 1986), 180, cited in von Kellenbach, *Anti-Judaism*, 105-107.

of horror culminating in a cathartic relief. It revolves around two divine commands. The first reads: sacrifice/kill you son; the second decrees: Do not touch the boy (Genesis 22:2,12). The final divine edict counterbalances, overrules and outlaws the first one. The codifier Umberto Cassuto represents mainstream Judaism promulgating that the story alludes to an internal polemic in the Hebrew Bible as regards human sacrifice. Opening with a command to commit human sacrifice, the story dialogises contemporary cults of human sacrifice, morally negating them (Leviticus 18:21, 20:2-5; Deuteronomy 12:30-31, 18:10).[16]

In the deep structure, the second divine command outlaws bloodshed in its religious praxis and murder in the social context, within the family or outside it. It lays down the basis of social structures, harnessing drives to inhibitions by enforcing laws. Genesis 22 therefore opens with the command to sacrifice a life which is unlawful, and culminates in prohibition on causing harm onto another. It is the ultimate voice of God, protector and creator of life as well as giver of laws that promulgates these principles. Intertextually, the narrative corresponds to laws that safeguard human rights for life, corporal integrity and social safety, resonated in the Ten Biblical Commandments (Ex. 20:1-17).

Paternal Abuse and Incest
Where do we see analogous relations between a 21st century case of incest, the Monotheistic God, biblical Abraham and Isaac, and God the Father and Jesus the Son? De Haardt conjectures such an analogy conceiving Hebrew monotheism to generate a mono-generative, non-relational God. Concomitantly, His creatures are encouraged to destroy relationality with their closest and dearest through murder and rape.

Is the Hebrew God a threat to relationality? At heart, the biblical deity is also the lawgiver of prohibitions on erasing sexual bars among kin, on rape and on inflicting harm. Concomitantly, the Hebrew Bible revolves around relationality mutually on both the social and religious strata, which the Hebrew Bible interrelates. Breaking the law is conceived as both social and religious offence. On the social and domestic strata, relationality is anchored in laws of permissible or illegitimate relations.

Interrelating cruelty of the strong and obedience of the weak is a relevant issue, especially when obedience is generated by fear rather than recognising

---

[16] Umberto Cassuto, *Commentary on Genesis* (Bialik: Jerusalem 1962), 82 [Hebrew title: פירוש על ספר בראשית א-ב]; Irving Greenberg, *The Jewish Way: Living the Holidays* (Summit Books: New York 1988), 19.

a legitimate authority. The issue that interlinks all three cases brought up by de Haardt is the demarcation between lawful paternal authority and unlawful paternal abuse of power, whether by violence or sexual assault. Paternal abuse is criminal and outlawed, and by being ethically immoral, is distinguishable from paternal authority ingrained in lawful responsibility to guarantee the welfare of one's ward. Endowed to parents, functionaries, teachers, or leaders, authority is anchored in legitimate and constitutional laws. Conversely, abuse of power defines exercising unauthorised, incontinent and unlawful use of force exerted against another person contrary to human rights. Abuse of power aims at forcing another person to act against his/her will and wellbeing.[17] Abusive power characterises crimes like rape, unlawful incarceration or murder, which are forbidden by law both within the family and without it in society (Exodus 20:2; Leviticus 18, 20, 19:29). Corresponding to biblical prohibitions, narratives show that the law does not exempt family members, rulers or kings as shown in the cases of crown princes like Shechem and Amnon, or rulers like Pharaoh, King Abimelech, King David, or King Ahab and his queen Isabel, who were all eventually punished for abuse of power (Genesis 34; 2 Samuel 13; Genesis 12; Genesis 20; 2Sam.11; 2 Samuel 13; 1 Kings 21, respectively). In corroboration, the Hebrew Bible does not exempt a master from abusing his or her slave; the mere inflicting of minor harm, such as striking out a tooth, results in immediate manumission; as a corollary, even sexual abuse of a slave woman is concomitantly outlawed (Exodus 21:26-27; Leviticus 19:20-22). By extrapolation, a father is unequivocally held accountable for harming or sexually abusing his offspring.

The Fritzl case shows a man working outside any legitimate authority with disrespect to God, law and human rights, within family or society. His crimes fall under symptomatic abuse of power inimical to parental authority, assigned to protect and enhance the welfare of his ward. Neither divine nor biblical paragons were guiding Fritzl, but his primal drives. There was neither logic nor theology behind his incestuous crimes. Preceding his crimes against his daughter and their mutual offspring, Fritzl had committed a violent rape, was tried and jailed; his victim was a complete stranger, arbitrarily attacked. Moreover, before or during that time, he had imprisoned his own elderly mother in an upstairs windowless room for 20 years up to her last day.[18] Taking her

---

[17] Ido Abraham, *Education after Auschwitz* (lecture course, Amsterdam University 1994).
[18] Angela Balakrishnan, "Josef Kept Sick Mother Locked in Attic, Leaked Papers Reveal," in: *The Guardian* (31 October 2008).

secrets with her to her obscure death, her abuse remained for conjectures. All the while, on what moral planet was Fritzl's wife living and keeping silent when her husband built torture rooms above and beneath her floor, when her daughter disappeared and a paralleled ghost family was sustained imprisoned in her house for 20 years? Where was her responsibility? And has androcentricity ever existed without the adoration and participation of women?

What interlinks the cases of Abraham and Fritzl is not a deity lending or legitimising an unlimited power of one human over another, but conversely, a deity that outlaws abusive paternity, manifested in the divine commandment: "Lay not thine hand upon the lad" (Genesis 22:12).[19] The Hebrew Scriptures tackle the issue of abuse by, on the one hand, conjuring literature of horror with God's dramatic intervention, and on the other hand, by endorsing prohibitive laws that thwart positions of power. Eventually, God levels down power relations precisely as an unchallenged sole creator of life who sanctions laws to protect it.

It is arrogant on the part of both 20th and 21st centuries feminism to conjecture that ancient society could not differentiate between paternal abuse and paternal authority, or that biblical society lacked moral conscience and blindly obeyed a deity that had none.

Extrapolating on the moral sensitivities of the Hebrew Bible, the Talmudic sages highlighted the plight of the weak, and were wary of the contingency of abusive power and violence to ramify from the domestic level to the social stratum. Rabbi Chassda says that a person should never impose fear over his house, as shown by the Mistress of Gibeah, whose husband had imposed excessive fear over her. Eventually, a fly fell one day into her husband's soup. Terrified of his reaction, the Mistress fled to her father's house and consequentially thousands died in the aftermath. Rabbi Jehuda says that a person who imposes fear over his house might end up transgressing prohibitions over incestuous relations or bloodshed (Babylonian Talmud, *Gittin* 6).[20] Notwithstanding having been written some eighteen hundred year ago, these Talmudic commentaries are still appropriate to our issue.

---

[19] Quotes from the Bible throughout the article are from King James Version.
[20] Ariel Slonim, "Excessive Fear," in: Kippah - *Beit Midrash* (*www.kipa.co.il*, 4 May 2006) [Hebrew].

The Cruel Deity of the Hebrews

As an antithesis of the pagan goddess, 20th-century neo-goddess feminism represents the biblical God as a cruel ruthless male deity and Jews as murderous wandering invaders, women-haters and destroyers of the atavist goddess and her idyllic matriarchy. These postulations draw on reductionist readings of the Hebrew Bible which turn, by mimetic repetitions into self-evident truths.[21]

Carol Christ perpetuates 20th-century neo-pagan feminist theology into the 21st century, attributing to the Hebrew Bible and its deity contingent cruelty that annihilated the golden times of the goddess and has been ramifying from the Hebrew Bible to the bloody crusades, medieval witch hunting, and genocide of Native Americans, to eventually bringing the Holocaust upon the Jews themselves. Perpetuating these postulations into the 21st century, Christ reverberates with her earlier work of the 20th century. Deprecating the Hebrew deity seems integrated in the propagation of the boundless goodness of the pagan goddess, whose demise is elucidated by antithetically foiling on the Hebrew Bible and patriarchy attributed to the Hebrews and their God.[22] In blaming the Jews for ramifying violence into the world, Carol Christ adapts centuries-long libels that have vilified the Jews for spreading evil in the world. As a corollary, reverting the causal guilt for the Holocaust unto the Jews shifts the blame away from the victimisers to the victims by vilifying the latter. Such argumentations resonate with hate theology, evoking the oldest libel of the *deicide* of Jesus, which, while having precipitated massacres and persecutions of Jews throughout the ages, were justified by accusing the Jews of culpability.[23]

Analogising the Hebrew Bible and the Hebrew deity with love of wars, powers of vengeance, cruelty, and genocide that have allegedly permeated the world is anti-Jewish in itself; academically and historically, it is displaced, inadequate and anachronistic.

Relating violence and war, ancient texts record the voices of their characters within their historical and temporal contexts, describing, and not necessarily propagating violence. Ancient tribal wars were reciprocally waged, and the

---

[21] Von Kellenbach, *Anti-Judaism,* 91-105, 107-111, 113-116.
[22] Carol P. Christ, *Laughter of Aphrodite: Reflections on a Journey to the Goddess* (Harper & Row: San Francisco 1987), 24, 75, 78, cited in von Kellenbach, *Anti-Judaism,* 113,120; Carol P. Christ, "Why women, men and other living things still need the Goddess: Remembering and Reflecting 35 years later," in: *Feminist Theology* 20 (2012), 242–256, here 242-255, 249-250.
[23] Von Kellenbach, *Anti-Judaism,* 24, 41, 47-49, 52, 115-120.

minor Israelites were historically unsuccessful in them, more often than otherwise being slaughtered and subjugated by their stronger neighbours as the book of Judges relates. Concomitantly, Moabite King Mesha dedicates the destruction and total massacre of the Hebrew population of Nebo to Ishtar-Chomesh, (KAI 181).[24] Beside recording an ancient war by a dispassionate authorship, this massacre ensues a blood sacrifice to the king's goddess, which thwarts re-constructionist neo-pagan promotion of an ancient peaceful goddess of women.

Further, feminist accusation of the Hebrew Bible, the Israelites and the Hebrew God for ramifying politics of genocide is anachronistic and displaced. In the first place, rabbinical literature of some 1800 years ago had already banned the Exodus call for war of annihilation as inapplicable in the aftermath of its concurrent time.[25]

In the second place, the comparison between genocide and tribal wars of ancient time is inadequate as it is drawn on a displaced juxtaposition of two kinds of killing: casualties of war waging between two armed groups on the one hand, and genocide executed on a group of an unarmed minority within the same society on the other hand. Logistically, these are two different categories of killing. The tribal wars of Joshua and Judges fall under wars between peoples engaged in mutual armed clashes, both calling for victory in battle and evoking their gods' aid. During wartime, existence depends on successfully neutralising the other, which is weighed by military power to inflict death and damage onto the enemy. Such killing falls under casualties of war mutually inflicted by nations on each other, categorised as lawful deaths still legitimised in our time. While WWII had cost around 70 million dead, these were considered war casualties; so were the victims of the atomic bomb of Hiroshima, and Nagasaki in 1945 or those caused by the US and British bombardment of Baghdad in 2003.

Genocide is defined as lethal and destructive acts unlawfully directed against an unarmed minority, precipitated by ethnic, religious or racial hatred. It is therefore the killing of the Jews and Gypsies, howbeit comprising some 10% of the fatalities of WWII, that was dubbed as genocide and unlawful killing, since it was not exercised between armed nations, but exerted by a

---

[24] Karel van der Toorn, *Family Religion in Babylonia, Ugarit and Israel: Continuity and Changes in the Forms of Religious Life* (Brill: Leiden 1996), 277.
[25] Daniel and Jonathan Boyarin, "Diaspora: Generation and the Ground of Jewish identity," in: *Critical Inquiry* 19 (1993), 693-725, here 610.

state against citizens in its midst. Whether during war or peace, genocide logistically falls outside the legitimate category of war casualties. As the people's protector, the biblical God undertakes the role of soldier promising victory to His people over their enemies, in accord with the functional role of ancient deities. Concomitantly, the Hebrew Bible demarcates between wartime killing and unlawful killing of minorities and outsiders in its midst. An adversary nation is defined as a military enemy and foe, *oieev* and *tsaar* (Numbers 35:23; Esther 7:6). A minority is categorised as *Ger,* a foreigner and stranger dwelling in the land among the people. The *Ger* resurfaces 92 times in the Hebrew Bible, and is declared protected and beloved by God and law, and guaranteed equal rights like the Israelites, independently of race, origin or religion (Numbers 15:15). As a corollary, collective punishment and destruction of a community or a city are also challenged in the Hebrew Bible. Abraham thwarts God's intention to destroy the population of Sodom as one: "Wilt Thou also destroy the righteous with the wicked?" (Genesis 18:23). In Jonah, God substitutes religious wrath with compassion for all living souls, human and animals all being His creation, and admonishes the prophet for aspiring to destroy the entire population of Nineveh city in God's name howbeit for following another religion (Jonah 4:9-11). In this spirit, counterfeiting Deuteronomy 13:13-17 that promulgate the destruction of a city, should it desert God's worshiping for another, the Talmud counter-decrees: *lo haya ve-lo yehiye* – it cannot happen and shall never be acted out in reality. The ruling is equally downsized to the domestic level, in order to outlaw punishing disobedient offspring (Sanhedrin 71a). Concomitantly, the cessation of the death penalty in Judaism became a common consensus since the beginning of the 1st century AD, and having been rarely carried out even in the few centuries before, it remained a mere Talmudic issue of value argumentation since then. Some researchers argue that the Jews lost their judicial authority to exert lethal punishment under the Roman Empire. Nonetheless, the Jewish nodal objections to death penalty have been construed around the concept of creation of both man and woman after the divine image. Accordingly, the isomorphic presence of God in humans is conceived as a wholistic representation in both body and soul. Consequentially, murder or the exertion of death penalty are conceived as damaging God's image and diminishing the divine presence on earth, thereby falling under sacrilege. By extrapolation, the infliction of pain, torture or maiming another human-being or oneself are equally outlawed. The cessation of death penalty accounts for the fact that homosexuals, "suspected" witches, adulterous persons, or criminals have *not* been executed in Jewish communities ever since.[26]

Attributing ramification of wars and genocide to the Hebrew Bible, the Hebrews and their deity by antithetic theology is displaced. The Canaanite wars took place some 2000 years (if at all) before the Crusades, and, by extrapolation, the massacres of Muslims and Jews alike were inspired by the riding-in-blood angels of *Revelations* (14:20; 19:11-15), and precipitated by Papal-awarded absolutions of sins for the killing of infidels.[27] Christian communities had appropriated the Hebrew Bible to execute people suspected of witchcraft and various religious inequities because they believed their measures to be the absolute truths. Such policy conjoined claims to an autonomous hegemony and to the absolute and true divine epiphany of Christianity. Its ruthlessness could not have been anchored in ignorance of the Judaic texts and spirit, or their diversity, internal dialogue and modifying interpretations of the Hebrew Bible and its laws. Medieval Church kept a close watch on its Jewish residents, and by conjecture, Christian theologians were well enough learned to know that Jews banned executions and corporeal punishments. Christian intolerance and cruelties should be owned by Christian responsibilities. Blaming the Jews for Christian atrocities is historically inadequate, academically unwarranted, morally displaced, ethically corrupt, and anti-Jewish.

Christa and Judaism

Lisa Isherwood promulgates the call to feminise the Christ in the Christa. Christa feminists postulate that the maleness of Jesus the Messiah has been the source of discrimination and exclusion of Christian women from both spiritual redemption and religious functions, as well as the cause of vilifying and disembodying women's corporeality in Christianity. In feminising Christ, Christa feminist theologians seek to liberate women from masculinised Christianity and validate their relationality to the divine through a feminised Messiah. Emulating Christ, Christa embodies feminised divinity and messianism in the

---

[26] Yair Lorberbaum, *In God's Image: Myth, Theology, and Law in Classical Judaism* (Cambridge University Press: New York 2015), 202; Beth A. Berkowitz, *Execution and Invention: Death Penalty Discourse in Early Rabbinic and Christian Cultures* (Oxford University Press: Oxford 2006).

[27] Christopher Tyerman, *God's War: A New History of the Crusades* (Harvard University Press: Cambridge MA 2006), 32-34,38, 54-59.

flesh and thus empowers the divine in women from without, enfleshing the female divine incarnated within them.

In "Christa – Women's Journey Home?",[28] Isherwood universalises the plight of women. In so doing, she glosses over the fact that even in its revolutionary evolution, Christa is exclusively bound to Christianity. Universalising Christa problematises the audience's diverse affiliations, resonating with Christian claims to a universalised epiphany of Jesus Christ.

Von Kellenbach conceives universalism to be oppressive towards a minority, being an imposition on the part of a major group to ramify its communal experience as a universal truth. Denying the particularity of a minority in its midst turns its identity invisible.[29] Universalism evokes the historically Christian politics towards the Jews; being unable to devolve its universal epiphany of salvation for the global mankind, Christianity had employed a theology of conversion and devaluation towards Judaism.

Announced by confluent universalism, Christa induces such propensities into feminism. As a majority, gentile feminists conjure a mind-set of conversion by assuming their plight and history to be akin to those of Jewish women. Reinforcing notions of female universalism and women's communality, Christa feminism, while unawares, glosses over an antithetic theology that deprecates values held dear by Jewish women. Christa's universalistic feminism seems to fall back on historical Christianity, utilising Judaism as an antithetic foil to reaffirm its own identity while devaluing Judaism. Universalising such an identity thus seems to adjoin with antithetic attitudes towards the Other.

Concomitantly, Isherwood slides from universalism to antithetic theology. Rectifying the need to feminise the messiah in Christa, Isherwood postulates that the male Christ that antagonises women originates in dualism born in Neo-Platonism and Jewish apocalyptic messianism; the latter is claimed to rebound with the biblical patriarchy and its warrior King Messiah.

Overarching such conceptualisations at face value, Isherwood does not corroborate her juxtaposition of Neo-Platonism and Jewish apocalyptic messianism. Nor does she warrant her claim that apocalyptic Judaism has been dualistic. Introduced as self-evident truths, these postulations leave no space for contention. Concomitantly, while tracing masculinisation of the Christian

---

[28] Lisa Isherwood, "Christa – Women's Journey Home?" in: *Catherina Helkes Lecture Series* (Utrecht, Netherlands, 23 April 2016) (unpublished article), 1-8.
[29] Von Kellenbach, *Anti-Judaism*, 128-129.

messiah in Judaism, her depiction of the Jewish Messiah shows a lacuna of warranted Jewish sources, like Raphael Patai's *The Messiah Texts*.[30]

Furthermore, Isherwood holds Judaism responsible for Jesus' maleness that had wronged Christian women. As a corollary, she dubs Jewish society as thoroughly patriarchal from biblical times to the present. With such inclusive postulations, Isherwood deems to establish that Hebrew patriarchy, the Hebrew Bible and Judaism have been the roots of Christian misogynistic evil by moulding Jesus' maleness after Jewish militant conceptions of Messiah the warrior king.[31]

The masculinisation of Jesus the Messiah is claimed to coincide with the biblical religion of the Hebrews that downplayed the goddess purporting to have the male monotheistic God superseded. By analogy, Christa feminism corresponds to neo-goddess feminism, whose exponents claim their goddess to have been suppressed and annihilated by Jewish patriarchy.[32] Analogous to the neo-goddess feminism, the Christa movement accentuates the revival of the feminine divine while positioning women as victims of the Hebrew God, Hebrew Bible and Judaism. By conjecture, Christa resonates with the libel of the *deicide*, juxtaposing the goddess' demise with holding Judaism responsible for Jesus' maleness that has eliminated the feminine divine in Christian messianism. By extrapolation, Judaism is held accountable for the consequential androcentricity of Christ; it has circumvented Christian women's religious participation, corporeality and redemptive spirituality, since for them Jesus embodies the ultimate messianic salvation through the incarnated divine in the masculine flesh.

Eventually, Isherwood's article slips into the pitfall of anti-Judaism shown in the previous articles and resonates with the Church's historical antipodean theology. Repatriating similar antithetic feminism, Isherwood's analogies suffer from confluent defaults. Between deconstructing Jewish history and sweeping tautological generalisations over the Hebrew Bible, Hebrew patriarchy, Jewish messianism and Judaism, she resonates with 20th century anti-Jewish feminism, likewise showing lacunae of emic biblical research and contextual insight into Judaism. In blaming Christian androcentricity on Jewish patriarchy of both biblical and contemporary Jewish society, Isherwood seems oblivious or indifferent to the radical evolvement Judaism has undergone in its history.

---

[30] Raphael Patai, *The Messiah Texts* (Wayne State University Press: Detroit 1988).
[31] Isherwood, "Christa," 1.
[32] Von Kellenbach, *Anti-Judaism*, 91-97.

The last centuries have culminated in the current appointments of women as rabbis, judges in religious courts, spiritual partners to rabbis and communal leaders in all Jewish communities in Israel and around the world, including ultra-orthodox synagogues.[33]

Isherwood's article reiterates 20th century anti-Judaism manifested by a strand of Christian and goddess feminism that has denunciated Hebrew patriarchy as the oppressor of goddess religions and the evil root of wrongs wrought upon both pagan and Christian women. Antithetic feminism downplays the fact that such wrongs were actually executed by their own Christian communities.[34] Like confluent neo-goddess and Christian feminisms, Christa feminism seems unable to uproot anti-Jewish propensities inherent in its historical Christian provenance. In the wake of goddess and Christian feminist theologies, Christa feminism misinterprets the aversion of Judaism to iconism, be it in masculine or feminine moulded visualisation, confusing it with annihilating the feminine divine.

Comparing Messiahs
As a point of disputation, mere comparison between the Christian Messiah and the Jewish Messiah precipitates antithetic theology. Resurfacing in Christian or Christa feminist theology of our time, such a comparison conjures the medieval contests held between Church officials and representatives of the Jewish communities entitled *Vikuach*. Forced on the Jews, such theological disputations were anti-Jewish in nature, staged to disrepute the Jews for rejecting the one true messiah, Jesus Christ, and to devalue the Jewish messiah.[35]

Aiming at validating the true messiah in Christa evokes the Church's theology of devaluation, antithetically decrying the Jewish messiah all over again. As a corollary, Isherwood represents the Hebrew Bible, Judaism and the Jewish messiah as the ramifying powers that have militarised and masculinised the Christian Messiah with devastating consequences for Christian women. Presenting the Jewish messiah as a militant warrior-king and Jewish society

---

[33] Sarah Zukerman, "Commentary on 'Assemble the people together, men, and women and children, and thy stranger who is within thy gates' (Deuteronomy 31:12)," in: *Kolech: Weekly Magazine of Feminist Orthodox Women* (Beit Hillel: Jerusalem) [Hebrew title: הקהל את העם]. (www.kolech.co.il, 7 October 2016)

[34] Von Kellenbach, *Anti-Judaism,* 24, 109-113, 120-124.

[35] Robert Chazan, "The Condemnation of the Talmud Reconsidered (1239-1248)," in: *Proceedings of the American Academy for Jewish Research* 55 (1988), 11-30; Simon Schama, *The Story of the Jews: Finding the Words: 1000 BCE to-1492-AD* (Penguin: Toronto 2014), 349-355.

as a hard-core patriarchy turns the Jewish messiah into the anti-thesis of Christa. As Judaism is held accountable for masculinising the incarnation of the messianic divine in the flesh for Christian believers, Judaism itself is deemed responsible for barring God to Christian women.

Blaming or accrediting the Hebrew Bible for Jesus' divinised kingship or male messianism are inaccurate. One nodal divide resides in the divination of humans. Ancient Israel adopted kingship from its neighbours who endorsed divinised kingship. Nonetheless, circumventing the divination of humans, Israelite culture did not divinise their kings who then had to abide by laws of nature, God and society. Concomitantly, the prophets chided Israelite kings and condemned and ridiculed foreign kings' claim to divination (Ezekiel 28). The epitome *Mashiach* – messiah is post-biblical. Its root "mashach" appears in the Hebrew Bible not as a nominal, but in the form of verb or adjective, originally referring to the anointment of living priests and kings with oil (Numbers 3:3; 1Sam. 15:17).[36] The epitome "mashach" has generated more divides than analogies between the Jewish messiah and the Christian one. The advent of Jesus the Messiah is anchored in the Evangelical appropriation of the Hebrew Bible and is self-evidently post biblical. Divinising the term *mashiach*, Christianity has transcended Christ into an integral entity of the divine Trinity to be worshipped as a theomorphic intermediary between humanity and God, as divinity incarnated in the flesh, and as the divinised Son of God. The Jewish messiah neither incarnates the divine nor functions as a theomorphic intermediary between humans and deity to reach the divine. While Jews believe in a future messianic time, they neither pray to nor worship the messiah. Eventually, the Jewish messiah could be anyone righteous and worthy to bring the messianic time, whilst concomitantly, the concurrent generation should prove worthy to receive it by accumulating good deeds and charity. A prominent legend relates that the messiah will rise from among the righteous ones who are hidden from everyone's eyes and sometimes even unknown to themselves.[37] Such legends democratise Jewish messianism, implying that the messiah could be any righteous person – man or woman. As a corollary, the 16th century community of Safed in northern Israel alludes to a feminised image of the messiah. Their *kabbala* transcended the eponymous foremothers Rachel and Leah into a two-faced embodiment of the *Shekhina*; Rachel representing Her maternal sorrow embracing the people's exile and

---

[36] Patai, *The Messiah Texts*, xxi.
[37] Scholem, Elements of the *Kabbala*, 10-11.

suffering, and Leah embodying the Messianic hope inherent in the *Shekhina*. The Safed community infused Sabbath prayers with ecstatic rituals aiming to attain a mystical union with the *Shekhina* through Rachel and Leah. With devotion and good deeds of *tikkun* – amendment – the Safed community aspired to enhance the coming of messianic times.[38] Messianic redemption in Judaism eventually does not depend on a messiah, not even on God, but on actions of both men and women aspiring to do good in the world. Women's participation in such messianism is self-evident.

Through the Antithetic Looking Glass
Being exposed to anti-Jewish propensities feels like entering a circus room full of distorting mirrors.

It is my conclusion that the articles discussed above show anti-Jewish propensities from three mind-sets: Christian, neo-goddess paganism and Christa feminism. Oversimplifying biblical patriarchy, they associate Hebrew religion, texts and society with hard-core androcentric utilitarianism. Such antithetic feminist theology presents the Hebrew deity as a solipsist, militant, cruel, tyrannical patriarchal male God, who is paradoxically, at the same time, also presented as disembodied and alienated from relationality with both divine and earthly femininity, nature and humanity – despite their being His Creation?! Such depictions correlate a realm run by loveless, patriarchal, debased, murderous, and daughter-rapist men. Thus vilified and dehumanised, the Hebrew religion, deity, Hebrew Bible, and Judaism are represented in a stereotyping antithesis to the ideals of feminist movements. The articles discussed above show that feminist anti-Judaism has re-entered the 21st century rebounding with their predecessors of the 20th century as well as with the historical anti-Judaism in Christianity.

Antithetic feminism puts Judaism and Jews on the defensive, which precipitates a religious war in lieu of a dialogue. Retrospectively, such propensities revert us back to the Middle Ages, when the Church declared the Talmud and rabbinical texts repudiating, adversary, anti-Christian and heretical. Entitled *Vikuach*, the Church had launched such theological polemics in the form of public disputations, "inviting" rabbis to debate with Church representatives as mentioned above. While such debates were aimed to prove the Jews wrong, the Jewish representatives wavered between being obliged to defend their faith

---
[38] Ibid., 134, 144-145.

and being wary to avoid offending Christianity for fear for their community and their own lives.[39] Re-positioning Judaism in theosophical contests in our time is bitter. It attests to the perpetuation of antithetic theology and its teaching of contempt affronting Judaism even today. Like the medieval debates, such contemporary disputations rebound with the recurrent issues: interpretations of the Hebrew Bible; the Hebrew godhead; validation of the Christian Messiah against the Jewish one; and living Judaism itself. In the following, some nodal points shall be discussed from Jewish perspectives.

Through the Emic Looking Glass
The Hebrew Godhead
"They figured thee in a multitude of visions; behold thou art One under all images."[40]

Contrary to feminist depiction of the Hebrew deity as a monolithic, androcentric, non-relational male etc., Hebrew texts exhibit diverse images of the divine whose worship is multi-layered. Karel van der Toorn postulates that ancient society endorsed pluralism quite like modern society, and that viewing ancient societies as an incorporate collective governed by a monolithic ideology is inaccurate: "The fallacious use of name-tags – such as 'Mesopotamian civilization' or 'Israelite religion' – should not make us forget that these designations cover in fact a diversity of practices, groups, and opinions."[41] Concomitantly, contemporary researchers depict the ancient biblical world as multi-cultural, diverse and religiously localised; its religious life straddled between coexistence with the peripheral cultures surrounding it and the indigenous family and clan cults of their own ancient ancestors. Warranted finds witness a colourful kaleidoscope of religiosity, recounting the worship of god El and Yahwism alongside female deities and divine consorts like Asherah, Anath, the queen of heaven, and their local variants. Local cults existed alongside fluid court cults shifting with various kings; all variants nonetheless fell under ancient Hebrew religion.[42] As a corollary, Reiner Albertz proposes

---

[39] Chazan, "The Condemnation," 54-59; Schama, *The Story of the Jews*, 349-355.
[40] "Hymn of Glory," Sabbath prayer, *The Standard Prayer Book*. Translated by Simeon Singer (1915). (http://www.sacred-texts.com/jud/spb/spb20.htm, 19 April 2017)
[41] Karel van der Toorn, "Ritual Resistance and Self-Assertion; the Rachabites in Early Israelite Religion," in: Jan Platvoet and Karel van der Toorn (eds.), *Pluralism and Identity: Studies in Ritual Behaviour* (Brill: Leiden 1995), 229-260.
[42] Gösta Werner Ahlström, *Aspects of Syncretism in Israelite Religion* (CWK: Gleerup 1963), 5; Raphael Patai, *The Hebrew Goddess* (Wayne University Press: Detroit 1974), 18-20; Saul

to circumvent terms like "popular religion", "official religion" proper or "syncretism". He considers dialectical terms like "popular religion" and "official religion" inapplicable since royal courts and commons alike practised pluralistic cults in Ancient Israel. Concomitantly, an official religion cannot be constituted where a monolithic cult is not established. Furthermore, syncretism becomes inapplicable as the Israelites shared Canaanite cults and deities with their neighbours.[43]

The Patriarchal God and the Female Divine
Antithetic Feminism has stigmatised the Hebrew deity as a patriarchal, single male or mono-generative father. Biblical research offers more balanced and multifaceted depictions.

The Patriarchal God correlates with the biblical term *elohei avot*, fathers' god(s); *avot* meaning ancestors and fathers; *elohei* signifying both plural and singular god(s). Most scholars identify this deity as the god El, a Mesopotamian deity – the moon god, deity of storm, clouds, mountain Sin or the steppes, who is accompanied by one or more female deities.[44] Some scholars conjecture that each biblical patriarch had a different god, alluding to the practice of domestic and localised religions revolving around the worship of eponymous

---

M. Olyan, *Asherah and the Cult of YHWH in Israel* (Scholars Press: Atlanta 1988), 34; Susan Ackerman, "And the Women Knead Dough," in: Alice Bach (ed.), *Women in the Hebrew Bible: A Reader* (Routledge: London 1999), 21-32; Susan Ackerman, *Under Every Green Tree. Popular Religion in Sixth-Century Judah* (Scholars Press: Atlanta 1992); Susan Ackerman, "The Queen Mother and the Cult in Ancient Israel," in: *Journal of Biblical Literature* 11.3 (1993), 385-401; William G. Dever, "Asherah, Consort of Yahweh? New Evidence from Kuntillet Ajrûd," in: *Bulletin of the American Schools of Oriental Research* 255 (1984), 21-37; William G. Dever, "Recent Archaeological Confirmation of the Cult of Asherah in Ancient Israel," in: *Hebrew Studies* (1982), 37-43; Van der Toorn, "Ritual Resistance," 229; Judith M. Hadley, *The Cult of Asherah in Ancient Israel and Judah: Evidence for a Hebrew Goddess* (Cambridge University Press: Cambridge 2000), 57.

[43] Rainer Albertz, "Family Religion in Ancient Israel and its Surroundings," in: John Bodel and Saul M. Olyan (eds.), *Household and Family Religion in Antiquity* (John Wiley & Sons: Hoboken, New Jersey 2008), 89-112.

[44] E. L. Abel, "The Nature of the Patriarchal God *El Sadday*," in: *Numen* 20, Fasc. 1 (1973), 48-59; Sigmund Mowinckel, "The name of the God of Moses," in: *Hebrew Union College Annual* 32 (1961), 121-133; Philip J. Hyatt, "YHWH as 'the God of my Father'," in: *Vetus Testamentum* 5, Fasc. 2 (1955), 130-136; Terence E. Fretheim, "Suffering God and Sovereign God in Exodus: A Collision of Images," in: *Horizons in Biblical Theology* 11.1 (1989), 31-56; Lester L. Grabbe, *Judaic Religion in the Second Temple Period: Belief and practice from the Exile to Yavneh* (Routledge: London 2002).

ancestors, male and female, who embody house spirits and family gods.[45] Such *elohei avot* – ancestors' god(s) – would represent the eponymous founders of tribes and could function as house spirits or minor deities of individual households or clans accompanied by their eponymous spouses. Jacob personifies the eponymous ancestor *Isra-el;* while Rachel and Leah could be conceived of as domesticated stories about eponymous mothers of tribes (Ruth 4:11-12, Jeremiah 31:15, Isaiah 53:7).[46]

Scholars find consensus in the postulations that monarchic Israel was polytheistic, worshipping YHWH and god El among others, of whom none was celibate. The cult and origin of the god YHWH are disputed. Karel van der Toorn postulates that prior to reaching Israel, groups of Edomites and Midianites already worshipped YHWH as their god around 14th century BCE.[47] YHWH appears in Hebrew inscriptions dating as early as the 8th century BCE, and was worshipped in both kingdoms of Judah and Israel, alongside Asherah for His divinised consort, well into the Babylonian exile.[48] The title Asherah could refer to a cultic object, a sacred tree, the female deity herself and/or all these together.[49] Some researchers conceive of YHWH's character and function as an inclusive deity;[50] a nationalised ramification of a local worship; or the input of the Persian exilic community who then established YHWH as a national deity in the 2nd temple built in 353 BCE by the returning Babylonian exiles under Ezra and Nehemiah.[51] Bob Becking proceeds to demarcate between Yahwism and Judaism, the latter evolving in the wake of the destruction

---

[45] Benjamin Halevi, "Additional Notes on Ancestors Worship," in: *Beit Mikra Journal to Research of the Bible and its World* (1975), 101-117 [Hebrew title: עקבות נוספים לפולחן אבות]; Karel van der Toorn, *Family Religion in Babylonia, Syria and Israel: Continuity and Change in the Forms of Religious Life. Studies in the History and Culture of the Ancient Near East* (Brill: Leiden 1996), 55-6,66; Reiner Albertz, "Family Religion," 98-99.

[46] As, for example, *rechela,* a mother sheep (Isaiah 53:7).

[47] Van der Toorn, *Family Religion,* 282-283.

[48] Ackerman, "The Queen Mother," 385–401; Dever "Asherah, Consort," 21–37; Emerton John A. "Yahweh and His Asherah: The Goddess or Her Symbol?" in: *Vetus Testamentum* 49.3 (1999), 315-337.

[49] Hadley, *The Cult of Asherah,* 4-30.

[50] Thomas L. Thompson, "How Yahweh became God: Exodus 3 and 6 and the Heart of the Pentateuch," in: *Journal for the Study of the Old Testament* 20, 68 (1995), 57-73.

[51] Ze'ev Weisman, " The Interrelationship between J and E in the Jacob Narrative – Re-examined," in: *Proceedings of the World Congress of Jewish Studies,* World Union of Jewish Studies (1985), 35-42 [Hebrew title: בחנים תיאולוגיים ומשמעותם לגבי התהוות הסיפורים על יעקב].

of the Second Temple in 70 AD.[52] As a reminder of a multi-layered past, both divine names Elohim and YHWH pronounced as *Adonai*, Lord, are still employed in contemporary Hebrew Prayer books.

While rejuvenating the divine presence in multifaceted images, Judaism has preserved its female divine, not suppressing but evolving it throughout the ages. Having seen Asherah outdated, Judaism has been replenished with new *hieros gamos* or divine marriage, seen in (re)newed mystical unions between God and divine consorts. We see God's female co-personification in divine bride and counterpart alternatively resurfacing in Wisdom, Sabbath, Torah or *Shekhina*, the latter conceived as immanent presence in the world and within humanity.[53]

Hebrew God-language
Judaic conception of God does not embrace incarnation. Nonetheless, according to Scholem, any God-talk in itself denotes anthropomorphic embodiment, since human perception works by images anchored in the ontological world.[54] Linguistically, Hebrew God-language refurbishes the biblical cosmology with duo-gendered deification. Alternatively shifting from feminine to masculine and from singular to plural images, Genesis 1 opens with a plural appellation of the divine, *Elohim*, grammatically appearing in a masculine singular nominal form, which is simultaneously plural. The second verse moves to *ruach*, the divine spirit in a singular feminine form. On creating humanity, God *Elohim* refers to Himself in first person plural.

The biblical codifier Umberto Cassuto postulates that in relating "Let Us make man in Our image(s), after Our likeness(es)" (Genesis 1:26), the plurality of God's likeness(es) and images alludes to a duo-gendered pantheon, with a female divine for partner and co-creator, creating together duo-gendered humanity after their respective male and female images.[55] Such linguistic subtlety is lost in most if not all foreign translations. Concomitantly, researchers

---

[52] Bob Becking, "Introduction," in: Bob Becking and Marjo Christina Annette Korpel (eds.), *The Crisis of Israelite Religion: Transformation of Religious Tradition in Exilic and Post-Exilic Times* 42 (Brill: Leiden, London 1999), 1-8.
[53] Scholem, *Elements of the Kabbala*, 102, 124, 218, 229, 230, 233, 234, 236, 262, 296-297; Patai, *The Hebrew Goddess;* Moshe Weinfeld, "Feminine Features in the Imagery of God in Israel: The Sacred Marriage and the Sacred Tree," in: *Vetus Testamentum* 46 (1996), 515-529; Baruch Margalit, "On the Issue of YHWH and his Asherah," in: *Beit Mikra: Journal for the Study of the Bible and Its World* 4.143 (1995), 376-391 [Hebrew title: לסוגית יהוה ואשרתו].
[54] Scholem, *Elements of the Kabbala*, 153.
[55] Umberto Cassuto, *From Adam to Noah* (Hebrew University Press: Jerusalem 1944), 28-29.

conjecture that the two Cherubim on the Ark were shaped as duo-gendered images in embrace, to envision a duo-gendered divinity (Exodus 25:18-20, 22; Babylonian Talmud, *Yoma* 54b).[56] The Hebrew godhead is thus conceived as divine presence described by verbal attributes that are corporeal and duo-gendered, by analogy, alluding to isomorphic relationality between the divine and humanity.[57]

Divine Relationality and Corporeality

Contending feminist depiction of the biblical God as mono-generative male and consequentially non-relational and disembodied, it is hereby postulated that the nodal point of the Hebrew Bible is the relationality between God, creation and humanity. In monotheistic representation, the biblical Creator precipitates multifaceted relations with the terrestrial world without intermediaries or intermediate means, bringing to fruition unmediated relationality between Creator and creation. Relationality between Creator and creation develops in three corresponding phases in Genesis 1: a. divine announcement of a phenomenon coming into being: Let there be; b. a phenomenon enfolding its immanent existence: and there was; c. God's seeing that it is good, generating ontological recognition by the Creator. In pronouncing "Let there be", the Hebrew God emancipates the creation from gods who embody and emulate natural phenomena devaluing their ontological presence. In seeing that it is good, God endorses the immanent existence of the created. The biblical Creator is simultaneously active and non-intrusive, relating to the creation not by controlling but by letting it evolve to deploy its inherent being. "Let there be" allows each part of the creation to survive and live by its inherent power to be, not outside its being, but endowing it its own talent, in its own innate terms within a creation that in itself revolves around its inherent being.

Rejecting pagan myths, Judaism does not erase relationality between deity and nature or between humans and nature. As the Hebrew Bible induces de-mythification of nature it conversely creates unmediated relationality between these factors. Nor does de-mythification mean breaking relationality with God. Whatever Judaism has rejected, invented or re-adapted from pagan cults and

---

[56] Patai, *The Hebrew Goddess,* 111-133; Marvin Hoyle Pope, *Song of Songs* (Doubleday: Garden City, N.Y. 1978), 153-158.

[57] Scholem, *Elements of the Kabbala,* 154-155; Howard Eilberg-Schwartz, "The Problem of the Body for the People of the Book," in: Alice Bach (ed.), *Women in the Hebrew Bible* (Routledge: New York 1999), 53-77.

myths, it had neither the aspiration nor the political power position to enforce conversion, change or destroy other peoples' cults and temples. Jewish monotheism has evolved as an internal process searching for self-definition for its own communities. These notions are extrapolations on the following Jewish thinkers.

The codifier Umbero Cassuto contends that Genesis 1 de-mythifies ancient myths that had identified natural phenomena with gods who functionally embody them. Anchoring nature in the ontologically phenomenal world, mythical images resurface in the Hebrew Bible henceforth as grand metaphors without mythifying natural phenomena proper.[58] Abraham Heschel postulates that it is the prophets' achievement to reject worshipping, mythically personifying or divinising natural phenomena. Counter to pagan cults, biblical texts de-mythify the earth, which theologically neutralises nature in lieu of sacralising it. Heschel promulgates that, ceasing to be our creating goddess mother, the earth becomes our created sister, and like humankind, abides by the confluent ontological laws. As a sibling within Creation, humans become the associates and partners of earth and all natural phenomena, recognising their mutual interdependence and vulnerability: "And thou shalt make a covenant with the stone of the field; and the beast of the earth shall be at peace with thee" (Job 3:23).[59] Analogously, as life must be protected by laws, so does the earth. Entitling all members of the household to rest on the seventh day, male and female, servants and slaves alongside domestic animals, the earth too is given a rest on both the weekly Sabbath and the entire seventh year (Ex.20:8–11; Leviticus 25:1–7). Commandments to protect the earth reside in the belief that like humanity, the earth is a subject of ontological creation and is neither divinised nor elevated above it. Prohibitions on moulding images of God ban worshipping concrete objects like the earth as a living god (Deuteronomy 5:4-5; 6:4). Neither does it mean a deity detached from relationality to humankind or corporality, but rather alludes to the idea of God's grandeur wavering above human grasp.[60]

What is shunned from moulded representation finds its form in the realm of the imagination, in verbal metaphors and illustrative images. It is in the space

---

[58] Umberto Cassuto, Commentary on *Genesis*, 13–14.
[59] Abraham Joshua Heschel, *God in Search of Man: A Philosophy of Judaism*. Translated by Azan Meir Levi (Magnes, Hebrew University: Jerusalem 1983),71–73, [Hebrew title: אלוהים מבקש את האדם].
[60] Ibid.

of the imagination that relationality of the biblical divine resurfaces in gendered attributes of God, surviving and evolving in re-adapted representations every generation anew. 1st century Judaism transposed the verbal image of divine indwelling among the people, the verb *shakhan* (Exodus 25:8), into a nominal image of feminine immanence of divine presence, entitled *Shekhina*. Alongside divinising Sabbath, the Torah and *Shekhina*, at times embodying both eponymous foremothers Rachel and Leah, images of female divine have been ubiquitously dominant in Jewish heritage.[61] Concomitantly, the Safed kabbala had domesticated the feminine divine presence. Interfacing Sabbath and *Shekhina*, a woman lighting her Sabbath candles identifies with the *Shekhina*.[62] *Shekhina* is still directly addressed in synagogues in Jewish prayers books of all contemporary streams in Judaism.

The Divine Image and Relationality: The Divine Revealed
21st century feminism lags behind 20th century feminism, interlinking the Hebrew deity, monotheism and biblical patriarchy with androcentricity and non-relationality between divine-humans-nature-man-women.[63]

Eluding the incarnation of God in human flesh, divine image in Judaism may seem a self-contradicting and unsolvable issue, offering a mystical, image-less depiction while revolving around revelations of divine presence within the world;[64] it is conceptualised in divine presence, "God revealed" – *hamitgale*.[65] Nonetheless, such divine presence is all about relationality. The concept of "divine revealed" overarches several concepts: the divine image after which humans are created; divine indwelling among the people; and God's duo-gendered personifications. The divine presence is relational to the world and humanity, and it merges both ontological and mystical demarcations.

Divine presence offers relationality among humans in mutually recognising the divine image in each other, in the belief of all humans having been created by God and after divine likeness and image (Genesis 1:27). Conceiving the divine image in oneself and in others adverts sacred relationality. Relationality by the divine image alludes to bonding among members of kinship sharing a sacred homological token. Such a conception resonates

---

[61] Scholem, *Elements of the Kabbala*, 259-307; Patai, *The Hebrew Goddess*, 96-110.
[62] Scholem, *Elements of the Kabbala*, 134, 144, 145.
[63] von Kellenbach, *Anti-Judaism*, 78-82, 85, 120, 137.
[64] Scholem, *Elements of the Kabbala*, 153-157.
[65] Ibid., 157, 165, 190, 276.

with ancient tribal kin constituting their communality by sharing a sacred totem for mutual recognition. The belief in divine image endowed by God to all humans turns them akin to both God and each other like family members. As a corollary, God reverberates with a divinised ancestor who serves kin members to trace a unifying provenance for their relational bond and communal identity. As Esau and Jacob reunite, 20 years of lethal sibling rivalry, exile and alienation melt into mutually empathetic recognition among brothers, whereby Jacob says: "I have seen thy face, as though I had seen the face of God" (Genesis 33:10). A few millennia later, in a Dutch concentration camp during WWII, a Jewish woman named Etty Hillesum writes in her diary: "I love people so terribly, because in every human being I love something of You (God). And I seek You everywhere in them and often do find something of You."[66] Finding relationality in mutual recognition of the divine image in the Other, biblical Jacob and Etty Hillesum intertextually evoke the recurrently interrelated biblical conceptions of the divine image and likeness in humans (Genesis 1:26-27); divine indwelling among people and on earth (Exodus 25:8); love of God (Deuteronomy 6:4); and God's commandment to love one another equally as oneself (Leviticus 19:18). By extrapolation, as Judaism searches the divine revealed neither in engraved images nor in supernatural miracles or even angels, life itself turns into a divine revelation, both divinely sacred and ontological. Abiding by such conceptions, monotheism bids unmediated relationality, both societal and mystical, between deity and humans and among humans themselves. Such relationality has existential, ethical, societal, and mystical ramifications. The following is brought as corroboration.

Following Yair Lorberbaum, the biblical conception of divine image constitutes a re-adaptation of ancient ideas about relationality between the divine and humanity. That the ancient conception promulgates that similitude of the divine induces divine presence, in the world and in humans. Originally, the ancient world had endowed a godly image exclusively unto kings, and, considering them divine, elevated them above other humans and beyond the laws of nature and society. The Hebrew Bible has revolutionised and democratised the concept of divine image, attributing it to all humans, men and women, commons and kings alike. On the one hand, the divine presence infuses life with sacrality; on the other hand, endowing divine image to all

---

[66] Etty Hillesum, Klaas AD Smelik and Arnold Pomerans, *Etty: The Letters and Diaries of Etty Hillesum 1941-1943* (Wm. B. Eerdmans Publishing: Grand Rapids, MI 2002), 514.

humans makes them equal before the laws of both nature and society. Creating humans after the image of God turns the divine image into a phenomenon both corporal and mystical, a divine presence incorporated in one's body and soul, which blurs the dichotomies between them. The divine image conjectures relational isomorphism between deity and humans, inducing unmediated interactive relationality between humans and divine. Rabbinical Judaism has accordingly extrapolated on isomorphism between God and humans to ban corporeal punishment and death penalty. Believing that humans substantiate extensions of divine presence, they conceived the infliction of pain on another human-being as hurting God. Since humans ontologically ramify the divine image on earth, destroying one human-being at the hand of another diminishes the divine presence in the world. By extrapolation, the presence of God in the world mutually depends on humans fulfilling the divine image.[67] Democratisation of the divine image is meaningful for gender reading. Democratising the divine in humanity resurfaces in both stories of creation. In the first story of creation, in Genesis 1, God creates both genders after a divine simile which seems ontological and corporal. In the story of Eden, the Fruit of Knowledge of good and evil alludes to moral conscience. Emulating ethical talents, it is acquired from God by both man and woman. In juxtaposition, the two stories of creation represent the divine in humans as ontological, ethical and mystical embodiments. By analogy, democratising the divine image turns the woman into an autonomous entity, both morally and corporally. Consequentially, the divine image affords the woman the recourse to unmediated relationality with the divine; a direct relationship independently of intermediaries even where androcentricity tends to be predominant. A classic example resurfaces in Hannah's prayer and vow, independently undertaken without her husband or the temple priest, Eli, negotiating for her (1Samuel 1:9-13; 2:1-10). This point leads to the issue of biblical patriarchy and women.

Patriarchy
Wavering between two axes, antithetical feminism either idealises a matriarchal society or vilifies a patriarchal system whose nascent bed is claimed by proponents of the matriarchal theory to be the Hebrews. Academically, the concept of pre-historical matriarchy is unwarrantedly born in romantic ideas of the

---

[67] Lorberbaum, *In God's Image*, 166-167; Yair Lorberbaum, "In God's Image," *JTS Library Book Talks Online.* (www.jtsa.edu/library, 2 March 2016).

19th century.[68] By analogy, so are antithetical notions regarding biblical patriarchy. For a start, a neutral and academic definition of "'patriarchy" is called for.

Simon Duncan postulates that patriarchy is highly differentiated in its structural, contextual, historical, and geographical ramifications. Moreover, on the ground, patriarchy inter-relates with other structures, systems and processes, including matriarchy. Patriarchy shifts with circumstances and socio-historical conditions and wavers with particular interpretations by individuals, families and communities. It is unwarranted, therefore, to regard patriarchy as a monolithic system spreading like "ethereal blanket floating over the world."[69] In this light, antithetic feminism reiterates tautological conceptualisations. By extrapolation, it is inaccurate to attribute the origin or responsibility for patriarchy to one particular culture, or claim that it overshadows all fabrics of society ever since, due to that culture. It is incorrect to admix ancient Israeli society with contemporary Judaism or represent both as epitomes of androcentric patriarchy. Moreover, it is unwarranted to retroject issues of Christian androcentric patriarchy onto Jewish contexts. Drawing an analogy for example, between biblical patriarchs and the patriarchal Church would be displaced since the biblical fathers inhere in the domestic and rural ancient Israel, while Church Patriarchs constitute a medieval super-structure anchored in a Christian centralised society.

The basic unit of biblical society was *Bet Av*, "a father's house" by title and representation. However, it had incorporated the extended family, men and women affiliated by blood or marital ties and bound by communal interests and land. Such extended units were not particular to ancient Israel; they have been archaeologically witnessed in Celtic finds as well, for example.[70] Commonly, a *Bet Av* would be headed by the elder male pointing to patriarchy; however, matriarchal systems intersected and modified it. Women like Zelophehad's daughters and Naomi headed their own houses (Numbers 27; Ruth 1-4). Concomitantly, a woman may remain at her father's house and on her natal land, eventually contracting either endogamous conjugation with one

---

[68] Cynthia Eller, *Gentlemen and Amazons: The Myth of Matriarchal Prehistory, 1861–1900* (University of California Press: Oakland, CA 2011).

[69] Simon Duncan, "Theorising Differences in Patriarchy," in: *Environment and Planning A*, 26:8 (1994), 1177-1194.

[70] Shimon Dar, "The Relationship between the Dwelling Place and the Family in Ancient Israel," in: *Research in Ancient Israel in Antiquity* (1996), 151-157 [Hebrew title: הזיקה בין מבנה-המגורים ובין המשפחה בארץ-ישראל מאז תקופת המקרא ועד תקופת התלמוד].

of her father's paternal kin or a bond of "*beena* marriage" importing a husband from outside the tribe. Under such circumstances, a woman's status would fall under a matriarchal paradigm. Intersecting the patriarchal system, it would allow a woman to inherit her natal land and perpetuate her family line (Numbers 27: 1-5, 36:6-12 Ruth 1-4).[71] Sheshan, a sonless man, arranges exogamous marriages for two of his daughters, and leaving the third on his natal land, marries her to their house slave, which entrenches her recourse to the family's inheritance and line (1Chron. 2:34-35). Job bestows land unto his daughters, by extrapolation, having them marry under matriarchal constructions, either with an endogamous or *beena* bridegroom (Job 42:15). While living under biblical patriarchy, wives and female members of all degrees were equally guaranteed rights to shelter, provision, the seventh day rest and protection from sexual abuse, down to maidservants or even captive brides, who are either offered marriage within the family, or set free, but are forbidden by law from being sold forward (Ex. 21: 7-11; Deuteronomy 21 10-15).

Even where patriarchy was the norm, individuals and families would interpret and manoeuvre their affairs according to their own convictions, though within the customs and laws of their time. It is arrogant of modern women to assume that biblical families or fathers were indifferent to the wellbeing and interests of their daughters or other female family members. Acting like a paragon of patriarchy, Laban, for example, also acts as a father and pursues Jacob to the border of Canaan in a desperate attempt to retrieve his daughters back home, and finally conceding, makes Jacob swear never to take additional wives over his daughters, concerned that this would cause them great distress, while the contemporary norms evidently allowed it (Genesis 32:50). Indeed, a daughter of the time married at her father's permission; but so did sons. Abraham and Judah arrange their sons' marriages, acting as *paterfamilias* (Genesis 24, 38). However, when heading a familial unit, a woman acts as a matriarch and arranges her ward's marriage according to the family's incorporated interests. Hagar arranges a bride for her son Ishmael when, by conjecture, she leads a matriarchal household residing with her natal tribe (Genesis 21:21).

---

[71] Julian Morgenstern, "Beena Marriage (Matriarchat) in Ancient Israel and its Historical Implications," in: *Zeitschrift für die Alttestamentliche Wissenschaft* 47.1 (1929), 91-110; Julian Morgenstern, "Additional Notes on 'Beena Marriage' (Matriarchat) in Ancient Israel," in: *Zeitschrift für die Alttestamentliche Wissenschaft* 49.1 (1931), 46-58; Thalia Gur-Klein, *Sexual hospitality in the Hebrew Bible: Patronymic, Metronymic, Legitimate, and Illegitimate Relations* (Routledge: Oxford 2013), 171-173, 179-181, 193, 198, 209, 212-215, 217, 219-221, 223-224, 235, 239, 242, 247-249, 251-254, 265-266, 268.

Naomi plans Ruth's marriage instructing her to glean in Boaz's field, and eventually directs her to lie at his feet on his drunken night at the threshing floor so as to induce him to marry her. Ruth for her part has abandoned her native family, land, gods, and culture to accept Naomi's maternal authority with mutual understanding that it enhances their communal status and their family's interests (Ruth 1-4).

A Self-Retrospective Look at the Mirror
The medieval *Vikuach* contests between the Church and Jewish representatives were defamed for the assistance of Jewish converts whose self-deprecating distortion of Judaism had served Christian accusations on a silver platter. Internalising antithetic and non-emic propensities against their own Jewish communities eventually enhanced the converts' acceptance in their new community.[72] Unawares, some Jewish feminists repeat such history, acclimating propensities of antithetic Christian and neo-pagan feminism. At heart, the divide resides in a gap between emic insight and comprehensive knowledge on the one hand, and adopting alien value judgement on the other. In the following, points of anti-Judaism which resurface in Jewish feminists' texts shall be discussed.

Her taking up the banner of anti-Judaic tendencies in feminism notwithstanding, Judith Plaskow claims that biblical family laws fail to forbid incestuous abuse of either daughter or granddaughters; as a corollary, she promulgates that biblical texts purport the protection of the strong and masculine in lieu of the weak and feminine in society.[73] Such allegations distort and circumvent the biblical spirit that conversely promulgates protection for the weak members of society, widows, orphans, the poor, and the foreigner (Malachi 3:5). Plaskow's postulations are unwarranted and furthermore misrepresent the strict family bars on sexual relations among kin stipulated in Leviticus 18 and 20, bars that aim at restraining male family members and protecting feminine family members from sexual abuse. Incest laws fall under prohibitions by inclusion, extension and extrapolation. By inclusion, incest laws endorse strict bars on sexual contact between kin whether related by blood or marital affinity

---

[72] Schama, *The History of the Jews*, 350.
[73] Judith Plaskow, *The Coming of Lilith; Essays on Feminism, Judaism, and Sexual Ethics 1972-2003* (Beacon Press: Boston 2005), 121, 168 respectively; Thalia Gur-Klein, "On Feminist Propensity: Anti-Judaism in Plaskow's Reading of Hebrew Texts; a Contra-Reading," in: *Feminist Theology* 17.2 (2009), 254-260.

down to three generations in either direction, paternal or maternal (Leviticus 18:6-20).[74] By extension, if a granddaughter is barred for sexual relations, even more so a daughter whether related by marital or blood affinity. By extrapolation, the prohibition on concurrent relations with both daughter and mother mutually outlaws sexual contact with one on account of relations with the other. If a man is married to a woman, her daughter is forbidden unto him, be she his natural child related by blood or step daughter related by marital affinity through his wife who is her mother. Simultaneous relations with both woman and daughter also mean that being married to one imposes bars on relations with her mother, on account of her being a man's mother-in-law (Leviticus 18:17; 20:14). Extrapolating on the biblical texts, the Talmud shows uncompromising abhorrence of incestuous relations equating it with bloodshed. The sages thus decreed that if a person is commanded either to commit incest or kill another (innocent) human being, or otherwise be killed, howbeit under the threat of death, such a person should still refuse to commit either murder or incest, and rather let himself be killed; only when pursued by a murderer or perceiving a murderer in action, one is allowed to strike that person in order to save life (Babylonian Talmud, *Sanherdrin* 74a; 8:7 respectively).

Furthermore, Plaskow promulgates that the Jews in *Esther* were acting on a broader warrant for genocide,[75] reversing the roles between the persecuted Jews and their persecutors, who were the ones given a genocidal licence to exterminate the Jews. Moreover, the king would not revoke Haman's decree to annihilate the Jews on that designated day. He merely allowed them to carry arms for defence, which by conjecture had been forbidden unto them so as to expose them to harm. In the following, with the threat of genocide hanging over their heads, the Jews were allowed to fight in self-defence specifically only against their attackers, youth or old, which they did while avoiding looting (Esther 8 and 9). Like confluent anti-Judaic propensities in antithetic feminism, Plaskow's postulations perpetuate historical anti-Semitic libels that misrepresent the Hebrew Bible and Judaism, vilifying the Jews as perverts, blood thirsty, cruel, and exploiters of the weak. She concomitantly reiterates a feminism that proclaims the Hebrew God, God-language and divine figuration

---

[74] Stephen F. Bigger, "The family Laws of Leviticus 18 in their Setting," in: *Journal of Biblical Literature* 98.21 (1979), 187-203; Louis M. Epstein, *Sex Laws and Customs in Judaism* 12 (Ktav Pub. House: New York 1968); Louis M. Epstein, *Marriage Laws in the Bible and the Talmud* (Johnson Reprint Corporation: London 1968).

[75] Plaskow, *The Coming of Lilith*, 114.

to be masculinised and void of female factors, metaphors and imagery.[76] These issues have been argued to be unwarranted and biased, but coming from a Jewish feminist theologian, they seem to emulate self-deprecation and ignorance of one's heritage.

Concomitantly, Carol Och propagates that the Hebrew God orders Abraham to kill his son so as to teach him obedience for thwarting His intention to annihilate Sodom's population. In demanding blind obedience, God moreover is said to sever Abraham's former alliance with the pagan goddess; whereby God demands that he (Abraham) renounces the most fundamental tenet of matriarchal religion, and kill his own child in lieu of maternal love nurtured by the goddess.[77] Och reverberates with anti-Jewish libels that delineate the Hebrew God as a bloodthirsty tyrant and Jews as His morally blind followers, who, being hostile to the primordial goddess, turn heartless fathers and child killers; the pagan goddess, by conjecture, reverberates with boundless love.[78] Och circumvents the very moral fibres of Genesis 18 and 22 which thwart collective annihilation and human sacrifices (discussed above), both of which she distorts. Like the Christian and neo-pagan feminists discussed above, Och presents the Hebrew deity as an antithesis of the primordial goddess; and, highlighting God's command to Abraham to sacrifice Isaac, she blots out the second command which comes to contradict it and abrogate human sacrifice. Concomitantly, Och is oblivious of Jewish exegesis.

Asphodel P. Long straddles between rediscovering the feminine divine in Judaism and antithetic feminism, blaming the Hebrews for suppressing goddess' religions, howbeit conceding that they have tried, but failed and left it for the Church Fathers to root out.[79] Since the *Shekhina*, the female divine immanence is still included in all prayer books of every Jewish stream until today, such claims show Judaism to have preserved a goddess religion befitting its spirit and worship.

As a corollary, Melissa Raphael exalts the *Shekhina* as divine presence in humanity, while conjuring an unmodified statement saying that "Orthodox male discourse, in interpretive and practical dominance privileges masculinity

---

[76] ibid 121,168 respectively; Gur-Klein, "On Feminist Propensity," 254-260.
[77] Carol Och, *Behind the Sex of God* (Beacon: Boston 1977), 45-46; cited in von Kellenbach, *Anti-Judaism*, 102.
[78] Ibid.
[79] Asphodel P. Long, "Anti-Judaism in Britain," in: *Journal of Feminist Studies in Religion* 7.2 (1991), 125-133, here 131.

as the primary image of God".[80] Since the statement is not supported by showcases or warranted citations, it remains ambiguous. Whether irony or criticism, it disconcertingly stereotypes Orthodox Jewry. Unambiguous is Cynthia Ozick, whom Raphael brings up. Ozick analogises the Nazi extermination system with the socio-historical position of Jewish women whom she claims likewise suffered misogynistic policy of annihilating silencing, exclusion, erasure, and suppression of their talents and activities at the hand of Jewish men.[81] Appropriating the Holocaust and the Nazi racial and extermination policy against men, women and children to highlight social discrepancies is morally reprehensible and displaced. The latter falls under the category of social evolution to be argued, protested, revolutionised, and renewed, while the former inheres in irreversible crimes against humanity and genocide. *Per analogiam*, Ozick puts Jewish men on a par with the Nazi deportation, persecution and mass killing at the hand of the *Einsatzgruppen*, the *death squads and/or the gas chambers*. Comparing the social status of Jewish women with the Nazi Holocaust shows contempt towards the actual Shoah victims; the comparisons are unethical and unwarranted, and academically convey a narrow insight or knowledge about Jewish women.

Jewish heritage has never silenced women's voices and roles. It is the female grief and lamenting voices of Rachel and Zion that communicate the people's suffering to God and the world (Jeremiah 31:15; Lamentations). And ever since the biblical Deborah, a wife, mother, judge, and spiritual leader, Judaism counts prominent women like the 2nd century Talmudic scholar Bruriah (Tractate *Pesachim* 62b); the learned daughters of 12th century codifier Rashi, who became themselves biblical codifiers;[82] diarists like Glukel von Hameln in the 17th century,[83] and Etty Hillesum in the 20th century, both showing deep knowledge of Jewish sources and Judaism;[84] or Hannah Rochel Verbermacher in the 19th century, known as the Maiden of Ludmir, who by her learning and charisma became a holy rabbi with a Hassidic

---

[80] Melissa Raphael, *The Female Face of God in Auschwitz: A Jewish Feminist Theology of the Holocaust* (Routledge: London 2003), 3.

[81] Cynthia Ozick, "Notes toward Finding the Right Question," in: Susanah Heschel (ed.), *On Being a Jewish Feminist: A Reader* (Schocken: New York 1995), 120-151; Cited in Raphael, *The Female Face*, 21.

[82] Judith S. Antonelli, *In the Image of God: A Feminist Commentary on the Torah* (Jason Aronson, Incorporated: New Jersey, London 1997), xxix.

[83] Bertha Pappenheim, *Die Memoiren der Glückel von Hameln* (Beltz Gelberg: Weinheim 2013).

[84] Hillesum, Smelik and Pomerans, *Etty*.

community of her own.[85] These women, among others, show that Judaism has produced learned and courageous women who were creative thinkers, scholars, political and religious leaders, and excellent writers. The Jewish community reciprocated with reverence. Furthermore, there has never been a prohibition or ban on women's education and learning in Judaism. Based on Deuteronomy 31:10-13, which specifically commands to gather all the community, women and children to be taught God's Torah, the Talmud and rabbis encouraged learning among women.[86] As a corollary, in order to forward grass roots knowledge of Torah and Judaism among women and laymen, the rabbis had produced *Tze'ena U-Re'ena*, a compilation of Women's Bible in Yiddish with Talmudic exegesis which has been most popular in Jewish houses ever since.[87] On the social strata, Jewish women were engaged in charity and social work,[88] which in the end of the day was valued as highly as Torah study if not more. The Talmudic case of Mar 'Ukba and his wife teaches that charity coming from a pure heart gains a woman a divine revelation, showing her to be more highly appraised than her learned husband (Babylonian Talmud, *Kethuboth* 67:72).[89]

Conclusion

The Jewish feminists quoted above resonate with anti-Jewish Christian and neo-pagan feminism of both the 20th and 21st centuries. Both Jewish and non-Jewish women discussed here are educated and established scholars and/or teachers. As the Talmud says: if a flame has caught up with the cedars, what shall the moss on the wall do? (Babylonian Talmud, *Moed Katan* 25:3).

---

[85] Nathaniel Deutsch, *The Maiden of Ludmir: A Jewish Holy Woman and Her World* (University of California Press: Oakland, CA 2003).
[86] Sarah Bekerman, "Gather the People: men, women and children," in: *Kolech, Online magazine of Religious Women* (www.kolech.org.il, 7 October 2016).
[87] Sol Liptzin, *A History of Yiddish Literature* (Jonathan David Publishers: Middle Village, NY 1972), 10-11; *Zennah u-Reenah. Frauenbibel: Nach dem Jüdisch-Deutschen Bearbeitet von Bertha Pappenheim Erstes Buch Moses* (Jüdischer Frauenbund: Frankfurt 1930); Margalit Shilo (ed.), *Voices of Jerusalem Women: Writings of Jewish Learned Women of the Nineteenth Century* (Dinur Centre: Jerusalem 2006) [Hebrew title: הקול הנשי הירושלמי: כתבי למדניות מן המאה התשע עשרה].
[88] Beth S. Wenger, "Jewish Women and Voluntarism: Beyond the Myth of Enabler," in: *American Jewish History* 79.1 (1989), 16-36.
[89] Admiel Kosman, *Femininity in the Talmud* (Hakibbutz Hameuchad: Tel-Aviv 2008), 40-42, 53-54, 62-63, [Hebrew title: נשיות בתלמוד]; *Mar* – an archaic title in Aramaic for a revered/esteemed/learned man.

Anti-Judaism in our century shows that teaching of contempt must still be recognised and replaced by teaching of respect. A synonym for recognition of the Other, it ought to cover respect for living Judaism as well as towards its ancient past and the dead who cannot speak for themselves. In the end of the day, I do not wish to perpetuate mutual alienation, but to open hearts to the moral concerns and multifaceted depth and beauty of Judaism.

Thalia Gur-Klein MA in English Literature and Yiddish Culture, Leiden University; MA in Jewish Studies, Hebrew Bible, Talmud, and Feminist Theology, Amsterdam University. Published several articles about Jewish women, and a book titled *Sexual Hospitality in the Hebrew Bible: Patronymic, metronymic, legitimate and illegitimate relations* (Routledge, 2014). Her current research deals with veneration of saints in Judaism: from Jewish holy women to sexual objects of holy Jewish men.

Elisabeth Schneider-Böklen

Elisabeth Cruciger – Nun, Minister's Wife and First Lutheran Poetess[1]

The hymn *Herr Christ, der einig Gotts Sohn* [Lord Christ, the only son of God] originating from the time of the Reformation is still sung today. It was written by Elisabeth Cruciger, a nun from Pomerania who had already been convinced by Johannes Bugenhagen of Martin Luther's theology. In 1524, she married Caspar Cruciger, one of Luther's co-workers, in Wittenberg, and in that same year her hymn was first published. Elisabeth Cruciger's text combines biblical theology, parts of the patristic thinking and religious experience of female mysticism. Besides her hymn, a letter exists which is mentioned in another one written by Joachim, a baptised Jew in Stettin. In this letter Cruciger shows a very profound knowledge of the new Lutheran doctrine of Justification, and also empathy for Joachim's spiritual situation. Elisabeth and Caspar Cruciger were married by Martin Luther in 1524. A document detailing the ceremony, discovered in 1717, reveals an anti-romantic view of marriage.

Das Lied "Herr Christ, der einig Gotts Sohn" aus der Reformationszeit wird bis heute gesungen. Es stammt von Elisabeth Cruciger, geborene von Meseritz (ca. 1500–1535) einer Nonne in Pommern, die um 1522 durch Johannes Bugenhagen von Luthers Theologie überzeugt wurde. 1524 heiratete sie Caspar Cruciger, einen von Luthers Mitarbeitern in Wittenberg. Ihr Lied wurde 1524 das erste Mal gedruckt, der Text verbindet biblische Theologie, patristisches Gedankengut und die religiöse Erfahrung weiblicher Mystik. Neben ihrem Lied gibt es einen Brief von ihr, der in einem Brief eines getauften Juden Joachim aus Stettin von 1524 zitiert wird. Darin zeigt sie eine tiefe Kenntnis der lutherischen Rechtfertigungslehre wie auch Empathie für Joachims geistliche Situation. Ein Porträt von Elisabeth Cruciger findet sich vermutlich im Epitaph der Familie Cruciger "Jesus segnet die Kinder" aus der Werkstatt von Lukas Cranach d. J. von 1560.

---

[1] This text is based on a lecture given at the 21st Annual Meeting of the Society for Reformation Studies in Cambridge (9-11.4.2014). Thanks to Mary Ratcliffe for her help in translating into English!

Elisabeth Cruciger, née von Meseritz, is one of the almost forgotten women of the Church; however, only "almost", because in the German Protestant church her hymn "Herr Christ, der einig Gotts Sohn" [Lord Christ, the only son of God] has for many years been the required hymn in the service held on the last Sunday after Epiphany.[2] The paper shall take a brief look at Elisabeth Cruciger's life and work, aiming to show that her life – as a nun and also as a married woman – was determined in the first place by her deep faith and relationship to the God Father, the Son and the Holy Spirit, expressed by the feeling of love, rooted in Church practice by praying, singing, living with Scripture and the Sacraments. All of these points are also to be found in her song.

The last 15 years have seen the publication of several new scholarly articles about Elisabeth Cruciger's life and her hymn. In 2001 Mary Jane Haemig started a new discussion about the reasons for which Elisabeth Cruciger had not always been recognised as the author of the hymn,[3] Then in 2002, in an article published both in German and English, Albrecht Classen praised Elisabeth Cruciger as a religious poetess and also as a theologian of great importance, although mostly neglected in literary studies.[4] These opinions about Elisabeth Cruciger were well summarised by Linda Maria Koldau in 2005.[5] In 2011, Micheline White published an article about the reception of Elisabeth Cruciger's hymn in England, where it had already been translated into English at the time of Reformation.[6]

Her Life as Nun

Elisabeth was born in Pomerania (today Poland), on the estate of Meseritz, located southeast of the town of Treptow (nowadays Trzebiatów) and northwest

---

[2] Various interpretations may be listened to on www.youtube.de.
[3] Mary Jane Haemig, "Elisabeth Cruciger (1500?-1535): The Case of the Disappearing Hymn Writer," in: *The Sixteenth Century Journal* 32, No. 1 (2001), 21-44.
[4] Albrecht Classen, "Elisabeth Creutzigerin oder Crucigerin," in: Albrecht Classen, *Mein Seel fang an zu singen. Religiöse Frauenlieder des 15.-16. Jahrhunderts. Kritische Studien und Texteditionen (Studies in Spirituality, Supplement 6)* (Peeters: Leuven/Paris/Sterling/Virginia 2002), 258-265.
[5] Linda Maria Koldau, *Frauen-Musik-Kultur. Ein Handbuch zum Sprachgebiet der Frühen Neuzeit* (Böhlau: Köln 2005), 419-423.
[6] Micheline White, "Women's Hymns in Mid-Sixteenth-Century England: Elisabeth Cruciger, Miles Coverdale, and Lady Elizabeth Tyrwhit," in: *ANQ: A Quarterly Journal of Short Articles, Notes, and Reviews* 24, No. 1-2 (2011), 21-32, 23.

of Schivelbein (Świdwin), in about 1500.[7] In her childhood, she entered a convent for nuns, probably Premonstratensians, in Marienbusch Abbey (which no longer exists), near Treptow. There, a nun's education in late mediaeval piety may have acquainted Elisabeth von Meseritz with chants. In her years at Marienbusch, she also learnt something about the most important biblical and theological matters of interest (in Latin). There she most probably led a spiritual life with a mystical relation to Jesus Christ, embedded in the daily monastic prayers and services. The song she wrote later, in 1524, obviously reflects both.

In 1517, Johannes Bugenhagen arrived at the monastery of Belbuck, near Marienbusch, as a Bible teacher. Later on, Bugenhagen was impressed by Martin Luther's theology,[8] and it is also probable that Elisabeth von Meseritz was affected by this new thinking and belief. The emergence of her evangelical thinking can be detected in a letter dated 1524 which she wrote to Joachim, a baptised Jew in Stettin (Szczecin). A rough translation of an excerpt reads as follows:

> Dear brother, grace and peace. I understand, dear brother, that we are living reluctant to accept God into our lives and not able to receive God's grace (although we are redeemed by the blood of Christ)... But console yourself, dear brother, look, I have asked God by a gentle request before His divine eyes, I wish you and give you grace and peace through His power... (Christ) will cover our injustice, so that we will not be accused by anybody. Therefore, enjoy yourself and console yourself, my dear brother, (as I do). So receive this letter and get consolation from it, as it pleases God, that we may console ourselves and kiss each other with the kiss of God's love..."[9]

Though Elisabeth von Meseritz wrote this letter only in 1524, it reflects the influence of the reformatory body of thought in the years before. This may be seen in the following:

1. Her ability to express her thoughts and beliefs focussing on the doctrine of justification ("Christ will cover our injustice..."), which leads to "enjoy yourself and console yourself," meaning a deep emotion.

---

[7] Hans Volz, "Woher stammt die Kirchenlied-Dichterin Elisabeth Cruciger?" in: *Jahrbuch für Liturgik und Hymnologie* 11 (1966), 163-165.
[8] Anneliese Bieber, *Johannes Bugenhagen zwischen Reform und Reformation* (Vandenhoeck: Göttingen 1993), 18.
[9] Otto Clemen, "Ein Brief eines getauften Juden in Stettin aus dem Jahre 1524," in: *Pommersche Jahrbücher* 9 (1908), 175-180, here 179 (translation into English by the author).

2. She writes confidently (in the reformatorian "priesthood of all believers"): "I have asked God by a gentle request before His divine eyes, I wish you and give you grace and peace through His power..."
3. She has no problem sending Joachim kisses in her letter: "It is a pleasure to God that we may console ourselves and kiss each other with the kiss of God's love." As mentioned above, the loving relation to God is the most important point, integrating body, soul and mind. Although the kiss she mentions will be the traditional "kiss of God's love" according to 1 Pet., or the "holy kiss" in Rom. 16,16 and 1 Cor. 16,20.

In 1521, Bugenhagen went to Wittenberg to study directly under Martin Luther. The abbot and several monks from Belbuck Monastery left with him. It is not quite clear why they departed; perhaps it was not only for the Lutheran ideas but also because of the fact that the Pomeranian Duke was "land-grabbing" Belbuck.[10] Elisabeth von Meseritz also left Marienbusch and went to Wittenberg, where she could live with Bugenhagen's family. Bugenhagen, although a priest, had already married Walpurga (Triller?) in 1522.[11] This complete change from a purely female environment must have been a big step for Elisabeth von Meseritz: to leave the nunnery that in every respect had been a home and a safe place for her entire life in order to face uncertainty. What happened then to her parents, brothers or sisters is not known, or rather not yet researched. It is at the end of this period of her life – about 1524 – that she must have written her hymn, "Herr Christ, der einig Gotts Sohn".

Her Life as a Minister's Wife in Martin Luther's Circle of Friends
On 14th June 1524, Elisabeth married the theologian Caspar Cruciger (the Elder), a 20-year-old student and assistant to Martin Luther; a text of the marriage ceremony conducted by Martin Luther exists. This text was first printed

---

[10] Norbert Backmund, *Monasticon Praemonstratense* (de Gruyter: Berlin 1983), 330; Hans Hermann Holfelder, "Bugenhagen," in: *Theologische Realenzyklopädie* (de Gruyter: Berlin 1981), 7, 356; Hermann Hoogeweg, *Die Stifter und Klöster der Provinz Pommern* 2 (Saunier: Stettin 1925), 68-71 [Kloster Belbuck], 758-769 [Kloster Marienbusch].
[11] Theodor Diestel, "Ein Schreiben der Witwe Bugenhagens," in: *Zeitschrift für Kirchengeschichte* 11 (1890), 483; Inge Mager, "Theologenehefrauen als 'Gehilfinnen' der Reformation," in: *Cistercienser Chronik* 120/2, (2013), 175-193, about Walpurga Bugenhagen, 176-180.

in 1717, but quotes Spalatin as the author.[12] This wedding was a far cry from being a romantic ceremony "in front of the parish church in Wittenberg." Almost without exception, it was the difficult times of family life which were mentioned: "misery, sorrow and hard work," quoting also Genesis 3, 19 to the bridegroom: "In the sweat of thy face shalt thou eat bread," and Gen. 3:16 to the bride: "in sorrow thou shalt bring forth children." Then, both had to say yes, Doctor Martin Luther put the rings on their fingers and thus ended the ceremony by quoting Gen. 1:28: "Be fruitful, and multiply." Two points here are interesting:

1. No word of the submission of the bride, but very realistic duties and tasks for both the bridegroom and the bride, founded in Scripture.
2. Sexuality means children and fertility – nothing more.

Since Elisabeth von Meseritz was of noble birth, Johannes Bugenhagen wrote in a letter to Georg Spalatin that he had not been able to reply any sooner because he had to prepare Elisabeth's wedding, and that Spalatin should please bring some venison for the wedding breakfast as they had to prepare food for about 10 tables, taking into account the bride's noble family – even though none of them would come![13]

Caspar Cruciger became a very successful assistant and writer to Martin Luther (It was said: *"Lutheranos Scribam habere omnibus Pontificiis doctiorem"* [The Lutherans have a writer more learned than all the pontificals!]).[14] Then, he became a School Director in Magdeburg and following that again a preacher and professor in Wittenberg.

What had Elisabeth's life as Cruciger's wife been like? A detailed picture of her personality and private life has not been handed down; only a few pieces of the puzzle are available. Here are only two examples: Elisabeth Cruciger was occasionally mentioned in correspondence between her husband and Luther. Thus, in a letter dated 21 December 1532, Martin Luther wrote to

---

[12] Johann Joachim Müller, "Was heut zu Tage bey Copulationen vor Ceremonien gebrauchet werden, ist bekannt; wie es aber zu des seeligen D. Luthers Zeiten damit ergangen, zeiget folgender von Spalatio gefertigter Aufsatz," in: Johann Joachim Müller, *Entdecktes Staats-Cabinet* (Jena 1717), 8. *Eröffnung*, 218-219.

[13] Rudolf Thommen, "Drei Briefe des Johannes Bugenhagen," in: *Mitteilungen des Instituts für Österreichische Geschichtsforschung* XXI (Innsbruck 1891), 154-159, here 158.

[14] Johann Caspar Wetzel, *Historische Lebensbeschreibung der berühmtesten Liederdichter* (Roth-Scholz: Herrnstadt 1719), I, 391.

Caspar Cruciger that his wife, Katharina and Elisabeth were exchanging gifts. Elisabeth bought Katharina golden jewellery and so Martin Luther sent Elisabeth something similar, a necklace.[15] In another letter from Johannes Bugenhagen to Martin Luther of 24 January 1532, Elisabeth is mentioned as an intelligent and sensible (*"prudens"*) woman.[16]

Nearly every word that Martin Luther spoke at his Table Talks (Tischreden) has been recorded. But that does not prove that he alone was talking in those days: on the contrary, the intellectual academic elite, (young) men and also sometimes the wives of Luther and his friends took part in the discussions.

So Elisabeth Cruciger is mentioned in Martin Luther's Table Talks. She once asked what to do in a (Catholic) church when the priest has raised the host. Martin Luther answered: "Liebe Els, nimm nur den Pfaffen nicht vom Altar, lösch auch die Kerzen nicht aus!" [17] [Dear Els, do not remove the priest from the altar, do not snuff out the candles!][18] This shows that Elisabeth Cruciger was perhaps an occasional guest at the Table Talks ("Dear Els" being a familiar form of address), and that she may also have been involved in the theological debates there, although there is no other proof or source in the Table Talks of her participation. Surely, she had the natural right to be a member at Luther's table in Wittenberg, like Katharina von Bora, the so-called "*doctorissa*",[19] who is also quoted as speaking Latin.[20]

Elisabeth had two children: in 1525 a son Caspar, called The Younger, who later becme a theologian and a follower of Philipp Melanchthon,[21] and a daughter, Elisabeth, who first married the rector Kegel in Eisleben and after his death Johannes, Martin Luther's son.

Elisabeth Cruciger died on 2 May 1535, probably only 35 years old.[22] Later on, Martin Luther referred to this and praised her as a great example of faithfully dying, saying to Caspar Cruciger in a Table Talk: "We must let *Dei misericordiam* [God's Mercy] be bigger than our *calamitates* [troubles,

---

[15] D. Martin Luthers *Werke: kritische Gesamtausgabe* [hereafter WA] (Böhlau: Weimar 1883), BR 6: *Letter Nr. 1981 of 21 December 1532,* 396.
[16] Otto Vogt, *Dr. Johannes Bugenhagens Briefwechsel* (Saunier: Stettin 1888), 123.
[17] WA TR 1, Nr. 803, 382-383.
[18] Translation into English by the author.
[19] WA TR 5, Nr. 5567, 247.
[20] WA TR 4, Nr. 4860.
[21] Friedrich Wilhelm Bautz, "Elisabeth Cruciger," in: *Biographisch-Bibliographisches Kirchenlexikon* (Bautz: Nordhausen 1990), I, 1171-1172.
[22] WA BR 7, 384, footnote 5.

calamities], for your dear wife was dying with such a seriousness of faith, that I would like to be with her. Oh, if I had jumped over the creek, I would never want to come back"![23] Caspar Cruciger himself must have been very sad, as Philipp Melanchthon wrote in a letter to Camerario, dated 23 May 1535: "Cruciger took Sebaldus as a companion with him, that he will lift his mourning, for Cruciger lost his wife."[24]

Her Indirect Living-On in her Husband's Booklet about Marriage
"Childbearing is also a way of serving God" wrote Elisabeth's husband, Caspar Cruciger in a booklet about 1. Tim. 2:15 (How wives also become blessed) after her death in May 1535.[25]

The text was translated into German in 1538 by Georg Spalatin and printed in Erfurt. Here, one may risk saying that Caspar Cruciger must have written the text not only because he was a well-educated theologian and Bible expert, but also as the result of a good and fulfilling marriage to Elisabeth Cruciger. And as for the theme of "Gender and Sexuality", here proof may be found for the thesis mentioned above: that Elisabeth's life – as a nun and additionally as a married woman – was determined in the first place by her deep faith and relationship to Christ, integrating (not repressing!) sensual feelings and sexuality.

Let it be put this way: she lived her life in this manner, and he wrote it down. Caspar Cruciger described the five virtues of a wife according to St. Paul: bearing children, love, faith, sanctification, and moderation:

- Bearing children: for Caspar Cruciger, that was a duty to the Church and the occupation and vocation of a wife; he wrote in addition of the difficulties and hard work involved in raising children;[26]
- Love: meaning living with love to God and one's neighbour. This applies to everyone, and for a wife it may mean, according to Caspar Cruciger, that she may love both God and her husband – for instance, staying with him

---

[23] WA TR 2, 78, Nr. 1377, 14-17.
[24] Carl Gottlieb Bretschneider, *Corpus Reformatorum* (Schwetschke: Halle 1835), II, No.1276, Philipp Melanchthon to Joachim Camerario from 23 May 1535.
[25] Caspar Cruciger, *Herrn || Doctor Cas=||par Creutzigers ausle=||gung/ vber Sanct Pau=|||lus spruch zum Thimotheo/|| wie die Eheweiber...* (Christoffel Golthammer: Erfurt 1538); original without numbered pages, hereby numbered by author. (http://digitale.bibliothek.uni-halle.de/vd16/content/titleinfo/995895, 8 October 2016)
[26] Ibid., [24]

in hard times – as well as showing love to her children. Furthermore, she shall also love the poor;[27]
- Faith: meaning trusting in Christ to receive His forgiveness for sins and thus becoming God's children and brothers and sisters in God and to one another?;[28]
- Sanctification: meaning that marital sexuality is holy and chaste. Therefore, Caspar Cruciger rejected both adultery and celibacy, and called marriage a wonderful thing;[29]
- Moderation: meaning a wife's (public) moderate behaviour in eating and drinking, in dressing and living. (It should not be forgotten, that in the 16th century there was no social concept of privacy as we know it today).[30]

To date, no pictures of Elisabeth Cruciger have been unearthed, but a certain idea of how she may have looked can be discerned from the memorial plaque for the Cruciger family produced by Lukas Cranach the Younger's workshop in 1560 ("*Jesus segnet die Kinder*") – perhaps Elisabeth is the married woman behind Caspar Cruciger.[31]

Her song *"Herr Christ, der einig Gotts Sohn"*[32]

1. *Herr Christ, der einig Gotts Sohn*
   Vaters in Ewigkeit,
   aus seim Herzen entsprossen,
   gleichwie geschrieben steht,
   er ist der Morgensterne,
   sein Glänzen streckt er ferne
   [33]*vor andern Sternen klar;*

2. *für uns ein Mensch geboren*
   im letzten Teil der Zeit,
   daß wir nicht wärn verloren
   vor Gott in Ewigkeit,
   den Tod für uns zerbrochen,

---

[27] Ibid., [12-13]
[28] Ibid., [12]
[29] Ibid., [15-16]
[30] Ibid., [19-20]
[31] http://www.lucascranach.org/digitalarchive.php, 7 February 2017.
[32] Martin Luther et al., *Enchiridion oder Handbüchlein geistlicher Gesänge und Psalmen* (Loersfeld: Erfurt 1524), 47.
[33] Ibid.

den Himmel aufgeschlossen,
das Leben wiederbracht:

3. laß uns in deiner Liebe
und Kenntnis nehmen zu,
daß wir am Glauben bleiben,
dir dienen im Geist so,
daß wir hie mögen schmecken
dein Süßigkeit im Herzen
und dürsten stets nach dir.

4. Du Schöpfer aller Dinge,
du väterliche Kraft,
regierst von End zu Ende
kräftig aus eigner Macht.
Das Herz uns zu dir wende
und kehr ab unsre Sinne,
daß sie nicht irrn von dir.

5. Ertöt uns durch dein Güte,
erweck uns durch dein Gnad,
den alten Menschen kränke
daß der neu' leben mag
und hie auf dieser Erden
den Sinn und alls Begehren
und G'danken hab zu dir.[34]

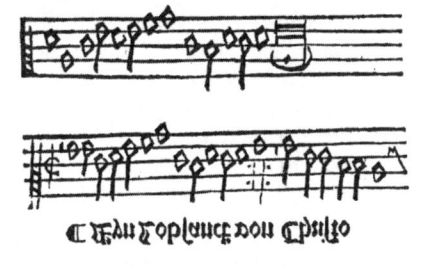

Figure 1: Herr Christ, der einig Gotts Sohn im Erfurter Enchiridion (1524) 33

Micheline White gives a line-by-line literal translation by Johannes Wolfart:[35]

1. Lord Christ, the only son of God
of his father in eternity
From his heart sprouted
As it is written
He is the morning star
who extends his radiance further
than other bright stars.

2. For us a person born
in the last part of time

---

[34] *Evangelisches Gesangbuch, Ausgabe für die Evangelisch-Lutherischen Kirchen in Bayern und Thüringen* (Evangelischer Presseverband für Bayern: München 1994), Nr. 67.
[35] White, "Women's Hymns," 30.

> The mother did not lose
> her maidenly chastity
> He broke death open for us
> unlocked heaven
> brought life again.
>
> 3. Let us in your love
> and knowledge increase
> That we may remain in faith
> and serve in the spirit so
> that we here may taste
> your sweetness in our hearts
> and thirst constantly for you.
>
> 4. You creator of all things
> you fatherly power
> Reign from end to end
> mighty in your own power
> Turn our heart to you
> and turn away our senses
> so that they do not err (or wander) from you.
>
> 5. Kill us with your goodness
> awake us through your grace
> Sicken the old man
> so the new one may live
> And here on this earth
> all senses and all desires
> and thanks (thoughts) will go to you.

Four extraordinary characteristics of Elisabeth Cruciger's poetry show her Lutheran thinking and feeling, and may also be partly linked to the context of "Gender and Sexuality" in a wider sense:

1. Biblical allusions

According to the reformatorian *"sola scriptura"*, Elisabeth Cruciger puts particular emphasis on citing the bible "as it is written", which is given a line of its own in her hymn. So, for instance, in the first stanza, like in Jn 1:18, the son is "from his (the father's) heart sprouted," as it is translated in the King James' Version: "the Son, which is in the bosom of the Father," or Jesus Christ called "the morning star" according to Rev. 22:16.

In the second stanza, she sings about the incarnation ("in the last part of time" according to Gal. 4:4), that is the Christmas story in the Gospels according to Mt. 1 and Lk. 1:26-56 and 2:1-21, and also the cross and resurrection in their meaning for man's salvation (according to 2 Tim. 1:10, Rev. 2:7).
In the third stanza, she prays "Let us in your love ...increase" according to 1 Pet. 2:2, or "that we serve in the spirit so" according to Jn 4:24; also, "that we here may taste / your sweetness in our hearts," which is rooted in Ps. 34:9 (vulg.) and 1 Pet. 2:3.
In the fourth stanza, Elisabeth Cruciger praises Christ's deity and reigning according to Rev. 11:15; the demand "turn our heart to you / and turn away our senses" may be rooted in Ps. 119: 36 and 37 (*"inclina – averte"*).
And the fifth and last stanza describes the spiritual change according to St. Paul's old and new man (Rom. 6:6, Eph. 4:22 and Col. 3:9-10).

2. The (Early) Christian tradition
As in the Credo or the hymns (sung at daily prayers in the nunnery), in the second stanza the words "The mother did not lose her maidenly chastity" are part of the credo: "born of the Virgin Mary" – which Miles Coverdale in the 16th century translated: "yet kepte she maydenheade unforlorne [not lost],"[36] but nowadays in the German hymnal, the Virgin Mary is no longer mentioned at all. According to Christa Reich, it was only in 1932 that Wilhelm Thomas and Konrad Ameln changed the phrase to its current state.[37] The words about Christ mentioned above in the first stanza are also to be found in Prudentius's hymn *"Corde natus ex parentis"* (4th century).[38] However, Christa Reich prefers to regard a sermon given by Ambrosius (for the consecration of a virgin, his sister) as the more direct source for the biblical thoughts used by Elisabeth Cruciger, as, for instance:

Hunc, inquam, dilige. Ipse est quem pater ante luciferum genuit ut aeternam, ex utero generavit ut filium, ex corde eructavit ut verbum. Ipse est in quo complacuit pater, ipse est brachium, quia creator est omnium...patris virtus [see stanza 4], *quia*

---
[36] Ibid., 24.
[37] Christa Reich, "Liedanalyse 'Herr Christ, der einig Gotts Sohn'," in: *Liederkunde zum Evangelischen Gesangbuch* 2 (Vandenhoeck: Göttingen 2000), 48-54.
[38] Waltraut Ingeborg Sauer-Geppert, "To the song 'Herr Christ, der einig Gotts Sohn'," in: Christhard Mahrenholz and Oskar Söhngen, *Handbuch zum evangelischen Kirchengesangbuch, Liederkunde* 1 (Vandenhoeck: Göttingen 1970), 100; Prudentius' hymn is found in: *Analecta hymnica medii aevi* 50, Nr. 26, 25.

divinitatis in eo corporaliter habitat plenitudo. Quem pater ita diligit, ut in sinu portet, ad dexteram locet... ut virtutem noverit.[39]

As for other allusions to hymns, Micheline White uncovered several more Latin sources in Elisabeth Cruciger's hymn.[40]

3. Mystical devotion
The mystical devotion of many nunneries in mediaeval times with its very emotional bridal mysticism and inner love to Christ is also found in the third stanza: "that we here may taste / your sweetness in our hearts and thirst constantly for you." Yet, there are, of course, biblical roots such as Canticum Canticorum or Ps. 34:9 (Vulgata): *"Gustate, et videte quoniam suavis est Dominus."*[41] However, Elisabeth von Meseritz may also have been thinking of tasting and thirsting not only in a physical but also a spiritual way at Holy Communion.

4. The new evangelical doctrine
Beside *"sola scriptura"*, *"solus Christus"* – in the last stanza Elisabeth von Meseritz points out the effects of God's grace (*"sola gratia"*): "Awake us through your grace / sicken the old man / so the new one may live." (In the German poem, the noun used is *Mensch*, which refers to both males and females, unlike the English "man").

In the hymn, one can see the deep devotion of Elisabeth von Meseritz to God the Father, the son and the spirit, combined with the feeling of love while also

---

[39] Ambrosius, *De virginibus* 3,1,3/ Patrologia Latina 16, 232-233 (here cited according to Christa Reich, footnote 33, 49); underlining added by the author. ["Love Him I say. He it is Whom the Father begat before the morning star, as being eternal, He brought Him forth from the womb as the Son; He uttered him from His heart, as the Word. He it is in whom the Father is well pleased; He is the Arm of the Father, for He is Creator of all...the Power of the Father, because the fulness of the Godhead dwelleth in Him bodily. And the Father so loved Him, as to bear Him in His bosom, and place Him at His right hand...and know His power." Translation into English by Philip Schaff, from "Ambrosius, De Virginibus," in: *Nicene and Post-Nicene Fathers*, Christian Classics Ethereal Library, Series II, Volume 10, 844. (http://www.ccel.org/ccel/schaff/npnf210.pdf, 2 April 2017)]

[40] White, "Women's Hymns," 23.

[41] "Das gehört seit Augustin und Bernhard (von Clairvaux) zu den kennzeichnendsten Bildern der Mystik," [that has belonged to the most typical expressions of mysticism since Augustinus and Bernhard of Clairvaux], according to Martin Rößler, *Da Christus geboren war... Texte, Typen und Themen der deutschen Weihnachtslieder* (Calwer: Stuttgart 1981), 189.

integrating the senses, rooted in church practice of praying, singing, living with Scripture, and the Sacraments.

Final remarks
The hymn was first printed in the Enchiridion 1524, without naming an author,[42] and then, in 1531, Elisabeth Cruciger was named as the author.[43] Nevertheless, throughout the centuries there has been an ongoing controversy about her authorship of the hymn, until in 1966, Hans Volz ended the discussion by verifying that Elisabeth Cruciger was indeed its author.[44] Mary Jane Haemig demonstrated very carefully that the reason for not crediting Cruciger as the author previously had been rather complex, stating that an "unwillingness by scholarly circles to credit a woman and an unwillingness to credit Elisabeth Cruciger because of the activities of her husband and her son may have played a part."[45] The latter part of her remark refers to the fact that in the intra-Lutheran disputes of the late sixteenth century, mostly over the theology of Melanchthon and the "true" Lutheran theology ending with the Formula of Concord 1577, Elisabeth's son, Caspar Cruciger the Younger, a follower of Melanchthon at the university of Wittenberg, had been imprisoned in Wittenberg in 1576 and then exiled. However, this argument, concludes Mary Jane Haemig, "though plausible, [it] cannot be proved".[46]

Elisabeth Schneider-Böklen studied Protestant Theology in Tübingen, Berlin and Heidelberg, and in 1971 was ordained as a pastor. From 1973 she worked as a teacher of religion. In 1991 she published, together with Dorothea Vorländer, *Feminismus und Glaube*, and in 1995, *Der Herr hat Großes mir getan. Frauen im Gesangbuch*. From 1995 she served voluntarily as a pastor for the blind and visually impaired. In 2005 she finished her dissertation in Marburg about the 18th century Moravian Church songwriter, titled "Amen, ja, mein Glück ist groß. Henriette Louise von Hayn."

---

[42] Luther, *Enchiridion*, 20.
[43] Andreas Rauscher, *Geistliche Lieder* (Erfurt 1531).
[44] Hans Volz, "Woher stammt die Kirchenlied-Dichterin Elisabeth Cruciger?," in: *Jahrbuch für Liturgik und Hymnologie* 11 (1966), 163-165.
[45] Haemig, "Elisabeth Cruciger," 43.
[46] Haemig, "Elisabeth Cruciger," 34.

Natalia Salas Molina

Liderazgo protestante femenino, un desafío desde la Reforma

Miles de mujeres cristianas y hombres en latinoamericanas desconocen el alcance de la Reforma, como tampoco su legado en las construcciones de género y el posicionamiento femenino. El liderazgo religioso es un desafío constante para aquellas osadas mujeres que intentan alcanzar la cima. La Reforma ha sido un apoyo y a la vez un obstáculo para ellas gracias a su herencia en patrones de género. Ejercer roles femeninos de liderazgo es una tarea que ha sido invisibilizada en las diversas áreas sociales y presenta distintos grados de dificultades en las instituciones eclesiales. Cuando las mujeres descubren que es un espacio donde podrían participar se encuentran con el peso cultural de las exégesis bíblicas misóginas, con la tradición del patriarcado sobre el poder religioso y con mandatos sociales que refuerzan la idea que las mujeres están en lo privado-reproductivo y no en lo público-reconocido. Abrir espacio de poder eclesial para las mujeres es una tarea difícil ya que se requiere no sólo alcanzar el liderazgo, sino que hacerlo desde las competencias de su género, para seguir plasmando un evangelio inclusivo, democrático, amable y generativo.

Thousands of Christian women and men in Latin America do not know the reaches of The Reform, and they do not know its legacy in the construction of gender and the feminine position. Religious leadership is one of the hardships that brave women try to scale. The Reform is both their aid and hindrance, because of their inherited gender patterns. Exercising feminine leadership roles is something that has been occulted in many social areas and it presents a difficulty to ecclesiastical institutions. When women discover it to be a place in which they can participate, they also discover the cultural weight of misogynistic biblical exegesis which goes with the tradition of masculine control over religious power, keeping women in the private-reproductive ambit and not the public-recognised ambit. Opening up a place for women within ecclesiastical power is a difficult task because it not only requires reaching leadership, but also doing so through the competences of their gender, so as to make an inclusive, democratic, loving, and generative gospel.

El protestantismo cruzó el tiempo y las fronteras. Es así que tras siglos de su creación se instala en Latinoamérica, no sólo como religión a través de múltiples denominaciones evangélicas, sino también siguiendo pautas respecto a los roles polarizados de género y liderazgo que permanecen hasta hoy en el plano religioso.

Tras una Visita el año 2013 al museo y casa de Martín Lutero y su esposa Katharina von Bora en Wittenberg, llamada Lutherhaus, con gran asombro algunas mujeres evangélicas del sur de Latinoamérica descubrieron los roles privados y públicos que este matrimonio inauguró como modelo religioso protestante de familia pastoral, en especial les asombra conocer la vida pública de Katharina, que iba más allá de escapar de un convento, casarse y procrear hijos e hijas; ya que logran reconocer esta estructura del lugar femenino evangélico donde las mujeres participan activamente en lo espiritual, cultico y administrativo, que en la práctica opera no sólo como un sacerdocio universal de todos los y las creyentes, sino también por el ejercicio del poder en forma cotidiana y graduado en las congregaciones de fe evangélicas, en mujeres con o sin investidura, bajo la misma sombra del patriarcado, 500 años después.

Se conoce de las investigaciones de género como plantea Lamas,[1] que los seres humanos son capaces de resistir a las imposiciones culturales, que están presente en las culturas de manera hegemónica, lo que permite una modificación de sus conductas. Siguiendo este planteamiento surgen algunas interrogantes en torno al liderazgo femenino: ¿cómo los grupos eclesiales, fruto de la Reforma, quiebran o mantienen los patrones de género establecidos para que surjan o se frenen las lideresas eclesiales? ¿Cómo las mujeres circulan hacia el empoderamiento público, visibilizado y valorado en el ámbito religioso? ¿Qué formas de liderazgo y poder ejercen las mujeres en sus congregaciones? Reconocer este camino es una tarea compleja, que no se va a responder en un solo texto o conversatorio, ya que significa visibilizar las estructuras de las desigualdades de género, las distintas posturas teológicas y encontrar pistas para identificar como el posicionamiento femenino cristiano puede avanzar en iglesias católicas, anglicanas, bautistas, pentecostales, y otras hacia un liderazgo femenino religioso en mayor igualdad frente al masculino, porque aun cuando, unas pocas mujeres han logrado llegar a la cima, también es cierto que todavía la mayoría de ellas son excluidas por su género en diversos lugares del mundo. Por ejemplo, en Latinoamérica, en países como Argentina, Perú, Bolivia y Chile, la pastora Tenorio informa que en las iglesias y organizaciones afines, las mujeres juegan diariamente papeles importantes en el quehacer eclesiástico, además los centros teológicos han dado apertura a la preparación

---

[1] Marta Lamas, *Feminismo, transmisiones y retransmisiones* (Taurus: México 2006), 91-114.

teológica y ministerial de las mujeres, sin embargo, son pocas las iglesias que tienen pastoras y mucho menos pastoras ordenadas.[2] Por lo cual, ir tras las huellas de un evangelio que incluye a hombres y mujeres sin diferencias como lo planteó la Reforma es un desafío profundo.

Liderazgo femenino eclesial
La invisibilización de las tareas que realizan las mujeres no promueve ni fortalece el liderazgo femenino en distintos ámbitos como el político, el militar y especialmente el religioso, lo que según Perrot,[3] dificulta su posicionamiento concretamente. El androcentrismo cultural permanente ha obnubilado el liderazgo femenino, especialmente en la religión cristiana y sus diversas denominaciones. Los estudios sobre el liderazgo han intentado mantener un interés por el tema desde una perspectiva de género, explican Irby y Brown,[4] con algún grado de éxito pero sin trascender en la opinión pública, ya que, según Montecino,[5] en la cultura dominante occidental, las investigaciones basadas en los modelos analíticos y en la observación de la realidad, bajo prejuicios androcéntricos y etnocéntricos ubican a las mujeres jerárquicamente y asimétricamente en desmedro de sus pares masculinos, idea que se agudiza a la hora de investigar sobre lideresas eclesiales.

Desconocer los liderazgos de mujeres e ignorar los grados de influencia en sus seguidores implica perpetuar los límites misóginos en la cultura. Por ejemplo, la iglesia católica declara en su doctrina: "La función pastoral al interior de la Iglesia está normalmente vinculada al sacramento del orden (...). Esta no es otorgada por la espontánea elección de los hombres. (...) Por este motivo no se ve cómo es posible proponer el acceso de las mujeres al sacerdocio",[6]

---

[2] Hilda Tenorio, *Informe de la Red Peruana de Mujeres "Mision Común" M21* (Presentado al VII Encuentro Continental Latinoamericano de Mujeres, La Paz-Bolivia, noviembre 2012), 1.
[3] Michelle Perrot, *Mujeres en la ciudad* (Editorial Andrés Bello: Santiago 1997), 119.
[4] Beverly J. Irby and Genevieve Brown, *Constructing a feminist-inclusive theory of leadership* (Paper presented at the Annual Meeting of the American Educational Research Association, ERIC Document Reproduction Service N°. ED 384 103, San Francisco 1995), 2.
[5] Sonia Montecino, "Devenir de una traslación: De la mujer al género o de lo universal a lo particular", en: Sonia Montecino y Loreto Rebolledo, *Conceptos de Género y Desarrollo* (PIEG: Santiago de Chile 1996), 9-34, aquí 11.
[6] Sagrada Congregación para la doctrina de la fe. *Declaración sobre la cuestión de la admisión de las mujeres al sacerdocio ministerial* (Roma 1976), 6. (*http://www.vatican.va/roman_curia/congregations/cfaith/documents/rc_con_cfaith_doc_19761015_inter-insigniores_sp.html*, 2 febrero 2017)

idea que el Papa Juan Pablo II continuó como sigue: "declaro que la Iglesia no tiene en modo alguno la facultad de conferir la ordenación sacerdotal a las mujeres, y que este dictamen debe ser considerado como definitivo por todos los fieles de la Iglesia".[7] Esta declaración opera como una carta de navegación, "facultando a lo sagrado como fundamento de legitimación de cualquier forma de autoridad y no sólo de las autoridades religiosas, sino de lo masculino como autoridad",[8] amplía Rosales respecto a los roles de género. Bajo este disciplinamiento religioso intentar entrar en el complejo entramado de roles – considerados tradicionalmente masculinos – es una tarea que nunca termina para las mujeres, porque constantemente deben enfrentar resistencias y prejuicios para alcanzar o permanecer en estas posiciones, independiente de su formación, sus cualidades o sus capacidades, menciona Eagly.[9]

Sin embargo, la Reforma en sus fieles humedeció la tierra para que brotaran nuevas semillas que dieran frutos y flores diversas que están floreciendo bajo la sombra de viejos árboles que difícilmente les han permitido ver la luz e iluminar. No obstante, algunas de estas semillas de todas formas crecen en el tiempo, aun en la rueda de los mandatos masculinos explica Burggraf: "Durante cuatrocientos años, la masculinidad estuvo entre los 'requisitos indispensables' de los candidatos al ministerio pastoral. Hoy en día, sin embargo, existe el acuerdo común entre las Iglesias evangélicas de Alemania para ordenar también a mujeres".[10] A su vez: "la Iglesia Anglicana de Inglaterra consagró a Libby Lane como su primera mujer obispo, poniendo fin a 500 años de exclusividad masculina en la conducción de la institución eclesiástica",[11] dando señales concretas del avance de las mujeres en el liderazgo eclesial.

---

[7] Juan Pablo II, Carta Apostólica *Ordinatio Sacerdotalis* sobre la Ordenación Sacerdotal reservada sólo a los Hombres (Vaticano: 1994). (https://w2.vatican.va/content/john-paul-ii/es/apost_letters/1994/documents/hf_jp-ii_apl_19940522_ordinatio-sacerdotalis.html, 1 marzo 2017)

[8] Sharo Rosales, "Imaginarios religiosos del género", en: Mireya Baltodano y Gabriela Miranda (eds.), *Género y Religión: sospechas y aportes para la reflexión* (Universidad Bíblica Latinoamericana: San José Costa Rica 1998), 263-275, aquí 265.

[9] Alice Eagly, "Female Leadership Advantage and Disadvantage: Resolving the Contradictions," in: *Psychology of Women Quarterly* 31 (2007), 1-12.

[10] Jutta Burggraf, *Las pastoras luteranas en Alemania 2007.* (http://www.almudi.org/Inicio/tabid/36/ctl/Detail/mid/386/aid/600/paid/0/Default.aspx, 15 junio 2016)

[11] Acontecer Cristiano. Net. *Iglesia Anglicana de Inglaterra Consagra a su Primera Mujer Obispo* (27/01/2015). (http://www.acontecercristiano.net/2015/01/iglesia-anglicana-de-inglaterra.html, 31 enero 2016)

Esta apertura para el género femenino en relación al liderazgo fue una osadía que cruzó el Atlántico, según consta en una publicación de una página web referida en un artículo de Patricia Cuyatti: "La Iglesia Luterana en Chile (ILCH) ha ordenado a la Rev. Hanna Schramm como primera pastora lo cual es un paso histórico dado que todas las iglesias miembros de la Federación Luterana Mundial (FLM) en América Latina y el Caribe ahora ordenan pastoras".[12] Un avance para este país. No obstante subraya Henn, una investigación respecto a este tema por parte del Consejo Ecuménico de las Iglesias señalaba que: "entre las 239 Iglesias miembros, había 68 en las que se ordenaban mujeres. El estudio añadía que muchas de las comunidades que ordenaban mujeres en Europa occidental y en Norteamérica evitaban hacerlo en África, en Asia y en América Latina".[13]

Visibilizar esta desigualdad en el cono sur de América requiere observar la construcción histórica de una mujer evangélica, mestiza, tercera mundista, surgiendo producto del legado cultural, con un sello que refleja una identidad que transita cargada por signos adquiridos involuntariamente, esto produce una forma de moverse socialmente de acuerdo a las relaciones de género que se representan en ese juego relacional asimétrico con sus pares masculinos donde ellas constantemente van a remitir su conducta a aquellas reglas históricas de dominación y sometimiento.

Las mujeres son educadas bajo una educación misógina que contiene muy pocas lecciones respecto a la igualdad de género y enseñanzas que no empoderen a las mujeres en ningún plano, porque al hacer una simple revisión en la prensa de los cargos públicos en el mundo, la mayoría son exclusivos de los hombres. Por ejemplo, según el BBC Mundo,[14] en el contexto político en el año 2015 sólo 19 mujeres eran presidentas de sus países, es decir cerca del 10% mundial. Esta presencia femenina ha sido posible en Latinoamérica, gracias a la adquisición de capacidades para liderar y más grados de escolaridad, también por un aumento de la participación femenina en la vida pública, mayor democratización en la región, legislación positiva en el ámbito

---

[12] Patricia Cuyatti, "Iglesia Luterana en Chile Ordena Hanna Schramm como Primera Pastora", en: *Federación Luterana Mundial América Latina y el Caribe* (29/04/2014). (https://america-latinacaribe.lutheranworld.org/es/content/iglesia-luterana-en-chile-ordena-hanna-schramm-como-primera-pastora, 31 enero 2017)
[13] W. Henn, *Ordenación de las mujeres*. (http://mercaba.org/VocTEO/O/ordenacion_de_las_mujeres.html, 1 febrero 2016)
[14] BBC MUNDO, "¿En cuántos países gobiernan mujeres?" (http://www.bbc.com/mundo/noticias/2015/01/150112_mujeres_presidentas_mapa_az, 20 agosto 2016)

internacional y cuotas que garantizan un mínimo de presencia numérica explica Fernández.[15]

Siguiendo la idea anterior, pero en el ámbito religioso, aun cuando muchas mujeres tienen en la actualidad una escolaridad lograda y una alta participación, el contexto eclesial sigue siendo muy mezquino para ellas, en algunas denominaciones – hijas inmediatas de la Reforma o herencia de sucesivos quiebres de esta u otra iglesia evangélica. Como por ejemplo, la Iglesia Evangélica Pentecostal de Chile, donde las mujeres no pueden ejercer ningún liderazgo eclesial formal. Además, aclara Salas,[16] en aquellas organizaciones eclesiales donde se ha iniciado el nombramiento formal de mujeres como pastoras, generalmente son las congregaciones quienes lo han exigido. Por ejemplo, la primera Iglesia Metodista Pentecostal de Chile nombra pastora a la viuda Patricia Ubilla de la IMP de Ñuñoa, a solicitud de los miembros de la congregación, según consta en una acta pública de esa iglesia,[17] sólo después de más de un siglo de existencia y de tener una fuerte presencia e importancia en el país por su influencia pública y mediática...

Dios no hace acepción de personas: avances y retrocesos de los liderazgos femeninos

Hechos 10,34b, un texto conocido, plantea esta frase: "Dios no hace acepción de personas". Sin embargo, nadie nombra el versículo siguiente (35) que habla del temor a Dios y de su justicia, que también puede aplicarse al género femenino. Hay consenso respecto a avanzar en igualdad de derechos y las mujeres están intentando tomar aquellos elementos que pudieran ser una perilla para abrir la puerta del liderazgo y el ejercicio del poder con aciertos, prejuicios, miedos y desequilibrios que se tropiezan constantemente con elementos de la cultura y la religión actuando diariamente.

En el avance hacia la paridad genérica, Lutero planteó que hombres y mujeres deberían leer la Biblia, ordenanza no menor ya que para innumerables personas en el mundo hasta hoy ha significado salir del analfabetismo.

---

[15] Anna María Fernández Poncela, "Mujeres y política en América Latina: Dificultades y aceptación social", en: *Argumentos* 19/51 (Mayo/Agosto 2006), 117-143. (http://www.scielo.org.mx/scielo.php?script=sci_arttext&pid=S0187-57952006000200005, 15 julio 2016)

[16] Natalia Salas, *Mujeres Evangélicas en Chile. Contribuciones sociales y religiosas desde el género* (Academia de Teología Femenina María Magdalena, Santiago de Chile, 31 agosto 2013), 3. (Paper presentado en el Seminario de Teología y Género, Santiago).

[17] Acta de la Reunión extraordinaria de la Junta Oficial de Diáconos de la Primera Iglesia Metodista Pentecostal de Ñuñoa (Santiago, 15 de febrero 2017), 1-2.

Las exigencias de Lutero, en 1523, respecto a que se funden escuelas cristianas,[18] no sólo significó un mandato para su territorio sino que los y las evangelizadores llevaron este planteamiento a otras latitudes de la tierra, lo que permitió en aquellos países con altas tasas de pobreza y analfabetismo, que las niñas y mujeres pudieran aprender a leer y escribir, ya que el reformador pensaba que toda persona debía responder de su fe y entender las Sagradas Escrituras, y para esto cada iglesia en su localidad debía contar con una escuela.

Esta idea de evangelizar y alfabetizar llego hasta el fin del mundo en el siglo XIX, a través de misioneros y misioneras de formación luterana, anglicana, presbiteriana y metodista. No obstante, según Bazley,[19] realizar ambas cruzadas tuvo sus tropiezos en la socialización de géneros, ya que si los pueblos originarios consideraban sospechosa una nueva religión, el educar a las niñas en la lectoescritura en la etnia mapuche, por parte de los y las anglicanas, fue un nuevo desafío.

Tras acceder las mujeres a las escrituras y al conocimiento teológico asociado al género, que en América latina fue posible posterior a la teología de la liberación, según analiza Ivone Gebara,[20] se produjo un salto significativo al interpretar la Biblia desde la óptica del 50% de la humanidad olvidada y muda. Releer la Biblia con lentes de género promovió un cambio de posición: "De las bancas al púlpito", lugar de poder por excelencia porque es el espacio donde Dios habla imperativamente, también propició, según Salas, un cambio en la participación de las mujeres en el ejercicio de roles tales como "Obispas, pastoras, diaconas, administrativas, directoras de zona, superintendentas, capellanas, encargadas de oficinas de asuntos religiosos municipales, jefas del cuerpo femenino,"[21] resistiendo y mudando conductas eclesiales sobre los paradigmas patriarcales que han circulado en sus inconscientes colectivos transgeneracionalmente.

---

[18] Teófanes Egido (ed.), *Lutero/Obras* (Ediciones Sígueme: Salamanca 1977), 213-232.
[19] Barbara Bazley, *Somos Anglicanos* (Imprenta Editorial Interamericana: Santiago de Chile 1994), 108.
[20] Ivone Gebara, "III Semana Teológica: Construyendo nuestras teologías feministas", en: Mary John Mananzan e Ivone Gebara (eds.), *Tópicos '9: Aportes para una teología feminista: Semanas Teológicas en Chile* (Centro Ecuménico Diego de Medellín: Santiago de Chile 1993), 71-124, aquí 72.
[21] Natalia Salas Molina, *Género y liderazgo religioso en mujeres evangélicas chilenas* (Diss., Universidad de Chile 2015), 2.

Para dar este salto las mujeres fueron encontrando pistas en los diversos estudios teológicos y de género, como la noción de un discipulado de iguales en los primitivos movimientos cristianos misioneros planteada por Schüssler Fiorenza,[22] así también, los estudios de género indican que se necesita, "el análisis no sólo de la relación entre experiencia masculina y femenina en el pasado, sino también de la conexión entre la historia pasada y la práctica histórica actual,"[23] acota Scott. Entonces reconocer y visibilizar nombres femeninos, que aportaron, apoyaron y acompañaron en la historia del cristianismo es una tarea vital. Por ejemplo, en la Reforma participaron: Marie Dentière (Bélgica, 1495-1561), Argula von Grumbach (1492-1553), Ursula Münstenberg (nació entre 1491-1495 y murió en 1534), Elisabeth Cruciger (1500-1535), Elisabeth Von Brandenburg (1485-1555), Elisabeth de Brunswick (1510-1558), Margarita de Navarra (1555-1572), Juana de Albret (1528-1572), Renata de Ferrara (1510-1575), Catherine Zell (1497-1562) describe Lerín.[24]

Junto con lo anterior resulta crucial dar cuenta de las cuotas de poder con que participan las mujeres, por ejemplo, Katharina von Bora (1499-1552), a quien Lutero en 1545 le escribe una carta, resaltando sus roles asociados a tareas eclesiales, laborales y económicas: "A mi amable y querida mujer, Catalina Luther de Bora, predicadora, cervecera, jardinera y un montón de cosas más",[25] adjetivos que dan cuenta de su posición social. Otro ejemplo de poder eclesial femenino es la gobernadora suprema actual de la Iglesia Anglicana, la monarca británica, Isabel Alejandra María Windsor, destacando su longevidad en el poder frente a sus pares masculinos católicos: "desde la coronación de Isabel II, el 2 de junio de 1953, siete papas han estado al frente de la Iglesia Católica, Pío XII, Juan XXIII, Pablo VI, Juan Pablo I, Juan Pablo II, Benedicto XVI y Francisco".[26]

---

[22] Elisabeth Schussler Fiorenza, *Discipulado de Iguales. Una Ekklesia-logía Crítica Feminista de Liberación* (Editorial Pachamama: La Paz 2011), 87-88.
[23] Joan Scott, "El género, una categoría útil para el análisis histórico", en: James S. Amelang y Mary Nash (eds.) *Historia y Género: Las mujeres en la Europa Moderna y Contemporánea* (Ediciones Alfons El Magnanim: Valencia 1990), 23-56, aquí 44.
[24] Amparo Lerín Cruz, *Las Mujeres en la Reforma Protestante del Siglo XVI.* (http://luiseduardocantero.blogspot.cl/2012/10/las-mujeres-en-la-reforma-protestante.html, 5 octubre 2016)
[25] Documentos reformadores.com, *Cartas de Lutero: A Catalina Bora. Halle, 25 enero 1546.* (http://semla.org/portal/wp-content/uploads/2011/05/Cartas-Martin-Lutero.pdf, 14 febrero 2017)
[26] Ana Mellado, "El papel de la mujer en la iglesia enfrenta a católicos y anglicanos", en: *ABC Sociedad*, Londres 3/4/2014. (http://www.abc.es/sociedad/20140403/abci-anglicanos-catolicos-mujer-201404031701.html, 5 octubre 2016)

No obstante descubrir los aportes de la inmensa mayoría de mujeres al trabajo pastoral o evangelizador muchas veces es buscar una aguja en un pajar. "Las mujeres dejan pocas huellas directas, escritas o materiales".[27] En las historias oficiales de las iglesias evangélicas no se revelan sus aportes o la real dimensión de estos. Por ejemplo, el movimiento pentecostal en Chile, en sus orígenes a principios del siglo XX, participaron hombres y mujeres. Sin embargo, en las historias escritas, destacan mayoritariamente los nombres masculinos y sus imágenes fotográficas.

Estas omisiones femeninas se reflejan en los aportes de 2 mujeres: Mercedes Gutiérrez y Elena Laidlow. Mercedes Gutiérrez se destaca por formar el primer grupo de mujeres de la Iglesia Metodista Pentecostal llamado "Dorcas", nombre que identifica después de un siglo a multitudes de mujeres de esta denominación y miles de otras iglesias pentecostales, trascendiendo fronteras en diversos países de América del Sur y generando un espacio de liderazgo femenino frente a sus pares y sus congregaciones.[28] A su vez, Elena Laidlaw fue una de las mujeres con mayor incidencia en la proclamación de un nuevo movimiento espiritual en Chile, conocido, según Hoover como "Avivamiento pentecostal",[29] dejando importantes huellas que casi desaparecen. No obstante Elena Laidlaw ha recibido un homenaje póstumo en un cementerio, en el contexto del centésimo quinto aniversario del pentecostalismo nacional, que se realizó el 13 de septiembre de 2014, destacándose una placa con su nombre que no estaba escrito en la lápida de su tumba hasta ahora,[30] reivindicando su testimonio de lideresa cristiana, ya que su memoria fue enlodada por relatos erróneos: en un estudio, los investigadores Fontaine y Beyer la describen como "una mujer de dudosa reputación",[31] dejando esta marca en su biografía.

Esta situación de violencia biográfica se vivencia en otros ámbitos, como por ejemplo, el político. Latinoamérica es el escenario mundial donde por

---

[27] Michelle Perrot, *Mi historia de las mujeres* (Fondo de Cultura Económica: Buenos Aires 2009), 10.
[28] Salas, *Género y liderazgo*, 40.
[29] Willis Collins Hoover, *Historia del avivamiento pentecostal en Chile* (Centro de Estudios Pentecostales: Concepción 2000), 33-36.
[30] Corporación Sendas, *Reconocimiento póstumo a la hermana Elena Laidlow Brown* (Santiago de Chile 2014). (http://corporacionsendas.cl/noticias_01.php, 30 septiembre 2016)
[31] Arturo Fontaine Talabera y Harald Beyer, "Retrato del Movimiento Evangélico a la Luz de las Encuestas de Opinión Publica", en: *Estudios Públicos* 44 (Chile 1991), 4. (http://www.cepchile.cl/dms/archivo_818_118, 3 septiembre 2016)

primera vez se nombra una presidenta, y se define una elección presidencial con dos candidatas. Sin embargo los aportes de ellas se visibilizan pero a su vez se descalifican, ya que son víctimas de la violencia contra las mujeres políticas: "puede ocurrir antes, durante o después de las campañas electorales, del mismo modo que en el ejercicio de las funciones públicas para producir la renuncia de las mujeres en sus puesto",[32] debido a que su evaluación no está centrada en el desempeño o resultados sino en su género. Por esta razón, en algunas congregaciones evangélicas, aunque están presentes las indicaciones de inclusión de género "a veces, se pasan por alto o ignoran esas políticas por lo difícil que resulta encontrar mujeres para liderar y conseguir que las iglesias propongan a candidatas, o porque las mujeres sienten que no tienen la pericia necesaria".[33] Ellas reciben frecuentemente la indicación que están entrando en un terreno no apto para su género.

Finalmente la invitación a participar para las mujeres es una decisión compleja, implica no sólo resistir el paradigma patriarcal para liderar, sino plantear una nueva visión exitosa, tarea difícil porque se conoce que la percepción y evaluación de los liderazgos son diferentes para cada género y que mientras más asertivos son los liderazgos femeninos pueden ser también más rechazados, de acuerdo con algunos estudios de Harvard Business Review que describe López,[34] ya que los hilos invisibles de la cultura y sus categorías aparecen cuando las cualidades de liderazgo asociadas a su género no son consideradas positivas, motivo por el cual los estilos de liderazgo en el plano eclesial mantienen los lineamientos de la Reforma, es decir rasgos predominantemente patriarcales.

Sin embargo, a pesar de lo anterior, en estas últimas décadas, algunas liderezas en las diversas organizaciones han planteado liderazgos donde están presentes la creatividad, la sensibilidad y la comunicación, en un sistema de organización menos jerárquico, más horizontal, donde prima la intuición, la

---

[32] Marta Gaba, *Violencia contra las mujeres en política*, 8 octubre 2016. (http://www.martagaba.com/2017/02/violencia-contra-las-mujeres-en-politica.html, 28 febrero 2017)
[33] Federación Luterana Mundial, *¡No será así entre ustedes! (Mc. 10:43) Una reflexión en la fe sobre el género y el poder* (Federación Luterana Mundial: Una Comunión de Iglesias Ginebra 2010), 10. (https://www.lutheranworld.org/sites/default/files/Una%20reflexion%20en%20 la%20fe%20sobre%20el%20genero%20y%20el%20poder.pdf, 8 octubre 2016)
[34] Alejandra López Martínez, *Liderazgo femenino en la política, la importancia de la imagen* (Universidad Anáhuac México Sur: Ciudad de México 2000) 6-7. (http://www.alice-comunicacionpolitica.com/abrir-ponencia.php?f=1c35f714863da344ceaa2c4ad6e05b5e.pdf, 11 octubre 2016)

empatía, la disponibilidad para trabajar en equipo y el buen trato de ellas, señalan Torres y Ramírez.[35]

Las lideresas son agentes de cambio, según estudios de Gibson, Ivancevich, Donnelly y Konopaske: sus actos afectan y pueden transformar las competencias y/o las motivaciones de las personas en una organización.[36] Por lo tanto, su influencia desde los espacios considerados sagrados deberá difundir exégesis bíblicas bajo una mirada inclusiva de géneros, revalorar las figuras femeninas bíblicas como por ejemplo, María Magdalena la apóstola y la primera persona en ver a Jesús después de su resurrección.[37] Promover una teología que reflexione, acompañe y organice sistemáticamente las lecturas de los liderazgos bíblicos femeninos y visibilizar los roles femeninos eclesiales con autoridad permite iluminar a otras mujeres que intentan liderar desde otra vereda que no sea patriarcal. Esto es un viejo desafío con nuevas herramientas teológicas y sociales, tras las huellas de la Reforma.

Probablemente, millones de mujeres evangélicas latinoamericanas o de otros lugares jamás escucharon de la participación y colaboración de mujeres en la Reforma, ni de las pioneras de sus propias denominaciones foráneas o autóctonas, así también las actuales teólogas europeas o de otros puntos del planeta tampoco conocen a las mujeres lideresas de Latinoamérica u otros territorios, de tiempos remotos o las actuales: aun cuando hoy funcionan suficientes medios de comunicación, sin embargo en diversas latitudes hay pequeñas voces que intentan fomentar, visibilizar, empoderar y reivindicar a las mujeres.

Natalia Salas Molina Magíster en Estudios de Género y cultura, Universidad de Chile. Licenciada en psicología, Universidad Bolivariana. Relacionadora Pública, Universidad Diego Portales. Bachiller en Teología, Comunidad Teológica Evangélica. Pastora Iglesia Metodista Pentecostal San Bernardo-La Portada. Directora administrativa, Academia de Teología Femenina María Magdalena.

---

[35] L. Torres y K. Ramírez, *Las características del liderazgo femenino como herramienta necesaria para lograr la negociación y concertación requeridas actualmente en el ejercicio de la política* (Universidad Autónoma de Baja california, Facultad de Ciencias Sociales y Política: Baja california 2006), 2.
[36] James Gibson, John Ivancevich, James Donnelly y Robert Konopaske, *Organizaciones, Comportamiento, Estructura y Procesos* (Editorial McGraw-Hill: México 2011), 308.
[37] Jn. 20, 1-18.

Silvia Martínez Cano

Mujeres creyentes, culturas e Iglesias: Reformas para comunidades católicas vivas y en acción

Las mujeres, como parte fundamental de todas las iglesias cristianas, sueñan con unas comunidades ricas en equidad. Equidad porque sueñan con iglesias que den a cada una y a cada uno lo que necesita, que atiendan en las necesidades de cada creyente. Unas comunidades que celebren en comunidad de hermanas y hermanos. Las mujeres y los hombres creyentes quieren ser valorados en su singularidad, y que la iglesia católica sea justa en las oportunidades, las capacidades y el trato que da a todas y a todos sus miembros. La equidad subraya el carácter justo y misericordioso del Evangelio e invita a la implicación personal de cada uno de los miembros de la comunidad. En la iglesia católica se asiste a cambios, que en un principio pueden resultar pequeños, pero que pueden ser sustanciales en la forma de entender esta iglesia. Son propuestas más cercanas a las proclamadas en el concilio Vaticano II, que subrayan el avance hacia la igualdad y la cooperación dentro de la iglesia católica. También apuestan por un espíritu conciliador y más misericordioso, más comprometido con las heridas del mundo. Este estilo recuerda que las Iglesias son signos de transformación del mundo. Por eso, en este momento de maduración de la iglesia católica, propiciado por el cambio de pontificado, es bueno preguntarse por la presencia actual de las mujeres en ella y en la sociedad. No es una cuestión secundaria, como dicen algunos, que va después de hacer reformas eclesiales. No, es el corazón mismo de las reformas eclesiales, que pueden dar iluminación a las comunidades que forman las Iglesias. De la forma de presencia de las mujeres en la iglesia católica dependen en alto grado las otras reformas. Este artículo revisa la situación de las mujeres en la iglesia católica y las otras reformas vinculadas a la situación de las mujeres creyentes. También propondrá posibles vías de reforma dentro de la iglesia católica, vinculadas a su compromiso con el mundo y sus culturas desde la perspectiva de las mujeres.

As a fundamental part of all Christian churches, we women dream of a wealthy community in equity. Equity because we dream of a church that gives everyone what they need, a church that meets the needs of every believer. Communities of brothers and sisters in which we all are valued in our uniqueness and afforded fairness in opportunities, capacities and treatment. Equity underlines the just and merciful character of the Gospel and invites the personal involvement of each of the members of the community. In the Catholic Church, changes are witnessed which initially may be small, but can be also substantial in the way of understanding the Church. These are proposals closer to that which had been proclaimed at the Vatican II Council, underlining the progress towards equality and cooperation within the Church. Also, they opt for a conciliatory and merciful spirit, more committed to the wounds of the world. This style reminds us that churches are signs of transforming the world. Therefore, at this time of maturation of the Catholic Church, led by the change of pontificate, it is good to ask for the actual presence of women in the Catholic Church and in society. This is not a secondary issue, as some church-goers may say. No, it is the heart of ecclesial reforms that can provide illumination and guidance to equalising communities. Shaping the presence of women in the Catholic Church is highly dependent on other reforms. This paper reviews the situation of women and reforms linked to the situation of female believers in the Catholic Church. It also proposes possible avenues of reform within the Catholic Church, linked to its commitment to the world and its cultures from the perspective of women.

Las mujeres, como parte fundamental de la iglesia católica, sueñan con una Iglesia rica en equidad. Este artículo utilizará el concepto de equidad, y no igualdad. Equidad porque las mujeres cristianas católicas sueñan con una Iglesia que dé a cada una y a cada uno lo que necesita, que atienda en las necesidades y celebre en comunidad de hermanas y hermanos. Las mujeres quieren igualdad, sí, pero más aún equidad. Equidad significa, primero, valorar a cada una e a cada uno en su singularidad, es decir aceptando la diversidad de experiencias de fe y sus formas de expresión. Segundo, ser justas en las oportunidades, las capacidades y el trato que reciben los distintos miembros de una comunidad. La equidad subraya el carácter justo y misericordioso del Evangelio e invita a la implicación personal. Y tercero, la equidad permite ejercer liderazgos que emocionen y motiven a las comunidades para que hagan un seguimiento de Jesús verdaderamente evangélico. Estos liderazgos son independientes del género del que lo ejercite y actúan por el principio de autoridad reconocida por la propia comunidad.

Ahora que se asiste, con cierta sorpresa, a cambios y propuestas eclesiales más cercanas a las proclamadas en el concilio Vaticano II, es necesario preguntarse cuál debe ser la presencia de las mujeres en la iglesia católica actual y en la sociedad. En una entrevista a Joan Chittister[1] a raíz de la elección de

---

[1] "Conferencia de Joan Chitistter: a propósito de Francisco", en: *Mujeres y Teología de Madrid* (2 septiembre 2013). (http://www.mujeresyteologia.com/2013/09/conferencia-de-joan-chitistter-a-prop%C3%B3sito-de-francisco.html, 10 junio 2017)

Jorge Bergoglio como papa de la iglesia católica, la teóloga afirmó que por primera vez en muchos años las católicas y los católicos se encuentran en un "momento de oportunidad", un "kairós" que podría ser el comienzo de una renovación eclesial que en su momento anunció el concilio y que quedó enfriado por el pontificado de Juan Pablo II. Sin duda la década de los 10 del siglo XXI está proporcionando un espacio de diálogo eclesial que beneficia y sustenta a todas y a todos. Ello no debe ser despreciado, por lo que es importante pensar en ello con preguntas adecuadas y soluciones dialogadas. La cuestión de las mujeres en la iglesia católica es una cuestión que depende en alto grado de las reformas que se quieran llevar a cabo. Se debe preguntar cuáles son las cuestiones teóricas y prácticas para la iglesia católica de hoy y a la vez el papel que cada uno y cada una ocupa en ella. Pero no es una cuestión secundaria, como dicen algunos, que va después de hacer reformas y enfocar de nuevo la iglesia católica hacia caminos evangélicos. Es una cuestión principal que debe ser tratada urgentemente si se quiere que las reformas de esta iglesia tengan efectos eclesiales beneficiosos.

Por tanto, este eres un tiempo de diálogo que ha sido propiciado en gran medida por un cambio en la actitud de la institución eclesial jerárquica tanto en los debates internos como en la visión de las preocupaciones externas a la iglesia católica. El papa Francisco ha sido uno de los protagonistas de este cambio, con su forma de asumir la responsabilidad del pontificado y por la forma de responder a las demandas que las distintas comunidades cristianas católicas hacían desde hace tiempo. Pero también está siendo protagonista una parte de la gran comunidad de la iglesia católica, que desde hace décadas reivindicaba la aplicación de las propuestas del concilio. Ante las provocaciones del papa está respondiendo con audacia y esperanza.

El Concilio Vaticano II, unas reformas que no se plenificaron
La iglesia católica arrastra desde hace décadas unas reformas que no han terminado de hacerse reales. Los años posteriores al concilio fueron esperanzadores para todas e para todos, con grandes cambios en aspectos concretos, pero la complejidad de la profunda renovación era grande. Tras una primera recepción ilusionada del concilio en los años 70 y 80, los cambios eclesiales se paralizaron en elementos superficiales. Laicas, laicos y clérigos contribuían a la construcción de comunidades eclesiales, pero la estructura profunda jerárquica de la iglesia católica no variaba. La liturgia se renovaba, cambiaba de idioma y se adaptaba el lenguaje, se introducía música y alegría. Pero a la vez se hacían difíciles las relaciones parroquiales. En el ámbito teológico, se daba mucha

importancia a la hermenéutica bíblica como herramienta teológica principal y se aceptaban oficialmente los métodos histórico-críticos de exégesis. Se recuperaba la eclesiología de comunión y subrayaba el papel de la iglesia católica a nivel local y la figura episcopal. Se abría la posibilidad de fórmulas descentralizadas de gobierno con la gestión algo más autónoma de las conferencias episcopales y se establecían mecanismos de administración de las comunidades locales como los consejos parroquiales en la que participaban clérigos, laicas y laicos. Todo ello en una resistencia muy grande de amplios sectores del clero.

Sin embargo, los textos del concilio, aunque aperturistas en algunos aspectos, también tenían cuestiones ambiguas, que procuraban, con la negociación y la indefinición teórica, un difícil equilibrio entre dos estilos en tensión dentro de la iglesia católica. Son ejemplo de esta tensión las polémicas intervenciones de Pablo VI en los consensos conciliares en el tema de la autonomía y colegialidad de los obispos, subrayando las líneas primaciales del papado, pese a lo que se afirma en la *Lumen Gentium* (22-23). El posconcilio mostró la continuidad de dos eclesiologías yuxtapuestas: la de jurisdicción jerárquica y patriarcal de la época antimodernista, y la de comunión del Vaticano II. Esta realidad era un problema práctico, ya que la interpretación de los documentos conciliares podía justificar ambas posturas. De hecho lo ha ido haciendo a lo largo de las décadas. La eclesiología del Vaticano II ha sido muy débil, frente a la tradición eclesiológica jerárquica y centralista. Esta última ha terminado por imponerse. Schatz señala, con toda la razón, que la realidad práctica de las diócesis y la visión de sus obispos se ha impuesto frente a las teorías conciliares[2] y esto ha ido provocando un choque constante con el ambiente cultural aproximadamente democrático y tolerante de la globalización de las sociedades, aislando a la iglesia católica de la significatividad social. En el espacio intraeclesial, la deconstrucción de la estructura clerical y la construcción de comunidades incluyentes e igualitarias se convirtió en una tarea ardua, lenta, en la que se consiguen avances muy poco a poco. Se hubiera necesitado al menos un siglo y medio para una verdadera transformación eclesial, pero no dio tiempo a ello.

Con el pontificado de Juan Pablo II, la tensión entre estas dos concepciones dentro de la iglesia católica se inclinó hacia un control centralista no solo del gobierno de la misma, sino de la producción de pensamiento teológico

---

[2] Klaus Schatz, *El primado del papa* (Sal Terrae: S antander 1996), 231.

que conlleva una gran presión eclesial sobre los sectores eclesiales más hermenéuticos y dialogantes con los retos culturales en esos momentos. Un ejemplo es la condena a la Teología de la Liberación en 1984. Juan Pablo II, el primer papa mediático y con un carisma populista y cercano, se convierte en un auténtico icono popular que subraya la tendencia decimonónica a la "papolatría". Al mismo tiempo, de forma inteligente, desarrolla un programa de nombramientos episcopales de tendencia conservadora y centralista[3] en las distintas diócesis del mundo, especialmente en Latinoamérica, para controlar los lugares de producción teológica y reforzar una teología oficial más cercana a la visión del Vaticano I que del Vaticano II. Con esta política paraliza la democratización de la iglesia católica, reforzando de nuevo el poder del clero y verticalizando el gobierno con ayuda de las múltiples censuras a aquellos sectores eclesiales más aperturistas. En los últimos años de su pontificado, incluso se censuró a los grupos eclesiales más moderados, cerrando lugares eclesiales de diálogo y quitando competencias tanto a las congregaciones religiosas como a las laicas y a los laicos. Su pontificado, excesivamente largo, ha producido 40 años de desierto, en los que algunos se preguntaban si "¿se impondrá de nuevo en la teoría y en la práctica una eclesiología monárquica, de modo que los aspectos colegiales y conciliares recién descubiertos se verán relegados, como ya ocurriera en el siglo XV?"[4] Es probable que si no se construyen ahora instituciones sinodales claras y fuertes, la respuesta a la pregunta sea afirmativa.

Ante esta situación, se produjo una respuesta a la pluralidad religiosa, descrita por Peter Berger,[5] que comenzó a afectar a la cohesión eclesial interna. El concilio generó no solo praxis diferentes dentro de la iglesia católica, sino visiones muy dispares.

Algunos pensaron que la puesta al día de la iglesia católica fue un espejismo y que sólo ha servido para crear más crisis e indiferencia, muchas bajas dentro de la iglesia católica y mucha confusión en los fieles. Por eso, estos últimos veinte años hay sectores de la iglesia católica que defienden una vuelta a esa iglesia grande y jerárquica, que idealizan como la salvadora de todos los problemas eclesiales. Se expresan con grandes rituales y ceremonias, cuidando la

---

[3] Jesús Martínez Gordo, *La conversión del papado y la reforma de la curia vaticana* (PPC: Madrid 2014), 99-101.
[4] Schatz, *El primado del papa*, 232.
[5] Peter Berger, *Una gloria lejana. La búsqueda de la fe en la época de la pluralidad* (Herder: Barcelona 1994), 86-134; Peter Berger, *Los numerosos altares de la modernidad. En busca de un paradigma para la religión en una época pluralista* (Sígueme: Salamanca 2016), 17-101.

devoción y piedad sensiblera y reforzando las estructuras jerárquicas que tanta seguridad dan en un mundo desordenado. Las creyentes y los creyentes, sumidos en este caos social necesitan dirección y consejo y por eso se necesita un ministerio ordenado fuerte y decidido que sepa decir lo que hay que creer y cómo hay que creer.

No se puede negar que este modelo ha tenido y tiene éxito aún. Los grupos que han tomado esta postura dentro de la iglesia católica tienen fuerza, porque han sido apoyados desde la jerarquía. Son grupos compactos de creyentes seglares (mujeres y hombres), y clérigos, con una gran seguridad en el mensaje eclesiológico que defienden, y sabiéndose con respaldo de un grupo eclesial que protege y ayuda. Para algunas católicas e algunos católicos, tanto gente adulta como gente joven es alentador no tener dudas acerca de la fe y sus implicaciones vitales. Para las creyentes y los creyentes mayores porque recuperan lo que creyeron perder. Para las jóvenes y los jóvenes porque en el caos existencial en el que viven es una opción que no provoca dudas y es clara en la praxis y el comportamiento. Al lado de esta seguridad se encuentran los fracasos personales y psicológicos en muchos de las creyentes y los creyentes que salen de estos grupos de la iglesia católica. Genera bajas muy dolorosas cuando algunas y algunos descubren que no se puede vivir en una sociedad paralela a la real. Cuando se sale y se descubre el mundo, el vértigo es infinito.

Por otro lado, otro sector menos visible se ha cansado de esperar las reformas internas que esbozaba el concilio y reniega de la tradición más cercana de la iglesia católica y su jerarquía. Pone todos sus esfuerzos en denunciar una iglesia injusta, corrupta y patriarcal y se atrinchera en comunidades populares donde vive la fe a veces al margen de la institución, otras, en conflicto constante con la jerarquía. Rechaza el diálogo con las jerarquías y pone su acento en el compromiso social hacia los pobres como elemento fundamental del proyecto de Jesús. Son comunidades que han cuidado especialmente la cercanía con las alejadas y de los alejados de la iglesia católica y se han esforzado en trabajar en red con otros entornos eclesiales abiertos al cambio estructural de la misma.

Y mientras que sucedía esto una gran masa de creyentes (mujeres y hombres) vivía su religiosidad de una forma sociológica más que desde una experiencia propia y madura, favoreciendo el abandono de lo religioso en las familias y en los entornos sociales. En el caso de España se ha pasado de un entorno mayoritariamente católico a una pluralidad religiosa que va en aumento en las nuevas generaciones. Crece vertiginosamente la indiferencia y un rechazo alarmante a la iglesia católica como institución, pero no tanto a la experiencia de Dios.[6]

Y así, se vivió en una iglesia católica incapaz de responder ante la división y el enfrentamiento interno,[7] incaz de sentarse a dialogar, arrogante ante la hermana y lo hermano diferente, e intransigente a la hora de tomar decisiones (*Evangelii Gaudium* 98). Una iglesia católica gobernada por el miedo al cambio, por el miedo a la pluralidad interna, por el miedo al recibir una respuesta que no se quiere oír ni discutir. Durante tres décadas se han tomado decisiones sin consenso, se ha censurado más que preguntado y se ha omitido y escondido, más que discutido las cuestiones importantes. Y esto ha dañado a la iglesia católica en general, como institución. Pero también a las comunidades que la forman, sufriendo en muchas ocasiones no sólo el acoso externo de críticas y agresiones que vienen de otros grupos sociales, sino también el acoso interno que enfrentaba sensibilidades y criterios a la hora de vivir el cristianismo. En definitiva, una crispación constante de las relaciones entre unos grupos de la iglesia católica y otros. Treinta años de desencuentros (las dos últimas décadas del siglo XX y la primera del siglo XXI) que continúan en la actualidad, constatando irremediablemente, que la Iglesia católica, en su interior también es, inevitablemente, plural.

El "kairós" de Francisco, retos y dificultades

El pontificado de Francisco ha desbloqueado esta situación inmovilista y crispada. Francisco ha movilizado una iglesia católica aletargada, con un viento fresco impulsado por el deseo de una reconciliación que la regenere. Ha provocado un "kairós". Y es que, en estos momentos de oportunidad, en los "kairós", la actitud es muy importante. Por poner un ejemplo. Cuando Francisco se instaló en la ciudad del Vaticano, comenzó a hacer vida en la Residencia de Santa Marta, comiendo con los demás residentes, y durmiendo allí como uno más. Cuando se conoció este hecho hubo voces primero de sorpresa (¿Un papa comiendo en un comedor comunitario?), después de justificación (No, es que está esperando a que acondicionen sus habitaciones privadas...), y posteriormente de indignación (¿Cómo es posible que se aloje en Santa Marta? ¡No es su lugar!). El gesto de Francisco propone una práctica comunitaria de la cercanía y la austeridad, una política cotidiana de misericordia como

---

[6] Fundación Santa María, *Jóvenes españoles* (SM: Madrid 2010), 27.
[7] Martínez Gordo, *La conversión del papado*, 188-189.

mejor manera de "ser" en el presente (*Evangelii Gaudium* 27). La actitud es importante.

Y hoy, gracias a Dios (¡nunca mejor dicho!), se vuelve a abrir la ventana del "aggiornamento". Es tiempo de comer juntos, es tiempo de diálogo, de una invitación cariñosa a formar parte de un proyecto de sororidad y fraternidad como es el cristiano. Es tiempo de ser comunidad de hermanas y hermanos. Tres años después de la elección de Francisco, esta actitud, el diálogo y la acogida, lejos de ser pasajera como algunos decían justificando determinadas acciones, ha hecho de este pontificado su hogar.

Los retos a los que se enfrenta Francisco no son pocos, y no se puede aventurar que aborde el principal problema de la eclesialidad de la iglesia católica, es decir, reestructurar a esta iglesia como una comunidad eclesial circular y democrática frente a la eclesialidad patriarcal y jerárquica que se vive hoy. Pero su deseo de una política eclesial de la alegría ilumina a muchos.[8] Francisco va abordando distintos temas no sólo con su actitud sino también dando pequeños pasos en la gestión y gobierno de la gran maquinaria eclesial, pero se pregunta ¿hasta dónde llegarán sus reformas? ¿Serán superficiales? ¿Abordará la puesta en práctica de la iglesia católica entendida como el Pueblo de Dios de la *Lumen Gentium* de verdad?

Su pontificado está marcado por una sensibilidad evangélica que detecta los lugares comunes entre diferentes. Desde una Teología del Pueblo, una de los desarrollos de la Teología de la Liberación en América latina, la política papal apuesta por defender la "unidad en la diversidad"[9] buscando esos lugares donde renovar las dinámicas de comunicación entre católicos (mujeres y hombres), enfrentando la división con misericordia y comprensión, preservando la unidad. Y además, se hace presente y traza acciones comunes tanto en lo intereclesial como en lo extraeclesial (*Dignitates Humanae* 1). Las reformas en los dicasterios de la Curia romana con la incorporación de hombres y también mujeres con distintos posicionamientos en la iglesia católica son un ejemplo de este trabajo.

Otro rasgo fundamental de las opciones teológicas y pastorales de Francisco es su dimensión profética, dedicando tiempo y esfuerzos en denunciar en los ámbitos públicos aquellas realidades heridas. Es frecuente que se posicione

---

[8] Rafael Luciani, "La opción teológico-pastoral del pontificado de Francisco", en: *Razón y Fe* 1411-1412 (2016), 459-471, aquí 470.

[9] Juan Carlos Scannone, "El papa Francisco y la teología del Pueblo", en: *Razón y Fe* 1395 (2014), 31-50, aquí 43-44.

denunciando situaciones de injusticia como la "vergüenza" de Lampedusa o la tragedia de los refugiados sirios o la frontera de México con Estados Unidos. Está utilizando los medios oficiales y multimedia para abanderar, a lo largo del año de 2016, una campaña de denuncia de distintos temas de importancia para el mundo, grabando un mensaje personalmente cada mes, e incitando a la acción y participación en el cambio social: el diálogo interreligioso, el respeto a la creación, las familias en necesidad, las dificultades de los pequeños agricultores, las mujeres en la sociedad, la solidaridad en las ciudades, la dignidad de los pueblos indígenas. No sólo está desarrollando la dimensión de crítica y denuncia de la profecía frente las injusticias, sino que también desarrolla la importante dimensión del anuncio, invitando las católicas y los católicos a ser creativos ante los problemas, a realizar un cambio de mentalidad, una participación teológica y política diferente, adaptada y dialogada con las culturas actuales.

Otro rasgo de este tiempo es la honradez y la transparencia. Francisco está saneando con discreción pero con mano firme el interior de la institución. Está poniendo los medios para actuar sobre la corrupción que se ha desarrollado durante 30 años en el Banco Vaticano, un territorio de unos pocos, donde el amiguismo y los intereses han primado sobre la ética y el buen uso de una herramienta financiera. Intervenir ha significado reconocer de forma humilde un problema interno que es la falibilidad de los miembros (mujeres y hombres) de la Iglesia (*casta meretrix*), y por tanto de la propia iglesia católica de forma pública. Los casos de pederastia, que fueron escondidos en el pontificado de Juan Pablo II, se han comenzado a tratar en una nueva Comisión específica para la protección de la infancia formada, entre otros, por dos víctimas de abusos sexuales por parte de sacerdotes. Con ello pretende intervenir en distintos niveles de la iglesia católica[10] pidiendo perdón en público a las víctimas, ser solidario con su sufrimiento y acompañarlas en su doloroso proceso personal.

La Teología del Pueblo recupera el concepto de "civilización de la pobreza", de Ignacio Ellacuría, proponiendo un estilo de austeridad, en el sentido de una apertura a Dios desde la sencillez y una participación solidaria con los pobres en la lucha por la justicia.[11] La famosa frase de Francisco "Cómo me gustaría una Iglesia pobre y para los pobres" recoge este rasgo que después ha sido

---

[10] José Luis Segovia Bernabé, Anónimo y Javier Barbero Gutiérrez, *Víctimas de la Iglesia. Relato de un camino de sanación* (PPC: Madrid 2015), 25-26.
[11] Ignacio Ellacuría, *Escritos Teológicos* (UCA: El Salvador 2000), 300-303.

desarrollado en la encíclica *Laudato Si'* publicada en 2015. Recoge en ella una propuesta hacia una ecología integral, que tiene en cuenta no solo el clamor de la tierra y de los seres que la habitan, sino las causas humanas que desencadenan este clamor (*Laudato Si'* 138). La situación del planeta está en relación directa con el sufrimiento de las personas, estableciendo la necesidad de actuar en la injusticia de las sociedades para que la vida del planeta se pueda preservar.

En este proceso de cambio de mentalidad que algunos se atreven a llamar una "Teología de cambio epocal"[12] existe una intención institucional clara de la participación de todos. En el verano de 2016 Francisco sorprendió con la formación de una comisión para el estudio del acceso al diaconado de las mujeres. Es la respuesta a una petición realizada por distintos colectivos de mujeres creyentes desde hace décadas que se verbalizó de forma directa en el encuentro con las superioras generales de las congregaciones femeninas (12 de mayo 2016). Parece que ha escuchado también las reivindicaciones de la Asociación Católica Romana de Mujeres Sacerdotes (ARCWP) que en el 3 de junio de 2016 se manifestaron en Roma pidiendo el acceso de las mujeres vocacionadas al ministerio sacerdotal. La comisión que hará este trabajo está formada por teólogos y teólogas (¡primera vez que se forma una comisión en el que el 50% son mujeres!) con distintas visiones y sensibilidades.

Parece que comienza a haber una intención clara de poner en práctica la colegialidad episcopal, pero también eclesial. Sin duda las muestras de una iglesia católica más colegial se orientan a nuevas dinámicas específicas de las comunidades cristianas católicas: quién tiene voz, quién participa, quién toma decisiones, cómo se toman esas decisiones.

En definitiva, los cambios que se van percibiendo en este "kairós", van acompañados de lugares comunes entre diferentes, de la dimensión profética, la honradez y transparencia, la austeridad, y la participación de todas y de todos. Esta propuesta, puede marchar un antes y un después en la forma de ser iglesia católica para el presente y el futuro. Por ahora, se está notando, pero se pregunta si tendrá continuidad no sólo en otros pontificados, siendo vulnerables a los cambios papales, sino también en este mismo, ya que hay una clara oposición a Francisco en algunos grupos de la iglesia católica ultra-conservadores que se han aliado para expresar públicamente, en documentos, pensamiento teológico y en ámbitos multimedia su desaprobación y clara oposición.

---

[12] Gerardo Daniel Ramos, *Introduciendo una teología del cambio epocal* (Credo Ediciones: Saarbrücken 2015).

No todas las católicas y católicos están dispuestos a aceptar un cambio eclesial. Los cambios sociales de la pluralidad se viven con miedo y las consecuencias que suponen en nuestra praxis individual y comunitaria provocan inseguridad ante la costumbre de un excesivo dogmatismo sobre la Verdad cristiana. La Iglesia, se construye en las culturas y también vive inevitablemente esa pluralidad. En la iglesia católica hay grupos eclesiales que se aferran a la herencia histórica como única forma de ser cristianos. Otros quieren cambiarlo todo porque no les es suficiente. Otros no son conscientes de lo que está sucediendo y otros simplemente están desorientados. La pluralidad de la iglesia católica es algo inevitable porque tiene que ver con un cambio de paradigma global del mundo.

Entender la pluralidad eclesial como un rasgo propio y positivo de la iglesia católica es una tarea en la que la propuesta institucional papal pretende involucrar a todas y a todos. Pero para ello debe haber en las comunidades católicas y en la jerarquía la voluntad y el esfuerzo que querer escuchar y dialogar. La pluralidad eclesial, no es un elemento extraño en la Iglesia,[13] ya existió en los primeros siglos, quizá con unas diferencias muy superiores a las del presente, y se crearon mecanismos de encuentro y diálogo como los sínodos, los concilios, las decisiones asamblearias en las diócesis, etc. Sentir al católico y a la católica que piensa diferente como hermano o hermana en la fe, dotó a la iglesia católica de una gran creatividad para resolver sus problemas eclesiales y sociales, pero también de una gran fuerza evangelizadora, mostrando una iglesia católica atractiva y acogedora. Tampoco las situaciones de crisis son extrañas para la iglesia católica. De ellas se ha sacado fuerza para asumir el Evangelio con todas sus consecuencias y reconducir a las comunidades creyentes y la Iglesia universal por los caminos de Jesucristo.

Reformas para un cambio teológico y epocal en la iglesia católica
Las mujeres católicas están percibiendo los cambios muy suavemente, pero es verdad que muchas de ellas consideran que no es suficiente si se quiere dar respuesta a las culturas y su necesidad de justicia, especialmente para los más empobrecidos, mayoritariamente mujeres.

La principal demanda que realizan las mujeres no es tan siquiera la "unidad en la diversidad", ni la equidad, sino la igualdad dentro de la propia iglesia católica. Por ahora, esta igualdad se da muy puntualmente, porque no se ha

---
[13] Rafael Aguirre (ed.), *Así empezó el cristianismo* (Verbo Divino: Estella 2013).

tocado el principal problema que la bloquea que es la estructura eclesial dominada por los varones célibes. Sin la intervención en este tema estructural, todas las reformas parciales pueden quedar invalidadas.

Reformas *Ad intra*
El problema estructural desigual de la iglesia católica está ligado al problema del poder de una jerarquía patriarcal masculina, que tiene como principal herramienta el ministerio sacerdotal como articulador de las comunidades católicas.

No se puede negar que la propuesta de Francisco tiene sus dificultades de puesta en marcha. Lo primero de todo eres la herencia eclesial ya mencionada. Segundo, la resistencia de algunos sectores conservadores de defender una eclesiología preconciliar como se describió en el apartado anterior. Desde Roma se insta a un giro hacia lo evangélico, pero todavía no está claro si ese giro es sólo teológico o tiene implicaciones eclesiales.

Desde la perspectiva que aquí se presenta y que es la de muchas teólogas católicas, existen dos dificultades en las reformas actuales que pueden paralizar estos cambios, y que afectan directamente a las mujeres creyentes católicas.

a) ¿Participación de las mujeres?
La primera es la idea que está presente en la parte de la jerarquía católica de que debe haber más participación de las mujeres en la Iglesia. Hay que puntualizar que la gran mayoría de creyentes activos y comprometidos en labores de la iglesia católica son mujeres. Las mujeres "ya" participan en la Iglesia católica, pero no se las ve. Las labores de catequesis y cuidado de la comunidad, de Cáritas y de otras instituciones recaen frecuentemente en las mujeres, presentes en la construcción cotidiana de esta iglesia católica. No necesitan ser "reinsertadas" en ella, pues ya son iglesia. Lo que necesitan es que se reconozca esta labor y se cuente con sus criterios e intuiciones, se les confíe la organización en los momentos que sea necesario y formen parte de los grupos de reflexión y decisión de la iglesia católica. Parece que con Francisco se asiste a una recuperación del diálogo con las mujeres creyentes católicas que había quedado bloqueado por la ambigua declaración de Juan Pablo II sobre la negación del sacerdocio femenino y una Carta Apostólica (*Mulieris Dignitatem*) que reiteraba modelos femeninos poco realistas, y francamente machistas, para esta época. El reto está más allá del debate sobre el sacerdocio femenino, punta del iceberg de una problemática mayor. Está en una revisión profunda de la antropología cristiana y sus consecuencias en las relaciones

entre hombres y mujeres creyentes.[14] El trabajo conjunto, como ya se ha atrevido a hacer Francisco, no debilita ni empobrece la iglesia católica, sino que la hace más creativa y capaz en el Amor de Dios. Pero sin esta profundización no es posible una visibilización real de las mujeres en los espacios de decisión y poder de la iglesia católica.

Es necesario pensar desde un reparto de poder equitativo, y abandonar el pensamiento de "inserción" de las mujeres, ya que es un pensamiento machista y androcéntrico, que pone en el centro la visión masculina y monopoliza el poder. Pensar en estos repartos de poder obliga a reformular las relaciones entre hombres y mujeres y también posibilita la reflexión teológica sobre el sacerdocio común de los y las creyentes.[15]

Es por tanto inevitable, dentro de ese sacerdocio común, plantear la participación de las mujeres en el ministerio sacerdotal. Supone el cambio comunitario a un servicio vocacionado y coordinado. Favorecería una lectura inclusiva de la tradición histórica cristiana donde la diakonía de las mujeres y sus liderazgos femeninos fueron efectivos y positivos. Reivindicar el sacerdocio de la mujer no es un acto de rebeldía, ni un ansia de poder, ni de ruptura con la iglesia católica, es una consecuencia de amor hacia la gran comunidad eclesial, una expresión del amor de Dios a su pueblo[16] que se da también en las manos y el corazón de las mujeres que buscan una iglesia según el evangelio, renovada y conciliar. Sin embargo, hay que subrayar que no es una reivindicación de un sacerdocio jerárquico y patriarcal como el que en la autoridad se desarrolla frecuentemente en la iglesia católica, sino que la participación de las mujeres en el ministerio sacerdotal, supone una revisión del sacramento y las implicaciones eclesiales que éste tiene.

La revisión del ministerio llevaría a una revisión de las diferencias de célibes y mujeres y hombres laicos permitiendo la suya presencia en las diócesis, no tanto en la participación que es mayoritaria sino en la organización y toma de decisiones que es minoritaria. Desde las instrucciones del concilio, muchas comunidades católicas se han sostenido y han sido el centro de la comunidad eclesial en muchos lugares, compartiendo con sacerdotes y religiosos y religiosas una visión de "Pueblo de Dios" fresca y fructífera. La cuestión no está

---

[14] Entrevista a Ivone Gebara 26 de marzo de 2015 (http://blog.cristianismeijusticia.net/?p=12066, 10 de junio de 2017).
[15] Junkal Guevara, "Todo el pasado se quiere apoderar de mi, y yo me quiero apoderar del futuro", en: *Sal Terrae* 1212 (junio 2016), 515-528, aquí 521.
[16] Suzanne Tunc, *También las mujeres seguían a Jesús* (Sal Terrae: Santander 1999), 158.

en la "participación en la iglesia", no se trata de "reinserción", se insiste, sino en una gestión eclesial compartida, equilibrada, donde las mujeres y los hombres creyentes sean escuchados y pero también participen en las decisiones que se toman, formando parte de comunidades y diócesis que se estiman y se quieren y valoran lo que el otro tiene que aportar.

Sería, por tanto, una deconstrucción de una eclesiología basada en una jerarquía de poder y seguida de una construcción de una eclesiología de comunión comprometida (una comunidad ecológica integral, según *Laudato Si'* 137-162) a través de la descentralización y democratización de la organización de la iglesia católica en la línea que apuntaba el concilio, pero teniendo en cuenta la realidad del siglo XXI (*Evangelii Gaudium* 16). Un lento proceso,[17] que se está realizando más en concreciones organizativas que en reflexiones profundas por ahora. De esta manera se realiza un traspaso subsidiario de tareas y decisiones al colegio episcopal, repartiendo entre todos el poder y las responsabilidades.[18] Pero no al laicado. La apuesta de Francisco por la colegialidad episcopal, fue expresada en la Exhortación Apostólica *Evangelii Gaudium* (32) afirmando que las conferencias episcopales pueden aportar una múltiple y fecunda contribución a la práctica de la colegialidad para que se realice concretamente (*idem* 30-31), pero faltaría prolongarse también a las relaciones entre clérigos y las mujeres y los hombres laicos.

El ejercicio de esta colegialidad implica otro nivel de subsidiariedad en la gestión de las diócesis, si realmente se pretende una democratización eclesial. Pasa por una revisión de su gobierno, donde se tenga en cuenta la pluralidad de los creyentes y donde se reimagine su estructura administrativa-geográfica, según sensibilidades, grupos eclesiales y situaciones sociales, fijándonos menos en lo territorial y más en formar comunidades católicas de referencia, en conexión directa con el obispo. Este cambio de modelo es importante especialmente en los contextos urbanos donde la propia estructura de la ciudad supone una dificultad añadida.

Sin duda, sería útil poder trabajar codo con codo con los obispos reimaginando estos órganos diocesanos de participación. Los consejos diocesanos podrían tener un papel protagonista en la activación de un diálogo diocesano a todos los niveles. Al igual que el papa Francisco está abierto a la escucha de

---

[17] Santiago Madrigal, "El concilio Vaticano II: remembranza y actualización", en: *Revista Teología* 117 (2015), 131-163, aquí 159. (http://bibliotecadigital.uca.edu.ar/repositorio/revistas/concilio-vaticanoremembranza-actualizacion.pdf, 10 junio 2017)

[18] Martínez Gordo, *La conversión del papado*, 192-193.

distintos colectivos católicos y las opiniones que estos puedan dar,[19] sería de desear que esta actitud se propagara en las diócesis y comunidades, haciendo crecer el talante dialogante y de escucha.

Esta situación favorecería la revisión de las tareas de servicio en las diócesis y comunidades católicas, que son fundamentales para las dinámicas comunitarias de esta iglesia. El reparto de labores catequéticas, asistenciales, sacramentales, de gestión y administración, debe ser ecuánime, de tal manera que no se establezca una discriminación de tareas por razón del sexo, que no tienen en ningún caso base teológica, sino que asume injusticias culturales. Es pertinente que se hagan repartos ecuánimes entre mujeres y hombres, en función de su vocación y compromiso complementando perspectivas y experiencias. En definitiva, que en la iglesia católica se hable de un "discipulado de iguales", seguidoras y seguidores de Jesús[20] donde los repartos de poder se piensen a través de relaciones empáticas, sin rivalidad ni competitividad.[21]

b) ¿una teología de la mujer?
El segundo planteamiento quizás erróneo de las reformas actuales es la afirmación de Francisco, extensible a su política institucional y teológico-pastoral, de la necesidad de "una teología de la mujer" en el ámbito católico. Hace tiempo que las mujeres creyentes llevan reflexionando sobre Dios dentro del ámbito católico. Desde los años 60-70 se comienza a escribir con metodologías feministas y desde una profunda reflexión hermenéutica de los textos de la Escritura sobre las mujeres y su experiencia de Dios. Teólogas como Mary Daly[22] y Rosemary Radford Ruether[23] en Estados Unidos, Catharina Halkes[24] en Centroeuropa o Kari Elisabeth Borresen[25] en Norteuropa, Ivone Gebara[26] en

---

[19] Santiago Madrigal, "Un pastor al servicio del Vaticano II", en: *Estudios Eclesiásticos* 350 (2014), 574-576.
[20] Elisabeth Schüssler Fiorenza, *Discipleship of Equals. A Critical Feminist Ekklesia-logy of Liberation* (SCM Press: London 1993), 104-116.
[21] Guevara, "Todo el pasado", 522.
[22] Por ejemplo: *Beyond God the Father: Toward a Philosophy of Women's Liberation* (Beacon Press: Boston 1973).
[23] Por ejemplo: *Sexism and God-Talk: Toward a Feminist Theology* (Beacon Press: Boston 1983).
[24] Por ejemplo: "History of Feminist Theology", en: *Year Book of the European Society of Women in Theological Research*, 1 (1993), 11-37.
[25] Por ejemplo: *Subordination and Equivalence. A Reprint of a Pioneering Classic* (Kok Pharos Press: Kampen 1995).
[26] Por ejemplo: *Intuiciones ecofeministas: ensayo para pensar el conocimiento y la religión* (Trotta: Madrid 2000).

Brasil, Elsa Tamez[27] en Méjico, Maria José Arana[28] e Isabel Gómez-Acebo[29] en España llevan 50 años escribiendo desde perspectivas y desarrollos teológicos diferentes. Existen asociaciones de teólogas en distintos lugares del mundo desde los años 80, por ejemplo, la ESWTR (que es ecuménica e interreligiosa) o la Asociación de Teólogas Españolas (ATE) y otras en diferentes países. ¿Cómo es posible que se hable de la necesidad de una "teología de la mujer" todavía si ya existe? Se puntualizan dos cuestiones.

En primer lugar, resulta asombroso ver que Francisco distingue entre las distintas particularidades de las culturas, cuando habla de la Teología del Pueblo, para comprender la experiencia cristiana y no distingue entre las distintas comprensiones que tienen las mujeres creyentes desde sus culturas, pero también desde su sexo y género. Con ello muestra que su visión de las mujeres sigue correspondiendo a una sublimación de las mujeres en un solo sujeto pasivo homogéneo propia de la teología preconciliar (años 50), donde se define a la mujer dentro de unos parámetros de feminidad más tradicional en el binomio maternidad/virginidad. No tiene en cuenta sus situaciones, aunque es consciente de ellas y de sus sufrimientos de una manera paternalista, tratándolas con minoría de edad. No hay en sus palabras, hasta ahora, un cuestionamiento de las relaciones entre hombres y mujeres ni de una revisión de la antropología teológica que mantiene las mujeres en segundo plano. Pese a que en el Vaticano II se rechazó las discriminaciones por razón de sexo (*Gaudium et Spes* 29), y se defendió la igualdad en el trabajo (*idem* 34), en la familia (*idem* 49) y la participación igualitaria en el apostolado (*Apostolicam Actuositatem* 9), en la práctica no hay cambios antropológicos o eclesiales para las mujeres, por ahora.

Los estudios exegéticos han dado muchos frutos en lo que se refiere a la comprensión de las mujeres tanto en los textos del Antiguo Testamento que justificaban la inferioridad de las mujeres, como en las relaciones de Jesús con las mujeres y su postura frente a su vida y liberación. También se ha estudiado las relaciones de hombres y mujeres en las primeras generaciones del cristianismo y las polémicas resultantes de los liderazgos de mujeres. Pero en la práctica, de nuevo, estos descubrimientos no están afectando a las estructuras eclesiales de la iglesia católica.

---

[27] Por ejemplo: *Luchas de poder en el cristianismo primitivo* (Sal Terrae: Santander 2005).
[28] Por ejemplo: *La clausura de las mujeres: una lectura teológica de un proceso histórico* (Mensajero: Bilbao 1992).
[29] Por ejemplo: *Lucas* (Editorial verbo Divino: Estella 2008).

En segundo lugar, cuando se habla de "teología de la mujer" ¿de qué se habla? La teología de la mujer no se define por la autoría femenina de la misma o por la reflexión teorizada o esencialista sobre la mujer. Hay teología hecha por mujeres que reproducen los modelos, pensamientos y conceptos teológicos masculinos y patriarcales. Hay otras teologías que se desmarcan de este continuismo preconciliar preocupándose de una reflexión encarnada en las experiencias de las mujeres y los sujetos sufrientes y sometidos. Estas, las teologías feministas, hechas por mujeres y por hombres, aparecen en el tercer tercio del siglo XX cuando las mujeres se constituyen en sujeto teológico y comienzan a hacer teología desde su experiencia y la de otras, que se reúnen a compartir la fe, a leer la Escritura y hacer crítica de su propia comunidad con el deseo de mejorar la vida de las mujeres en general y de los oprimidos. Su perspectiva crítica se desarrolló, y se desarrolla hoy, en un doble sentido: primero, respecto a los conceptos, valores, normas y estereotipos de una sociedad patriarcal y excluyente, y segundo, respecto a las consecuencias de las teologías patriarcales en la vida de las mujeres, en la Iglesia y en la sociedad.[30]

Las teologías feministas no son una teología del genitivo, o sea, no es teología de o sobre la mujer. Tampoco reafirman lo femenino en la teología. También no hay necesidad de teologías desencarnadas. Haciendo una lectura con perspectiva de género de lo que pretende la política de Francisco (por ejemplo, en la *Evangelii Gaudium*) se trata de dar cauces a las mujeres con su propia cultura y sus propias experiencias para que puedan construir y expresar su vivencia de Dios y puedan empoderarse a través de Jesucristo en el contexto histórico que habitan.

Por eso se debe hablar de "Teologías" de las mujeres en plural, ya que, por ejemplo, la teología ecofeminista de Ivone Gebara[31] no es lo mismo que la teología coreana de las "minjung dentro de los minjung" de Chung Hyun Hyung.[32] Las teólogas exploran las situaciones y matices de la vida de las mujeres en distintos lugares, y tratan de sintetizar cuál es la experiencia liberadora que experimentan las mujeres frente a la injusticia, el sufrimiento o la opresión acompañadas por Dios. La crítica a los modelos patriarcales, ha ido

---

[30] Lucía Ramón Carbonell, "Introducción general a la historia de las teologías feministas cristianas", en: Mercedes Arriaga Flórez y Mercedes Navarro Puerto (eds.), *Teología Feminista I* (Arcibel: Sevilla 2007), 101-177.
[31] Ivone Gebara, *Longing For Running Water: Ecofeminism And Liberation* (Augsburg Fortress Press: Minneapolis 1999); Gebara, *Intuiciones ecofeministas*.
[32] Chung Hyun Hyung, *Introducción a la teología femenina asiática* (Verbo Divino: Estella 2004).

acompañada de propuestas teológicas y otros lenguajes y narrativas que dan y pueden dar luz a muchas personas en el mundo.

Muchas teólogas católicas reivindican el camino que ya se ha hecho, para que se tenga en cuenta este "kairós" eclesial. Sería deseable que el nuevo modelo de "unidad en la diversidad" tuviera en cuenta los muchos descubrimientos hechos por las mujeres creyentes.

c) Otras reformas pendientes

Aparte de las reformas con respecto al tema del "Discipulado de Iguales" hay otras reformas que la iglesia católica debe abordar.

La primera tiene que ver con la desmoralización de la práctica religiosa. Es necesario retomar temas de la moral personal que quedaron enquistados tras el concilio y que necesitan una relectura para la vida cotidiana. Tras la publicación de la Exhortación Apostólica *Amoris Laetitia* en marzo de 2016, muchos teólogos y muchos creyentes se quedaron fríos al constatar que los cambios en los posicionamientos de la iglesia católica eran muy pocos. Sin embargo, este texto puede ser un inicio para mirar las cosas de otra manera. Un punto de partida para reflexiones sobre realidades personales y familiares a la luz del evangelio que puedan generar una praxis moral coherente con la misericordia de Dios. La afirmación polémica de Francisco sobre la homosexualidad: "Si una persona es gay y busca al Señor y tiene buena voluntad ¿quién soy yo para juzgarla?",[33] abre paso hacia una praxis no discriminatoria de la que todas y todos pueden participar. El texto también abre el debate sobre los modelos de familia y la necesidad de atender a las distintas realidades que se viven: separaciones, divorcios, familias reconstituidas, violencia doméstica (*Amoris Laetitia* 31-49). Esta explicitó el deseo de que las comunidades católicas cuiden y acompañen estas situaciones (*idem* 37), sin condenas y discriminaciones y en la medida de lo posible se acerquen a la vida celebrativa y cotidiana de las comunidades católicas como una y uno más,[34] pero no ahonda en la visión antropológica-teológica de estos modelos ni en las causas de la discriminación eclesial.

Otra de las cuestiones a abordar es la recuperación de un ecumenismo activo. Para estos tiempos de pluralidad y fragmentación es necesario el

---

[33] RTVE.es / Agencias, "El papa Francisco: 'Si una persona es gay, y busca a Dios...¿quién soy yo para juzgarla'" (29 julio 2013). (http://www.rtve.es/noticias/20130729/papa-francisco-quien-soy-yo-para-juzgar-gais/726843.shtml, 10 de junio 2017)

[34] Carmen Peña, "Abriendo las vías de encuentro y acogida", en: Gabino Urribarri (ed.), *La familia a la luz de la misericordia* (Sal Terrae: Santander 2015), 187-215.

diálogo entre iglesias. Las teólogas llevan años practicando este ejercicio de inclusión.[35] En estos espacios las mujeres son protagonistas porque están pendientes de los problemas de convivencia cotidianos por su condición de vivir en las fronteras de las iglesias, de las sociedades, de las culturas. Las mujeres son lugares y sujetos teológicos privilegiados de conexiones,[36] de resistencia y de resiliencia, donde recuperar el sentido del mundo y el camino de Jesús.[37]

Por último, la necesidad de abordar la crisis celebrativa y litúrgica. Impulsar la capacidad de alegría y celebración es impulsar la vida de las comunidades cristianas. La clave puede estar en transformar las celebraciones con estrategias, lenguajes y rituales accesibles a las creyentes y a los creyentes, que permitan una comprensión de lo que se vive y expresa. Recuperar la noción de que la Tradición se va construyendo y renovando con el paso del tiempo porque está viva en las creyentes y los creyentes.

Reformas *Ad extra*

Las reformas de la iglesia católica también tienen una dimensión apostólica profunda que ha de ser revisada. Hay críticas agresivas de los nuevos grupos ateos[38] y de otros grupos de poder (determinadas políticas internacionales o ciertos lobbies económicos) que se sienten incómodos con las denuncias ante la pobreza y la injusticia del actual papa. Por otro lado, la incapacidad de diálogo sobre las cuestiones de las mujeres ha hecho que determinados feminismos radicales o transfeminismos descarguen toda su agresividad contra la institución eclesial católica, extremando posiciones por ambos lados.

Sin embargo, se ha de tratar con la intervención de la iglesia católica en el problema de la feminización de la pobreza. Ella no es sólo económica, recorre las distintas facetas de la vida, incluida la religiosa.[39] La equidad entre hombres y mujeres mejora la experiencia de Dios colectiva e individual y hace que la iglesia católica sea de verdad espacio evangélico donde las mujeres tomen

---

[35] Por ejemplo, el Foro ecuménico de mujeres y la Asociación de mujeres en estudios teológicos (ESWTR), ambas en Europa.
[36] Mercedes Navarro, "Mujeres y religiones: visibilidad y convivencia en el sur de Europa", en: Pilar de Miguel (ed.), *Atreverse con la diversidad* (Verbo Divino: Estella 2004), 95-139, aquí 124-125.
[37] Silvia Martínez Cano, "Jesús en las Fronteras. Otro mundo es posible desde Jesús", en: Instituto Superior de Pastoral (ed.), *Hablar de Jesús hoy* (Khaf: Madrid 2014), 141-178, aquí 177-178.
[38] John Haugh, *Dios y el nuevo ateísmo* (Sal Terrae y UPCO: Santander 2012).
[39] Rosa Maria Belda Moreno, *Mujeres. Gritos de sed, semillas de esperanza* (PPC: Madrid 2009), 31-35.

conciencia de su pobreza y se organicen para luchar contra ella. La apuesta por salir a las periferias de las comunidades, de las diócesis y de las sociedades[40] puede ser una de las claves de este pontificado si se escucha a muchas de estas mujeres. Los seres humanos rotos, oprimidos, abusados, damnificados, embrutecidos, humillados, abandonados, violentados, explotados, expulsados tienen rostro de mujer y rostro de hombre. Ser agentes del cambio de las fronteras de nuestro mundo también es parte de las dinámicas internas de la iglesia católica (*Gaudium et Spes* 88).

Ha de acompañar este trabajo la lucha contra la violencia, ponerse del lado de las víctimas. Las Iglesias en general, pueden hacer un papel mediador y reconciliador, desde dos perspectivas: como elementos de ruptura de la violencia institucional de los estados, grupos étnicos, sociales, culturales y religiosos y como puentes de diálogo y reconciliación para reducir los fundamentalismos y favorecer los mestizajes. Aquí el trabajo ecuménico e interreligioso es fundamental.

Las comunidades cristianas católicas deben convertirse en lugares de acogida para la perseguida, violentada o violada, divorciada, abandonada, engañada o simplemente ignorada. Acoger a las mujeres de las fronteras sociales es acoger a las familias y otros colectivos desfavorecidos. En ello hay un quehacer teológico que debe centrarse más en la persona, preocuparse menos en decir como se tiene que ser (espiritualidad moralista) y más en preguntar que necesitan los cristianos católicos (espiritualidad proactiva).

Ocupar los espacios eclesiales: conclusiones

Este es verdaderamente un momento de oportunidad para hacer un cambio teológico y eclesial en la iglesia católica, pero a la vez es necesario cuidar de la forma de hacer esos cambios, yendo a la raíz de los problemas. Por eso, es importante que las mujeres creyentes "ocupen" los lugares eclesiales y la producción teológica,[41] para construir comunidades eclesiales católicas más acogedoras, más justas y más evangélicas (*Gaudium et Spes* 83). Se impone una transformación de la iglesia católica para un mundo diferente. Desde la experiencia religiosa de las mujeres creyentes, que ven en otras mujeres y viven en su propia vida la desigualdad, la injusticia, la discriminación, se vislumbra con claridad una serie de retos que espolean a la iglesia católica en

---

[40] Ricardo Blázquez, *Del Vaticano II a la nueva evangelización* (Sal Terrae: Santander 2013), 47.
[41] Joerg Rieger y Kwok Pui-Lan, *Occupy Religion. Theology of the Multitude* (Rowman and Littlefield: Maryland 2013), 117.

su caminar histórico. Para ello, han de estar presentes una serie de principios básicos de construcción eclesial:

1. Principio de autonomía. Donde no haya minorías de edad de las mujeres creyentes ni de las laicas y los laicos frente al clero. Ser autónomos significa ser capaces de crear, innovar en reflexiones y en vivencias para que la fe fluya y esté viva. Y ejercitar la labor de cuidar y favorecer su desarrollo va a contribuir a una nueva red de articulaciones sobre la experiencia de Dios.[42]
2. Principio de integridad de la fe. Por un lado, dotar de coherencia holística a la experiencia religiosa, favoreciendo una vivencia de la Trinidad económica que dota de libertad en el amor y no de sometimiento a la autoridad. Por otro lado, incorporar la subjetividad y la alteridad como modelo trinitario de comunión.[43]
3. Principio de pluralidad. Se trata de propiciar una cultura de pensamiento creativo en el ámbito teológico. El trabajo comunitario de investigación sobre Dios amplia la visión y mejora el conocimiento profundo de la verdad salvífica,[44] incorporando a los métodos compilatorios y sintéticos tradicionales otros como los métodos relacionales o creativos recuperándolos de la marginalidad teológica actual y multiplicando la capacidad de hablar de Dios y de sentir a Dios, sin imponer un solo camino o una hermética dogmática.
4. Principio de tolerancia. Es, por tanto, necesario un diálogo intraeclesial, donde las múltiples visiones tanto eclesiológicas como teológicas de la experiencia de Dios se relacionen en armonía, se toleren y se enriquezcan unas a otras. Las teólogas apuestan por construir un diálogo teológico entre diferentes corrientes eclesiales y teológicas que puede favorecer el entendimiento y el respeto por accesos a Dios alternativos.[45]
5. Principio de inculturación. Es necesario revisar las categorías filosóficas que se utilizan para referirse al mundo, a la creación y al ser humano.

---

[42] Silvia Martínez Cano, "Teología, creación y creatividad", en: Carlos García de Andoín (ed.), *Tiempo de disenso. Creer, pensar, crear* (Tirant Humanidades: Valencia 2013), 301-329, aquí 316.
[43] Erico Hammes, "Trinidad divina versus autoritarismo", en: *Concilium* 332 (septiembre 2009), 83-94, aquí 87-88.
[44] Martínez Cano, "Teología, creación y creatividad", 317.
[45] Elisabeth A. Johnson, *La búsqueda de Dios vivo. Trazar las fronteras de la teología de Dios* (Sal Terrae: Santander 2008).

También es necesaria una revisión de la antropología teológica clásica, causa (por su descontextualización) de muchos de los problemas prácticos eclesiales entre hombres, mujeres y mundo.[46] No debe dar miedo al pensamiento crítico y creativo. Es necesario un cuestionamiento de los lenguajes y comprensiones con las que la iglesia católica se dirige al mundo. Pero también una generación de lenguajes entendibles, una inculturación de lenguajes,[47] entre fe-cultura (categorías culturales, transculturales y microculturales) que descolonice[48] el mundo de la perspectiva centralista europea, entre fe-cuerpo que recupera su potencial salvador, entre fe-universo que recupere una sabiduría ecológica (Ecosofía)[49] que nos permite entendernos como criaturas de Dios en un mundo en proceso de sanación.[50] Compasión creativa y creciente en justicia.

6. Vivencia desde la mística. Una mística de sanación de las identidades, de los cuerpos, de los que sufren, en especial de las mujeres. Ellas con su resiliencia y su empoderamiento pueden sanar la vida de la iglesia católica desde sus experiencias de ser salvadas por Jesús en la dificultad.[51] Ellas han sido verdaderas buscadoras de Dios entre normas y dogmas que se alejaban de la relación íntima del encuentro interior. La mística se arriesga en caminos interiores personales que se entrecruzan en lo comunitario y convierte la mirada y los sentidos para tiempos más humanos.[52]

No es posible una iglesia católica de la Misericordia sin una reforma interna que rompa la incongruencia interna de la misma. No es posible una reforma interna si la iglesia católica no se deja interpelar por los y las que sufren. Lo que está en juego es la supervivencia del proyecto de Cristo y la necesidad de ser protagonistas principales de este "kairós" de Dios. Es urgente dar espacio a la reflexión sobre las situaciones problemáticas de las mujeres creyentes que se presenten y a la vez favorecer un clima donde la experiencia de Dios no sea

---

[46] Luis Correa Lima, "Lenguaje de creación y género", en: *Concilium* 347 (septiembre 2012), 53-64, aquí 59.
[47] Lucía Ramón, *Queremos el pan y las rosas* (HOAC: Madrid 2001), 175.
[48] Enrique Dussel, "Descolonización epistemológica de la teología", en: *Concilium* 350 (abril 2013), 23-34, aquí 32-34.
[49] Heather Eaton, "La creación: Dios, los seres humanos y el mundo natural", en: *Concilium* 347, (septiembre 2012), 65-78, aquí 67.
[50] Ramón, *Queremos el pan*, 214-215.
[51] Maria Carmen Martín Gavillero, *Mujeres en el siglo XXI* (Sal Terrae: Santander 2010), 88-89.
[52] Ibid., 146.

inmutable y estática sino dinámica, abierta y colectiva de forma que la diversidad haga crecer en el Espíritu. Vencer el temor al ridículo y a cometer errores[53] dentro y fuera de la iglesia católica. No pretender apoderarse de Dios y su Verdad y confiar en la comunidad cristiana católica de hombres y mujeres al servicio de la humanidad y del mundo. En definitiva, dejar actuar a Dios en la vida y en las personas para la transformación del mundo.

Silvia Martínez Cano Doctora en Educación por la Universidad Complutense de Madrid, Licenciada en Teología Fundamental por la Universidad de Deusto y Máster en Artes visuales y Educación por la Universidad de Barcelona. Es artista plástica desde clave feminista y religiosa, www.silviamartinezcano.es. Es profesora de Artes y Educación en la Universidad Pontificia de Comillas, y profesora de distintas materias de Teología Fundamental en el Instituto Superior de Pastoral de la Universidad Pontificia de Salamanca. Sus áreas de investigación son interdisciplinares: Teología, estudios Visuales y Culturales, Educación y estudios de Género. Sus publicaciones más recientes son: "Mujeres desde el Vaticano II: memoria y esperanza (2014); "Jesús en las fronteras. Otro mundo es posible desde Jesús", en *Jesús Hoy* (2014); "Del hilo de Penélope al tejido de Sonia Delaunay. Apuntes sobre la construcción de los lenguajes teológicos", en *Resistencia y creatividad. Ayer, hoy y mañana de las teologías feministas* (2015) y "Recuperar la voz, ejercitar la expresión, liberar la pasión por Dios" en *Mujeres, mística y política. La experiencia de Dios que implica y complica* (2016).

---

[53] Walter Kasper, "Es tiempo de hablar de Dios", en: George Augustin (ed.), *El problema de Dios, hoy* (Sal Terrae: Santander 2012), 26.

Teresa Toldy

Someone is Missing in the Common House: The Empty Place of Women in the Encyclical Letter "Laudato si'"

Global climatic changes are one of the most tragic threats to our present life and to the future generations, calling for an accurate analysis of the situation and for fearlessness. Pope Francis' Encyclical Letter, "Laudato si'" (LS), is the first papal Encyclical to totally focus on environmental issues. The document had a huge impact and sparked a lively debate of its contents. Notably, it underlines the necessity of a humane, all-encompassing, ecology, able to face the challenges of the degradation of both nature and social ties. However, if, on the one hand, the text can be seen as a path-breaking document, on the other hand it does not emphasise the specific impacts of the ecological crisis upon half the human population: the majority of poor people around the world are women. The inexistence in LS of an approach that takes into account the "disaggregated data" on women's situation hinders LS' project of an "integral ecology". It also reflects what has already been called the "blind spot" (Katha Pollitt) of the "cultural revolution" Pope Francis appeals to in LS (114). The present article focuses on the discussion of what this "blind spot" seems to be. It starts with a brief reference to various reactions to the Encyclical, in order to illustrate both the polemic surrounding it and the blindness of many of these reactions to women's situations. The second part presents the Encyclical's notions of "Common Home" and "Common Goods" as the background for an integral ecology. The following part presents some "disaggregated data," gathered by international organisations. The aim of this section is to "attach women's faces" to some of the ecological problems raised in LS as if they have no gender and no sex. The last part of the article appeals to the necessity of implementing a critical approach to anthropocentrism (mentioned in LS), that is consistent with a critical approach to androcentrism (not mentioned in LS). Or, to put it differently, there will be no possibility of an integral ecology without a radical critique of anthropocentrism as a synonym for androcentrism.

Die globalen Klimaveränderungen stellen eine der tragischsten Bedrohungen für unser heutiges Leben und für die zukünftigen Generationen dar. Es ist notwendig, die Situation genau zu analysieren und ihr ohne Furcht zu begegnen. Die Enzyklika "Laudato Si" von Papst Franziskus, ist die erste päpstliche Enzyklika, die sich ganz und gar auf die ökologischen Fragen konzentriert. Dieses Schreiben hat immense

Teresa Toldy
Someone is Missing in the Common House: The Empty Place of Women in the Encyclical Letter "Laudato si'"

Auswirkungen gehabt und eine lebendige Debatte über ihren Inhalt ausgelöst. Es ist bemerkenswert, dass es die Notwendigkeit einer humanen und allumfassenden Ökologie unterstreicht, die fähig ist, sich den Herausforderungen der Zerstörung sowohl der Natur, als auch der sozialen Beziehungen und Bindungen zu stellen. Obwohl der Text auf einer Seite als ein wegweisendes Dokument gesehen werden kann, untergräbt er auf anderer Seite die spezifischen Auswirkungen der ökologischen Krise für mehr die Hälfte der Menschheit: die Mehrheit der Armen in der Welt sind Frauen. Diese Abwesenheit beeinträchtigt das aus Laudato Si erwachse Projekt maßgeblich, will es doch eine integrale, ganzheitliche Ökologie institutionalisieren. Der vorliegende Beitrag konzentriert sich auf die Debatte über, den ihr zu Grunde liegenden so genannte toter Winkel. Er präsentiert die Ideen und Vorstellungen der Enzyklika und den in ihr thematisierten ökologischen Problemen, die derart verhandelt werden, als würde es weder Gender noch Geschlecht geben, und versucht ihnen das fehlende Frauengesicht zu geben. Diskutiert wird die Notwendigkeit einer kritischen Analyse von Anthropozentrismus und Androzentrismus. Es wird gezeigt, dass keine integrale Ökologie möglich ist, ohne einer radikalen Kritik des Anthropozentrismus, als einem anderen Begriff für Androzentrismus.

Introduction

Global climatic changes are one of the most tragic threats to our present life and to future generations. When "times they are a-changing" (as Bob Dylan wrote and sang already in 1964) as they are now, there is the need to find new ways out of the many faces the global crisis assumes, that is, there is the need for accurate analyses of the situation and for fearless stands – it is time to think of new answers. Pope Francis' Encyclical Letter "Laudato si'" (issued on 24 May 2015; hereafter LS) is the first papal Encyclical to totally focus on environmental issues.[1] The document had a huge impact and sparked a lively debate of its contents: for some people the letter is too radical, for others it is anti-modern. Indeed, the Encyclical focuses on the crisis of the 'common home' of humanity, identifying the problems and indicating the path. Notably, it underlines the necessity of a humane, all-encompassing ecology, able to face the challenges of the degradation of both nature and social ties. It uses a language enabling a dialogue not only with theologians, but also with experts, politicians, scientists, and activists – even if some of them have reacted negatively to the document.

---

[1] The present text uses the English translation of the Encyclical Letter. Numbers in parentheses following LS are paragraph numbers, as in the original document. See http://w2.vatican.va/content/francesco/en/encyclicals/documents/papa-francesco_20150524_enciclica-laudato-si.html

Teresa Toldy
Someone is Missing in the Common House: The Empty Place of Women in the Encyclical Letter "Laudato si'"

However, if, on the one hand, the text can be seen as a path-breaking document, different from the previous encyclicals in its primary focus, on the other hand it does not emphasise the specific impacts of the ecological crisis upon half the human population: the majority of poor people around the world are women. The inexistence of an approach that takes into account the "disaggregated data" on women's situation hinders LS' proclaimed project of an "integral ecology". It also reflects what has already been called the "blind spot"[2] of the "cultural revolution" Pope Francis appeals to in LS (114). In fact, to put it in Michael Schuck's words, it is very sad that there is no mention at all of the "incomparable and disproportionate suffering of women all around the wold because of the ecological crisis of water and food scarcity, of contamination with environmental pollution and climate changes."[3] The Pope is not alone in this blindness: as the current text will show, many reactions to LS shared this same problem. They also gave no voice to women's problems.

The present article will focus on the discussion of what this "blind spot" seems to be: the non-awareness of the still existing "different rooms" for men and women in what Pope Francis envisages as a "Common Home," and of the different places at the table when talking about "Common Goods," that is, the lack of awareness of the fact that many of the ecological problems stem from the interconnection between the domination of women and the domination of nature.

The article starts with a brief reference to various reactions to the Encyclical, in order to illustrate both the polemic surrounding it and the blindness of many of these reactions to women's situations.

The second part of the article presents the Encyclical's notions of "Common Home" and "Common Goods" as the background for an integral ecology, followed by an analysis of what is considered in LS to be putting the world as a Common Home at risk. This brief presentation is necessary in order to present the main concerns of LS, as well as to prepare the ground for the core issue of the present article: raising the question of the inexistence of women in the description of the situation. The use of expressions such as "men and women", "humanity" or "human beings" is not sufficient in order to turn visible the

---

[2] Katha Pollitt, "If Pope Francis Really Wanted to Fight Climate Change, He'd Be a Feminist," in: *The Nation* (9 September 2015). (https://www.thenation.com/article/the-popes-blind-spot/, 27 September 2016)

[3] Michael J. Schuck, "Laudato si' – Die Enzyklikavon Papast Franziskus," in: *Concilium* 51.5 (December 2015), 610-613, here 613 (my translation into English).

specific impacts of the identified problems upon women, and to acknowledge that in many of the described situations, women were victims of men and of a patriarchal social and economic order.

The next part presents some "disaggregated data" gathered by international organisations. The aim of this section is to "attach women's faces" to some of the ecological problems raised in LS as if they had no gender and no sex.

The last part of the article appeals to the necessity of implementing a critical approach to anthropocentrism (mentioned in LS), that is consistent with a critical approach to androcentrism (not mentioned in LS). Or, to put it differently, there will be no possibility of an integral ecology without a radical critique of anthropocentrism as a synonym for androcentrism.

Reactions to the Encyclical Letter "Laudato si'"

> LS had a huge impact and sparked a lively debate with regard to its contents. Climate scientists Ottmar Edenhofer and Christian Flaschland, for instance, emphasise the novelty of a papal document being quoted in scientific journals, which, according to them, means not only the acknowledgement of the Pope's dialogic attitude, but also the accuracy of the state of knowledge reflected in LS: With a view to climate science, many scientists have confirmed that LS accurately summarises the state of knowledge on the climate problem as assessed by the Intergovernmental Panel on Climate Change (IPCC), whose reports reflect the current state of scientific knowledge.[4]

The General Secretary of the World Council of the Churches, Rev. Dr Olav Fykse Tveit, stated that the Encyclical's message has a worldwide significance in various ways:

> Care for peace, justice and the common good of the human family and the care for the wellbeing of all life in love and solidarity are concerns of all people, whatever religion we belong to. The Encyclical therefore is addressed to all people and not to Christians only, to all walks of life and not just to religious leaders, politicians, business men or women or scientists. Opening this wider horizon, the Encyclical has necessarily an ecumenical and inter-religious appeal and calls for intentional cooperation. We have also seen that many religious communities, locally and globally, have welcomed this text from Pope Francis. Hardly any document of any pope has been received with the same enthusiasm in other churches, perhaps more even than

---

[4] Ottmar Edenhofer and Christian Flachsland, "Laudato si': Concern for our global commons," in: *Thinking Faith* (23 September 2015). (http://www.thinkingfaith.org/articles/laudato-si%E2%80%99-concern-our-global-commons, 7 November 2016)

within the Catholic church itself. I do not know of any document that has united Christian churches so much in these last years. It is referred to everywhere.[5]

In fact, not only scientists, but also theologians, politicians and activists greeted the text as a courageous statement on the existence of dramatic climatic changes, and in favour of global and local politics of change. Barack Obama, for instance, declared that he welcomed the Pope's Encyclical, and "deeply admire[d] the Pope's decision to make the case – clearly, powerfully, and with the full moral authority of his position – for action on global climate change."[6] Others welcomed Pope Francis' text because of the links it establishes between ecological problems and human rights: Kumi Naidoo, executive director of Greenpeace International, asserted that "what's important about the way he's addressed climate change is it's brought together with inequality, social exclusion and poverty."[7] Laura Westra and Janice Gray wrote that there have been "few if any religious leaders and heads of state before Pope Francis" who "have dared to condemn openly and clearly capitalism, globalization and consumerism, as well as the clear consequences that follow upon ongoing overuse and abuse of the Earth."[8] Indeed, LS proposes an integral ecology, "since everything is closely interrelated" (LS, 137), that is, there are not two different crises (the environmental crisis and the social crisis): the world is confronted with "one complex crisis which is both social and environmental", since there are interactions between natural and social systems (LS, 139).

According to Leonardo Boff, the novelty of the text lies precisely not only in proposing an "integral ecology" in which "every fact and phenomenon is

---

[5] Olav Fykse Tveit, "Caring for Our Common Home: An Ecumenical and Interreligious Concern," WCC General Secretary, Geneva, 15 January 2016. (https://www.oikoumene.org/en/resources/documents/general-secretary/speeches/aring-for-our-common-home-an-ecumenical-and-interreligious-concern/@@download/file/Caring%20for%20our%20common%20home%20rev%20OFT.pdf, 10 November 2016)

[6] Danny Wiser, "Obama calls for world leaders to heed Pope Francis's message," in: *Catholic Herald* (19 June 2015). (http://www.catholicherald.co.uk/news/2015/06/19/obama-calls-for-world-leaders-to-heed-pope-franciss-message/, 21 November 2016)

[7] "Greenpeace's Kumi Naidoo Praises Pope for Linking Climate Fight to Inequality & Poverty," in: *Democracy Now!* (25 September 2015). (https://www.democracynow.org/2015/9/25/greenpeaces_kumi_naidoo_praises_pope_for, 15 November 2016)

[8] Laura Westra and Janice Gray, "Introduction: The common good and the May 2015 papal encyclical," in: Laura Westra, Janice Gray and Antonio d'Aloia (eds.), *The Common Good and Ecological Integrity: Human Rights and the Support of Life* (Routledge: London and New York 2016), 1-8, here 1.

connected," but also in the emphasis given to injustice as a result of production's voracity:

> Production's and consumerist's voracity produces two forms of injustice: an ecologic injustice that degrades ecosystems, and a social injustice that throws millions of people into poverty and misery. The Pope exposes this causal relation. That is why he proposes a change of paradigm in the relationship between everything, a change that represents something better for nature and something fairer for human beings, and for all the other inhabitants of our common home.[9]

On the other hand, there were also negative reactions to the text. Some of these reactions came from Catholics. Catherine Keller comments on this:

> It was interesting to watch powerful Catholic Republicans reacting to the Encyclical, like Rick Santorum and Jeb Bush, who normally love church hierarchy, scramble to restrict papal authority to private faith, stripped of political and of scientific meaning. Just like secular humanism does.[10]

If for some people the letter is too radical, for others it is anti-modern. R. R. Reno, for instance, considers Pope Francis' Encyclical to be "strikingly anti-scientific, anti-technological, and anti-progressive sentiments." Summarising, he considers the text to be "the most anti-modern Encyclical since the *Syllabus of Errors* of Pius IX," since it criticises anthropocentrism in the name of a theocentric orientation, as well as of "economic globalization, a signature feature of late modern world."[11] He admits to be "disoriented" after reading "Laudato si'," since even if John Paul II "denounced the culture of death," and Benedict XVI "spoke of the dictatorship of relativism," their teachings did not put in question "modernity's positive achievements" like Pope Francis does: their "criticism" was just intended to "restore religious and moral basis" of

---

[9] "Ecologia integral. A grande novidade da Laudato Si'. 'Nem a ONU produziu um texto desta natureza'. Entrevista especial com Leonardo Boff," in: *Adital*, (18 June 2015). (http://www.ihu.unisinos.br/entrevistas/543662-ecologia-integral-a-grande-novidade-da-laudato-si-qnem-a-onu-produziu-um-texto-desta-natureza-entrevista-especial-com-leonardo-boff, 12 October 2016). The following quotations from Boff are all from the same on-line source.

[10] Catherine Keller, "Encycling: One Feminist Theological Response," in: *Syndicate* (22 December 2015). (https://syndicate.network/encycling-one-feminist-theological-response/, 10 July 2016)

[11] R. R. Reno, "The Return of Catholic Anti-Modernism," in: *First Things* (18 June 2015). (https://www.firstthings.com/web-exclusives/2015/06/the-return-of-catholic-anti-modernism, 22 July 2016). The following quotations from Reno are all taken from the same on-line source.

modern progress, something that Pope Francis puts in question.[12] Reno thinks that this approach will lead Catholicism back to "its older, more adversarial relationship with modernity," since it links the problem of the existence of poverty, environmental problems and the indifference of rich people with "a global view of modernity as the epitome of godless sin." He is actually convinced that even if there is the need for repent, "when it comes to pressing ethical problems, revolution is a dangerous game to play."

Peter Forster and Bernard Donoughue consider LS a naïve text, a "gentle idealism" that "longs for a world in which cats no longer chase mice," because "to regard economic growth as somehow evil, and fossil fuels as pollutants, will only serve to increase the very poverty that he seeks to reduce."[13] On the other hand, there were aggressive reactions in the Australian press in which, for instance, Paul Kelly, the editor-at-large of *The Australian*, accused the Pope and his advisers of being "environmental populists and economic ideologues of a quasi-Marxist bent."[14] Christopher S. Carson's panic attack when Naomi Klein was invited to speak at a press conference on LS in Rome, lead him to say that "a radical anti-capitalist and an anti-population growth zealot are welcomed to the Vatican."[15]

Indeed, the Encyclical focuses on the crisis of the 'common home' of humanity, identifying the problems and indicating the path. Notably, it emphasises the necessity of a human, all-encompassing ecology, able to face the challenges of the degradation of both nature and social ties, and calls for an

---

[12] There is also a debate going on about the continuity or dis-continuity of Francis' teachings with the teachings of former Popes, a debate that reaches far beyond the scope of the present text. For some examples of this discussion *a propos* the Encyclical Letter analysed here, see William F. Byrne, "The Tragedy of Laudato si'," in: *Crisis Magazine: A Voice for the Faithful Catholic Laity* (24 June 2015). (http://www.crisismagazine.com/2015/the-tragedy-of-laudato-si, 25 July 2016), or "Ecologia Integral".

[13] Peter Forster and Bernard Donoughue, *The Papal Encyclical: A critical Christian response* (The Global Warming Policy Foundation: London 2015), 7.

[14] Paul Kelly, "Green-left Pope Francis endorses flawed view of progress," in: *The Weekend Australian* (24 June 2015). (http://www.theaustralian.com.au/opinion/columnists/paul-kelly/greenleft-pope-francis-endorses-flawed-view-of-progress/news-story/57e6f3fce440ad900ab09540acd73253, 24 September 2016)

[15] Christopher S. Carson, "Pope Francis's sinister 'science' advisors: A radical anti-capitalist and an anti-population growth zealot are welcomed to the Vatican," in: *Frontpage Mag* (3 July 2015). (http://www.frontpagemag.com/fpm/259339/pope-franciss-sinister-science-advisors-christopher-s-carson, 14 July 2016). And see Naomi Klein's Vatican press conference (https://www.youtube.com/watch?v=m_kNNpjyzo8, 16 June 2016)

"urgent need for us to move forward in a bold cultural revolution" (LS, 114), and not just for a spiritual individual change in the "hearts and souls" of economic and political agents. Actually, LS is a theological and political document. Even more precisely: it is an eco-political theological document that challenges allegedly a-political faith approaches to world problems. In this sense, Catherine Keller's opinion is strategically reasonable, in face of the trends (also inside the Catholic Church) to override the relevance of Pope Francis' teachings, and his efforts to open doors and to adopt as his main concern the option for the poor as the main gospel's message:

> For the most part, [...] the conservative majority of churches remains untouched by or actively reactionary toward the emergent networks of ecologically-minded Christians. Ecotheological traditions have their own deep ancestry and planetary networks, but they remain fragile minorities, affiliated with feminist, liberation, process, and other dissident traditions, and are prone to drift discouraged or disenchanted from the exhausted oldline institutions that support or tolerate them. The asymmetrical schism runs right through some old denominations, most manifestly through Roman Catholicism. Theology in its various ecological and interreligious registers keeps trying but has not been equal to the challenge.[16]

And she concludes: "This is why we need the Pope."

It is remarkable that apart from Catharine Keller (to whom this text will come back), none of these positive references and negative reactions to LS noticed that women were non-existent – both in LS and in their own stances on the text.

"Common Good," "Common Goods," and a "Common Home" – in search of an integral ecology

Pope Francis uses *Gaudium et spes'* definition of "common good." For *Gaudium et spes,* "common good" is "the sum of those conditions of social life which allow social groups and their individual members relatively thorough and ready access to their own fulfilment, that every political community should pursue."[17]

Respect for common good requires a social order based on distributive justice, since the lack of justice is at the root of social conflicts and violence

---

[16] Catherine Keller, "Encycling: One Feminist Theological Response".

[17] *Gaudium et Spes,* Pastoral Constitution on the Church in the Modern World, Second Vatican Ecumenical Council, (Holy See, 1965), Nr. 26.

(LS, 157). That is why LS emphasises the duty of solidarity and of a preferential option for the poorest, establishing a core link between common good and what can be called "common goods." According to the Letter, the option for the poorest results from the recognition of "the universal destination of the world's goods" (LS, 158), and should be at the centre of international political and economic discussions (see LS, 49). It can be said, that ecology as justice is the leitmotiv of the Letter: "true ecological approach always becomes a social approach; it must integrate questions of justice in debates on the environment, so as to hear both the cry of the earth and the cry of the poor" (LS, 49).

The duty to put the poorest at the centre of ecology also means the "subordination of private property to the universal destination of goods, and thus the right of everyone to their use" (LS, 93). This is considered to be "a golden rule of social conduct and the first principle of the whole ethical and social order" (Ibid.). The Letter states that "the Christian tradition has never recognized the right to private property as absolute or inviolable, and has stressed the social purpose of all forms of private property" (Ibid.). This means that private property cannot be seen as part of God's plan as such.

Pope Francis establishes a link between the need to understand the "natural environment" as a "collective good," as "the patrimony of all humanity," and "the responsibility of everyone" (LS, 95). This is why it is not possible for someone to consider himself an "owner" of that common patrimony. The document distinguishes between "owning" and "administering." "Administering" means acting "for the good of all" (Ibid.). "Owning goods" that should be shared by everyone for someone's own profit means denying the existence of others. Francis quotes the New Zealand bishops' question of "what the commandment 'Thou shall not kill' means," when "twenty percent of the world's population consumes resources at a rate that robs the poor nations and future generations of what they need to survive" (Ibid.).

The integral ecology proposed by Pope Francis includes the environmental, economic, social, and cultural ecology as well as what he calls "the ecology of daily life" (LS, 147). An environmental, economic and social ecology means that there is not only the need to recognise the existence of a link between society and environment, but also the need to "question certain models of development, production and consumption" (LS, 138). There is the need of an ecology taking into consideration the interactions within social systems and among them:

> Social ecology is necessarily institutional, and gradually extends to the whole of society, from the primary social group, the family, to the wider local, national and

international communities. Within each social stratum, and between them, institutions develop to regulate human relationships. Anything which weakens those institutions has negative consequences, such as injustice, violence and loss of freedom. (LS, 142)

Social ecology imbalance has an impact upon nature too: "every violation of solidarity and civic friendship harms the environment" (LS, 142), since it introduces forms of injustice that impact the way nature is considered and "used" as a resource, and reveals the loss of understanding of the existence of an interconnection between all human beings (with the same dignity).

LS' agenda of cultural ecology means, first of all, incorporating "the history, culture and architecture of each place [...] preserving its own identity" (LS, 143) and establishing "a dialogue between scientific-technical language and the language of people" (LS, 143). Cultural ecology also means respect for local cultures and cultural contexts. The document emphasises the relevance of preserving local cultures, and the engagement of locals in their own culture (see LS, 144) as well as in their own definition of quality of life, since "quality of life must be understood within the world of symbols and customs proper to each human group" (LS, 144).

Finally, ecology of daily life (see LS 147-154) means taking care of common spaces, a sense of belonging, solidarity, and openness among neighbours, harmonic cities and proper infrastructures (transports, housing, public spaces) built in order to proportion the well-being of their inhabitants. It is in the context of this ecology of daily life that Pope Francis inserts the topic of "sexual difference" (LS, 155) to which the present text will come back later.

The Letter proceeds to conduct an analysis of the motives that lead our planet to the present situation. It identifies pollution and climate change, loss of biodiversity, decline of the quality of human life, social degradation, global inequality, the existence of weak answers to these problems, and disagreement among scientists and experts as the main problems besetting "our common house."

Since the present article will not go into the technical details of the identified problems, it will just summarise the issues which, according to the Pope, explain the imbalanced and risky ecologic situation:

– a "loss of that sense of responsibility for our fellow men and women upon which all civil society is founded" (LS, 23)
– a "short-sighted approach to the economy, commerce and production" focused on the "service of business interests and consumerism" (LS, 32), and on obtaining "quick and easy profit" (LS, 36)

– a "growth of the past two centuries" that "has not always led to an integral development and an improvement in the quality of life" (LS, 46)

But most of all, the document considers the globalisation of the technocratic paradigm and the modern anthropocentrism to be the human roots of the ecological crisis. The globalisation of the technocratic paradigm "exalts the concept of a subject who, using logical and rational procedures progressively approaches and gains control over an external object" (LS, 106). The submission to a technocratic logic diminishes human beings' capacity for "making decisions", for freedom, and for "alternative creativity" (LS, 108). This paradigm "tends to dominate economic and political life" (LS, 109), since it is obsessed with profit at the cost of human beings. The Pope considers that this is what happens when "finance overwhelms the real economy" (Ibid.). The Letter is critical towards "some circles" that maintain that "current economics and technology will solve all environmental problems," and that "the problems of global hunger and poverty will be resolved simply by market growth" (Ibid.).

Modern anthropocentrism, on the other hand, is based, according to LS, upon "a Promethean vision of mastery over the world, which gave the impression that the protection of nature was something that only the faint-hearted cared about" (LS, 116). At this point, the Pope criticises what he calls a culture of "practical relativism" (LS, 122). This culture of practical relativism has the following features:

– it "drives one person to take advantage of another, to treat others as mere objects," by "imposing forced labour upon them or enslaving them to pay their debts" (LS, 123)
– it "leads to sexual exploitation of children and abandonment of the elderly who no longer serve our interests" (LS, 123)
– it allows "the invisible forces of the market to regulate the economy, and consider their impact on society and nature as collateral damage" (LS, 123)
– it leads to "stop investing in people, in order to gain greater short-term financial gain" (LS, 128)
– it is at the roots of "human trafficking, organized crime, the drug trade, commerce on blood diamonds and the fur of endangered species" (LS, 123)
– it "justifies buying the organs of the poor for resale or use in experimentation or eliminating children because they are not what their parents wanted" (LS, 123)

In face of these problems, Pope Francis considers that the existing answers have been weak until now, due to the submission of politics to technology and finance, and to "the alliance between the economy and technology" (LS, 54). In this point the Letter is critical towards what is considered to be "superficial rhetoric" and "sporadic and perfunctory expressions of concern for the environment" that boycott "any genuine attempt by groups within society to introduce change," considering them a "nuisance based on romantic illusions or an obstacle to be circumvented" (Ibid.).

The Pope thinks that "for new models of progress to arise, there is the need to change models of global development" (LS, 194). It is not enough to make partial changes – he calls for a redefinition of the very notion of progress:

> It is not enough to balance, in the medium term, the protection of nature with financial gain, or the preservation of the environment with progress. Halfway measures simply delay the inevitable disaster. Put simply, it is a matter of redefining our notion of progress. A technological and economic development which does not leave in its wake a better world and an integrally higher quality of life cannot be considered progress (LS, 194).

Hence, in order to redefine progress, it is important to "review and reform the entire system" (LS, 193), that is, to establish a dialogue between politics and economy in which politics are not dominated by economy (LS, 189).

There is someone missing in the common House: The need to look at "disaggregated data"

This short presentation of LS already gives an idea of the "blind spot" found in this document. In spite of its systematic critique of the current social and economic order, in spite of proposing an integral ecology, and in spite of the constant appeal to take care of the Earth as our "common house" in the name of "common good" and of common-use goods, the document completely ignores the specific impacts of these issues upon women. The invisibility of women in the document,[18] along with the use of the expression "men and

---

[18] The English translation of the Encyclical quoted in this article tries to use an inclusive vocabulary: it uses the expression "men and women" 11 times, the word "humanity" 46 times and the word "poor" 61 times. The word "woman" (in singular form) appears 5 times: 3 times in the context of the theology of Creation of man and woman, once in relation to the problem of refugees and once in a reference to Mary (in this last case, it is written with a capital "W"). Mary receives the epithet "Queen and Mother of all Creation" (LS, 241).

women" in problematic situations where men and women play or played different roles, ignores the relevance of "disaggregating data," that is of an approach, considered very important since the Platform for Action and the Beijing Declaration from 1996,[19] that enables a detailed analysis of the specific situation of women with regard to various topics. This approach would foster an even more realistic portrayal of the ecological problems the world is struggling with, because it would clearly show that poverty has a female face, since women and girls are the poorest of the poor in this world.

There is enough data to support a picture of women's situation that could shed light upon some of the "blind spots" of LS. One of them is nothing less than the recognition of the specific impacts climatic crisis and dangers have upon women and children, since, in developing countries, they are most of the time the ones that carry the responsibility of feeding the family.[20] The Welthungerhilfe website, for instance, describes women's situation in developing countries as being particularly harsh:

> In developing countries, women produce up to 80% of the food. But they only own around 15% of the land. 6.4 million km is the distance women in Sub-Saharan Africa cover every day to collect water. That is almost as far as traveling to the moon 16 times. Who is responsible for the wood and water supply in Africa? 90% are women and 10% are men. 6 in 10 girls in Sub-Saharan Africa receive primary education. 781 million adults worldwide cannot read or write. 63.5% of them are women. In January 2015, the share of women among the 243 heads of state and government worldwide was 22. The ratio is still low, but there is a 45% increase since 2009.[21]

According to the United Nations, women and girls "represent half of the poor in developing regions and slightly more than half in developed regions".[22] In 2015, women's access to own cash income was much lower than men's. In sub-Saharan Africa, for instance, 46% of married women earn any cash labour income, in contrast to 75% of married men. Another sign of poverty and of

---

[19] The Fourth World Conference on Women, Beijing, 4-15 September 1995. (http://www.un.org/womenwatch/daw/beijing/pdf/BDPfA%20E.pdf, 10 October 2016)

[20] See FAO document: "Women feed the world." (http://www.fao.org/docrep/x0262e/x0262e16.htm, 14 July 2016)

[21] Welthungerhilfe. (http://www.welthungerhilfe.de/fileadmin/user_upload/Themen/Frauen_und_Entwicklung/Infographic-women-facts-figures-2015-welthungerhilfe.png, 24 July 2016)

[22] United Nations, *The World's Women 2015: Trends and Statistics*. (http://unstats.un.org/unsd/gender/worldswomen.html, 29 September 2016)

women's economic dependency has to do with the fact of being excluded from economic decision-making within their own households: "1 in 3 women have no say about major household purchases,"[23] even if they are the providers of food security for the family.

> Many of the world's poorest people are women who must, as the primary family caretakers and producers of food, shoulder the burden of tilling land, grinding grain, carrying water and cooking. This is no easy burden. In Kenya, women can burn up to 85 percent of their daily calorie intake just fetching water.[24]

According to Voss Foundation, there are many situations in which the responsibility of providing water to the family puts women at risk, since, "while walking to get water, particularly when they must walk alone before or after daylight hours, women are vulnerable to rape and other violent attacks."[25] The containers they use to collect water weigh over 40 pounds. The fact that they carry them on their heads, over long distances, "has detrimental health effects, including back and chest pains, developmental deformities, arthritic disease, and miscarriages."[26]

When it comes to women's access to assets, in 52% of the developing countries the "law guarantees the same rights, but discriminatory practices against women exist", while in 28% the "law does not guarantee the same inheritance rights".[27] This also means that when talking about the unequal and iniquitous distribution of goods, it is necessary to name the dramatic disproportionate distribution of property between men and women.

"Day to day ecology" also has divergent meanings for women and men. According to Eurofond's 2016 report on "The Gender Employment Gap":

> In spite of more than 30 years of equal pay legislation, the gender pay gap has remained persistent across all Member States, regardless of the overall level of female employment, national welfare models or equality legislation [...]. A gender-segregated labour market, the difficulty of balancing work and family life, and the undervaluation of women's skills and work are some of the complex causes of the

---

[23] Ibid.
[24] United Nations Development Programme, *Gender and Poverty Reduction*. (http://www.undp.org/content/undp/en/home/ourwork/povertyreduction/focus_areas/focus_gender_and_poverty.html, 24 September 2015)
[25] Voss Foundation. (http://www.vossfoundation.org/women-and-water/, 25 September 2016)
[26] Ibid.
[27] United Nations, *The World's Women 2015*.

persistent gender pay gap. On average, in 2014, women in the EU earned 16.1% less per hour than men, according to Eurostat data. The gender pay gap exists even though women do better at school and university than men.[28]

Women's day to day life also includes caring for children and dependent relatives (since caring is still understood, in many parts of the world, as being women's duty). the need to reconcile work with family and private life has different meanings for men and women. According to the European Parliament, "in the EU as a whole women spend three and a half times as much time as men on domestic work (12.9 hours and 3.6 hours per week respectively) and almost twice as much time on caring activities (10.7 and 5.5 hours)".[29]

This leads the European Parliament to the following conclusion:

> Since women assume more family care responsibilities than men, work-life conflicts also perpetuate gender inequalities. During the early years of a child's life, women in particular seek to reduce the amount of time devoted to paid work. However periods out of work or in part-time work may reduce a woman's long-term job security, possibilities for advancement and training, present and future earnings and pension benefits.[30]

The inequality between men's and women's rights, when linked with climate changes, has specific impacts upon women, including with regard to their reproductive health. LS is critical of "forms of international pressure which make economic assistance contingent on certain policies of 'reproductive health'" (LS, 50). However, according to the World Health Organization:

> For girls and women, poor nutritional status is associated with an increased prevalence of anaemia, pregnancy and delivery problems, and increased rates of intrauterine growth retardation, low birth weight and perinatal mortality. According to the Food and Agriculture Organization (FAO), in places where iron deficiency is prevalent, the risk of women dying during childbirth can be increased by as much as 20%.[31]

---

[28] Eurofound (2016), *The gender employment gap: Challenges and solutions, Publications Office of the European Union* (Luxembourg 2016), 17.

[29] Library Briefing: Library of the European Parliament, *Work-life balance: Measures to help reconcile work, private and family life* (27/05/2013). (http://www.europarl.europa.eu/RegData/ bibliotheque/briefing/2013/130549/LDM_BRI(2013)130549_REV1_EN.pdf, 28 October 2016)

[30] Ibid., 2.

[31] World Health Organization, *Gender, Climate Change and Health* (http://www.who.int/globalchange/GenderClimateChangeHealthfinal.pdf, 25 September 2015), 17.

According to this report, "after a natural disaster women are more likely to become victims of domestic and sexual violence and may avoid using shelters as a result of fear."[32] Their vulnerability increases in the context of environmental migration and displacements. For example, women migrating inside Latin America (coming to Mexico from other countries), "while they are seeking safety, they often find more danger instead in the form of sex traffickers and in marginal, hazardous jobs."[33]

These examples and data bring to light the blind spots of LS, also when it comes to recognising that women are not only in the position of being victims of a social order and an ecological disorder, but are also agents of change. As UN Women Deputy Executive Director Lakshmi Puri at GLOBE International's annual legislators' summit said: "they are on the front lines of combatting climate change and finding solutions – whether in mitigation, adaptation, resilience building or in more sustainable production and consumption patterns and waste disposal".[34] However, participation of women in this combat also depends on their possibility of reaching places where their voices are heard, that is of involving themselves in the conception of programmes and not only in their implementation. According to UN/Women:

> Today, there is growing recognition of the differential impact of climate change on women. Their critical role as leaders and agents of change in climate action and management of natural resources is often overlooked in climate negotiations, investments and policies. For example, women account for only 20-25 per cent of the workforce in the modern renewable energy sector, and a 2015 study covering 881 environmental sector ministries from 193 countries found only 12 per cent of the ministers were women.[35]

The history if women's efforts to survive and to enable their families to survive should also be considered as being part of the "cultural ecology" mentioned by

---

[32] Ibid., 16.
[33] UN Women, *Annual Report 2015-2016*. (http://annualreport.unwomen.org/en/2016/what-we-do/economic-empowerment, 1 March 2017)
[34] UN Women, "*'Women and girls are essential climate actors'* — *Lakshmi Puri in Paris. Remarks by UN Women Deputy Executive Director Lakshmi Puri at GLOBE International's annual legislators' summit dubbed 'Towards Coherence and Impact' at the Assemblé Nationale of Paris, 4 December 2015.*" (http://www.unwomen.org/en/news/stories/2015/12/lakshmi-puri-at-globe-internationals-annual-legislators-summit, 5 September 2016)
[35] UN Women, *Women leading climate action.* (http://www.unwomen.org/en/news/in-focus/climate-change, 10 October 2016)

Pope Francis (LS, 143). It is also part of the "world patrimony". It "calls for greater attention to local cultures when studying environmental problems" since culture "is more than what we have inherited from the past" (ibid.). Culture is "also, and above all, a living, dynamic and participatory present reality, which cannot be excluded as we rethink the relationship between human beings and the environment" (ibid.).

A critical approach to anthropocentrism calls for a critical approach to androcentrism

Pope Francis considers "modern anthropocentrism" to be one of the roots of the ecological crisis, because it took "the technological mind" as the main approach to nature. Quoting Romano Guardini, LS asserts that "the technological mind sees nature as an insensate order, as a cold body of facts, as a mere 'given', as an object of utility, as raw material to be hammered into useful shape" (LS, 115). However, Pope Francis recognises that an "inadequate presentation of Christian anthropology gave rise to a wrong understanding of the relationship between human beings and the world" (LS, 116), based upon "a Promethean vision of mastery over the world" (ibid.). In fact, this arrogant anthropocentrism emphasised an approach to nature based on the notion of "dominion" instead of a "sense of responsible stewardship" (ibid.). The devaluation of nature leads to the devaluation not only of beings other than human but also to the devaluation of human beings themselves. This leads the Pope to assert that "there can be no ecology without an adequate anthropology" (LS, 118) and without the healing of "all fundamental human relationships" (LS, 119). Anthropocentrism leads to forms of "practical relativism" (LS, 122), which "sees everything as irrelevant unless it serves one's own immediate interests" (ibid.), where 'everything' includes other human beings, especially the most fragile ones.

The document associates an integral ecology that "does not exclude human beings" (LS, 124) with the "need to protect employment," and this need with the place given to man and women in God's Creation:

> According to the biblical account of creation, God placed man and woman in the garden he had created (cf. Gen 2:15) not only to preserve it ("keep") but also to make it fruitful ("till"). Labourers and craftsmen thus "maintain the fabric of the world" (Sir 38:34). Developing the created world in a prudent way is the best way of caring for it, as this means that we ourselves become the instrument used by God to bring out the potential which he himself inscribed in things: "The Lord created medicines out of the earth, and a sensible man will not despise them" (Sir 38:4). (LS, 124)

The absence of a critical approach to androcentrism is even more puzzling in the context of this critical view of anthropocentrism, since androcentrism means – to put it plainly – "the belief that the male or masculine view is normative."[36] And the roots of androcentrism, at least in the Western world, are strongly connected with a theology of Creation and a Christian anthropology that considered women to be lesser human beings in need of guidance by men, just as passive nature was understood to be owned and dominated by them, according to a misguided interpretation of Genesis' tellngs of the creation of man and woman:

> There is no explicit mandate for the domination of some humans over others, as male over female, or master over slave, in the Hebrew story. This fact allowed the Genesis story to be used as a potent basis for an egalitarian view of all humans as equal in God's image in later Christian movements that sought to dismantle slavery and sexism. But this later Christian usage of Genesis overlooks what was implicit in the Hebrew story and explicit in Hebrew law and exegesis. Adam is a generic human who is assumed to be embodied by the male patriarchal class who represent dependent humans, women, slaves and children, and rule over God's creation.[37]

Let us just take a brief look at Augustine's and Thomas Aquinas' anthropology and theology of Creation, not only because they provide very relevant examples of these misguided interpretations, but also because their theologies had an everlasting impact upon Catholic theology.

For Augustine, in spite of the equal resemblance of men and women with God, because of their spiritual souls (since the soul has no body and no sexual features), men's body matches their soul as human beings (*vir* also means *homo*), while women are identified through the difference between their body (*femina*) and their soul (*homo*). Augustine asks himself why God has not created a masculine help for Adam. And he finds the answer for this question in the reproductive role of women.[38] The role of the woman is to be a passive help: in the process of gestation, she contributes the substance of her passive body to harbour the active principle of male semen.

---

[36] Rebecca Moore, *Women in Christian Traditions* (New York and London: New York University Press 2015), 3.
[37] Rosemary Radford Ruether, "Ecofeminism – The Challenge to Theology," in: *DEP - Deportate, esuli, profughe. Rivista telematica di studi sulla memoria femminile*, 20 (2012), 22-33, here 25.
[38] See Augustine, Gen. ad litt. IX, 2,3; Civ. Dei, IXX, 24.

Thomas Aquinas considered men and women to belong to the same *homo* species. For him, the sexual difference is accidental and based upon corporeity (vir, femina).[39] So the soul, as essential formal principle (*forma substantialis*) of human body, is the same in both women and men. However, women are seen as underdeveloped men, as a "shortcoming" (*aliquid deficiens et occasionatum*), since it is the manly semen that gives shape to the child: women's contribution is only providing the material for that. According to Aquinas' interpretation of Genesis and to the Aristotelic philosophy that inspired him, the biological function of women is passive and receptive. The woman's organic inferiority is decisive for her condition as helper of the man. Summarising, the man is the origin and aim of the woman, just like God is the origin and aim of Creation.[40]

The second range of women in these theologies is also very strongly rooted in the link between women and sin, and in New Testament interpretations of passages in Genesis. According to Ruether:

> 1 Timothy expresses what became the most important Christian justification for sexism, namely, the idea that women are both subordinate in the original "order of creation" and have become doubly subjugated because of their priority in causing sin to come into the world. Thus, 1 Timothy 2:11–14 declares: 'Let a woman learn in silence with all submissiveness. I permit no woman to teach or to have authority over men; she is to keep silent. For Adam was formed first, then Eve, and Adam was not deceived, but the woman was deceived and became a transgressor.' This passage read in its context shows that the author of 1 Timothy is actually contending against an alternative tradition with his own church where women did teach and had somewhat independent ministries. But in Christian tradition, this passage was read as an absolute reflection of early Christian practice, to be normative for all time. This idea that women are both naturally subordinate, because of their secondary status in the order of creation, and to be forcibly subjugated, as punishment for Eve's revolt against her subordination, causing sin to come into the world, is repeated in various forms in classical Christian teaching.[41]

---

[39] See Thomas Aquinas, De ente et essentia II,11-13; VI,5.
[40] See Thomas Aquinas, Summa Theologica I, I,93,4 ad 1. See also Maria Fernanda Henriques e Teresa Toldy, "Desconstruindo antropologias assimétricas," in: *Impossibilia. Revista Internacional de Estudios Literarios* 4 (October 2012), 18-33. See also the seminal book by Kari Elisabeth Boerrensen, *Subordination et équivalence. Nature et Rôle de la Femme d'après Augustin et Thomas d'Aquin* (Universitetsforlage: Oslo-Paris 1968).
[41] Rosemary Radford Ruether, *Christianity and Social Systems: Historical Constructions and Ethical Challenges* (Rowman & Littlefield Publishers : Lanham - Boulder - New York - Plymouth 2009), 93.

Teresa Toldy
Someone is Missing in the Common House: The Empty Place of Women in the Encyclical Letter "Laudato si'"

The idea of women as having a especial role in caring contributed directly to the invisibility of women in public spaces and to a normative interpretation of women's roles as being mothers and wives.[42] The consequences of a Christian anthropology based on this idea, linking women with private space while men's destiny was to occupy the public space where decisions – including ones regarding women – were taken, did not disappear with modernity. On the contrary: modern anthropocentrism (criticised by the Pope) also meant an androcentric dichotomy (the "missing link" in Pope Francis' critique). Modernity emphasised the notion of men being linked with reason, and women, with emotions. The modern notion of reason – developed mostly by male philosophers – built itself upon the glorification and universalisation of male (western) features, one of them bein the ability to dominate nature. On the other hand, women were seen as "the other", the non-normative human being, emotional, unpredictable, in need of being controlled by male reason and by "a scientific approach," also at the hands of men. As Genevieve Lloyd states in her seminal work, "rational knowledge has been construed as a transcending, transformation or control of natural forces; and the feminine has been associated with what rational knowledge transcends, dominates or simply leaves behind."[43]

Going back to LS, one can see that the total lack of reference to the androcentric damages caused by a theology of Creation and a western philosophical philosophy in which women are seen as less than men seems to be the result of blindness to the structural male construction of what the Pope calls "anthropocentrism". Indeed, anthropocentrism is androcentrism, since the idea of dominating nature is based upon the same structural order in which women (linked with nature and not with culture) are beings that should be dominated. And that is why an inclusive language like the one used in LS – "men and women", "human beings", "humans" – is actually not inclusive, because it does not put in question androcentrism: without this radical critique of androcentrism, talking about "men and women" when analysing a world built mostly in accordance with male reason means involving women in structures that were not built by them. As Lloyd says, "Women cannot easily be accommodated into a cultural ideal which has defined itself in opposition to the feminine".[44]

---

[42] John Paul II's Apostolical Letter, *Mulieris dignitatem* (1988), is a good example of this.
[43] Genevieve Lloyd, *The Man of Reason: "Male" and "Female" in Western Philosophy* (University of Minnesota Press: Minneapolis 1984), 2.
[44] Ibid., 104.

Actually, this is very clear in the passage of the Encyclical letter where – to put it in Catherine Keller words – "we feminists run for the exits,"[45] or feel a kind of a slap to the face, namely the passage on "valuing" "femininity" and "masculinity" as part of "human ecology" (LS, 155). The notion of femininity and masculinity is here said to correspond to "the relationship between human life and the moral law, which is inscribed in our nature and is necessary for the creation of a more dignified environment" (ibid.). The text adopts the classical language of papal documents and traditional theology, according to which there is a "nature" defined by the Creator and inscribed in human bodies. Human bodies "establish us in a direct relationship with the environment and with other human beings," they are "God's gift" for "welcoming and accepting the entire world as a gift from the Father and our common home" (ibid.). Rejecting nature, defined as a mirror of God's will for man and woman, is considered to be a way "often subtly" to "thinking that we enjoy absolute power over creation" (ibid.). The document even quotes Pope Benedict XVI, who spoke of an "ecology of *man*" based on the fact that "man too has a nature that he must respect and that he cannot manipulate at will"[46] (cited in LS, 155). It is very interesting to see that Benedict XVI spoke of an "ecology of *man*" and not of an ecology of "men and women", since it emphasises both the traditional theology of Creation and the reference to "man" as the prototype of human being. It is in the context of such an understanding of a nature created by God that Pope Francis talks about the need of "valuing one's own body in its femininity and masculinity" (LS, 155), and reproduces the paradigm of complementarity of man and woman, that is, what he calls "an encounter with someone who is different" (ibid.). He also inserts the traditional essentialist approach based upon the existence of a male and female "specificity" – "we can joyfully accept the specific gifts of another man or woman" –, and criticises what, according to him, is "to cancel out sexual difference," because it means that human beings "no longer knows how to confront it" (ibid.).

This passage, reproducing the traditional understanding of sexual difference and complementarity as part of God's Creation, is inscribed in an Encyclical letter which does not mention the specific problems of women in flesh and blood (indeed, it is not enough to sow the expression "men and women" along

---

[45] Keller, "Encycling: One Feminist Theological Response".
[46] Pope Benedict XVI, "Address to the German Bundestag, Berlin (22 September 2011)," in: *AAS* 103 [2011:10], 668.

the document). This, in association with the invisibility of the differences in problems men and women have to face in dealing with the ecological crisis, confirms the "blind spot"[47] identified in such an important and innovative document, or what could be seen as a "myopic spot" in Francis' pontificate. All the more so, since Pope Francis seems to understand that women are important for the Church: see the creation of a Commission to study the topic of diaconate in the primitive Church (even if the pope has already repeated twice the refrain of forbidding women's access to priesthood developed by John Paul II), and most of all, his recognition of the relevance of the option for the poor as the main mission and identity of the Church. Nevertheless, the myopic spot is still there. As Katha Pollitt puts it:

> I know I risk being the feminist killjoy at the vegan love feast, but the world, unlike Vatican City, is half women. It will never be healed of its economic, social, and ecological ills as long as women cannot control their fertility or the timing of their children; are married off in childhood or early adolescence; are barred from education and decent jobs; have very little socioeconomic or political power or human rights; and are basically under the control – often the violent control – of men.[48]

Conclusion

In fact, the main problem with the Encyclical is that women and men do not share "a common home" in the same way, because this house is built upon a "modern" order (conceived upon the possibilities and advantages of "dominating nature", including women, as opposed to culture) and not upon a "common vision" shared by women and men.

Indeed, "Laudato si'" rejects the idea of progress based upon the modern idea of the domination of nature, but does not seem to be aware of the link between this domination and the domination of women. The document uses an inclusive language when referring to problems with impacts that are often different for men and women, and repeats the essentialist perspective on man and woman when talking about the "specific roles" of each of them.

However, Pope Francis seems to be the "doorman" of a Church in which the obsession with dogmatic thinking (Benedict XVI') and the obsession with sexual morals (John Paul II') is replaced by the notion of compassion and

---

[47] See Miriam Duigan, "In His Thoughts and in His Words: Francis on Women," in: *Conscience: The newsjournal of Catholic Opinion Francis' Blind*, XXXV, 4.4 (2014) 19-23.

[48] Katha Pollitt, "If Pope Francis Really Wanted to Fight Climate Change".

forgiveness.[49] It seems that Catholics are called to not let the doors he is opening close again.

Teresa Toldy PhD in Theology at the Philosophisch-Theologische Hochschule Sankt Georgen (Frankfurt). Teaches Ethics at Univ. Fernando Pessoa. Researches at Centre for Social Sciences (Coimbra Univ.) where she co-coordinates the Observatory on Religion in Public Space. Chair of the Portuguese Association of Feminist Theologies. Member of the Editorial Board of the Journal ESWTR. Publishes in the field of religion and feminist studies.

---

[49] Rui Estrada and Teresa Martinho Toldy, "Pope Francis' Emphasis on Charity," in: *Concilium* 4 (October 2014), 101-111.

Silke Petersen

„Luther 2017" – ein erster Blick in die neue Lutherbibel

Beim ersten Lesen einer neu erschienenen Bibelübersetzung haben Lesende zumeist eine Vorliebe für bestimmte Textstellen, die sie zuerst aufschlagen – dies gilt auch für meine eigene Lektüre. Im Folgenden wird es um solche Texte gehen, die mir auch deshalb am Herzen liegen, weil es sich um Schlüsselstellen feministischer Exegese handelt. Im Mittelpunkt stehen die Themen: Weibliche Amts- oder Funktionstitel, Fragen der Inklusivität bei Gruppenbezeichnungen, sowie „Christologisches". Angesichts der Kürze meines Beitrages können viele Aspekte der neuen Übersetzung nicht gewürdigt werden. Ausdrücklich sei darauf hingewiesen, dass sich dieser Beitrag nicht mit den institutionellen Hintergründen der neuen Version beschäftigt. Anzumerken ist allerdings, dass die mit der Bearbeitung betrauten Exegeten und Exegetinnen deutlich mehr Änderungen wollten, als nachher vom so genannten Lenkungsausschuss angenommen wurden. Ich möchte dazu einladen, an meinem ersten Leseprozess der revidierten Lutherübersetzung zu partizipieren, – im Wissen darum, dass es sich um einen vorläufigen Eindruck handelt.

When reading a new translation of the Bible for the first time, readers mostly have a preference for certain texts, which they open first; this also applies to my own reading. This paper deals with such texts, which are also important for being key points of feminist exegesis. The focus is on the following topics: feminine official or functional title, questions of inclusiveness in group names, and "Christology". In view of the brevity of the contribution, many aspects of the new translation cannot be appreciated. It should be emphasised that this contribution is not concerned with the institutional background of the new version. What is apparent, however, is that the exegeses and exegetes entrusted with the work called for significantly more changes than were subsequently adopted by the so-called Steering Committee.

Beim ersten Lesen einer neu erschienenen Bibelübersetzung haben Lesende zumeist eine Vorliebe für bestimmte Textstellen, die sie zuerst aufschlagen – dies gilt auch für meine eigene Lektüre. Im Folgenden wird es um solche Texte gehen, die mir auch deshalb am Herzen liegen, weil es sich um Schlüsselstellen feministischer Exegese handelt. Ich möchte dazu einladen, an meinem ersten Leseprozess der revidierten Lutherübersetzung zu partizipieren, – im

Silke Petersen
„Luther 2017" – ein erster Blick in die neue Lutherbibel

Wissen darum, dass es sich um einen vorläufigen Eindruck handelt. Im Mittelpunkt stehen die Themen: Weibliche Amts- oder Funktionstitel, Fragen der Inklusivität bei Gruppenbezeichnungen, sowie „Christologisches". Angesichts der Kürze meines Beitrages können viele Aspekte der neuen Übersetzung nicht gewürdigt werden.[1]

Amts- und Funktionstitel für Frauen
Klassische Stellen zu diesem Thema finden sich in der Grußliste des Römerbriefes: Natürlich gilt ein erster Blick in eine neue Übersetzung der Apostelin Junia in Röm 16,7. Hier ist erfreut zu vermerken, dass der langwierige Prozess,[2] den fiktiven Apostel Junias wieder zu der ursprünglichen Apostelin Junia zurückzuverwandeln, tatsächlich auch in der neuen Revision angekommen ist: Röm 16,7 wurde im Vergleich zu früheren Fassungen und in Übereinstimmung mit dem textkritischen Befund, den auch die neueren Ausgaben von Nestle-Aland inzwischen akzeptiert haben (sowie in Übereinstimmung mit der der älteren Kirchenväter-Tradition) korrigiert.

Die Freude über die Änderung in Röm 16,7 wird jedoch sogleich im Blick auf den Beginn des Kapitels getrübt: In Röm 16,1 ist Phöbe nach Ausweis des griechischen Textes als διάκονος (Diakonin) und als προστάτις (Patronin) qualifiziert.[3] Wir lesen nun allerdings bei Luther 2017: „Ich empfehle euch meine Schwester Phoebe, die den Dienst an der Gemeinde in Kenchreä versieht (…), denn auch sie hat vielen beigestanden, auch mir selbst". Da hätte frau sich mehr gewünscht, zumal die „Diakonin" inzwischen nicht nur in der „Bibel in gerechter Sprache" auftritt, sondern auch in der Revision der Zürcher von 2007 angekommen ist. Auch ist an dieser Stelle eine Änderung im Verhältnis zu den

---

[1] Dieser Beitrag beschäftigt sich nicht mit den institutionellen Hintergründen der neuen Version. Anzumerken ist allerdings, dass die mit der Bearbeitung betrauten ExegetInnen deutlich mehr Änderungen wollten, als nachher vom „Lenkungsausschuss" angenommen wurden; vgl. dazu und insgesamt u.a. die Themenhefte: „Die Revision der Lutherbibel für das Jahr 2017" (EvTheol 4, 2016) und „Martin Luther und seine Bibel" (BiKi 1, 2017) sowie: Melanie Lange / Martin Rösel (Hg.), „Was Dolmetschen für Kunst und Arbeit sei". Die Lutherbibel und andere deutsche Bibelübersetzungen, Beiträge der Rostocker Konferenz 2013, Leipzig/Stuttgart 2014.

[2] Bahnbrechend für die neuere Diskussion war hier: Bernadette J. Brooten, „Junia ... hervorragend unter den Aposteln" (Röm 16,7), in: Elisabeth Moltmann-Wendel (Hg.), Frauenbefreiung. Biblische und theologische Argumente, GT.S 12, München ²1978, 148–151.

[3] Genaueres zu diesen Bezeichnungen und ihrer Verbreitung im frühen Christentum bei Ute E. Eisen, Amtsträgerinnen im frühen Christentum. Epigraphische und literarische Studien, FKDG 61, Göttingen 1996, 154–192, bes. 156 Anm. 13 und 14, sowie dies., Artikel: Phöbe, in RGG 4, Bd. VI, Tübingen 2013, 1318.

älteren Versionen der Luther-Bibel zu verzeichnen (Luther 1545: „welche ist am dienste der Gemeine zu Kenchrea"; Luther 1984: „die im Dienst der Gemeinde von Kenchreä ist" gegenüber dem neuen „den Dienst ... versieht"). Das Kriterium der Treue zum Luther-Text, das in der Revision 2017 insgesamt eine große Rolle spielt, scheint also nicht so ausschlaggebend gewesen zu sein, dass es eine Änderung prinzipiell verhindert hätte – warum dann nicht gleich richtig?

Inklusivität bei Gruppenbezeichnungen
Auch hier zeigt sich ein gemischtes Bild: Zunächst ist erfreulich, dass unter anderem im ersten Brief an die Gemeinde in Korinth die häufig angeredeten ἀδελφοί (die „Brüder" in älteren Bibelübersetzungen) inzwischen durchgehend mit „Brüder und Schwestern" wiedergeben sind (so etwa in 1,10.11.26 u.ö.). Dies geschieht differierend von den älteren Lutherversionen, ist aber im Sinne des griechischen Sprachgebrauchs exakt, da ἀδελφοί sowohl rein männliche wie auch gemischte Gruppen bezeichnen kann (nur rein weibliche sind sprachlich eindeutig durch ἀδελφαί repräsentiert). Im Einzelfall ist also kontextuell zu entscheiden, ob auch Frauen angeredet sind, was im 1Kor insgesamt inhaltlich eindeutig gegeben ist.

Ein weniger erfreuliches Bild ergibt jedoch ein Blick ins Markusevangelium. In Mk 3,31-35, der Geschichte von den wahren Verwandten Jesu, treten eben diese auf, um mit Jesus zu reden. Dabei wechseln die Gruppenbezeichnungen in interessanter Weise, was die neue Version offensichtlich übersehen hat (oder übersehen wollte), da wir dort lesen: „Und es kamen seine Mutter und seine Brüder und standen draußen, schickten zu ihm und ließen ihn rufen. Und das Volk saß um ihn. Und sie sprachen zu ihm: Siehe, deine Mutter und deine Brüder und deine Schwestern draußen fragen nach dir." Wenn in zweiten Vers die Schwestern vorkommen, müssen sie auch im ersten anwesend sein, da es kaum anzunehmen ist, dass sie zwischen Vers 31 und 32 vom Himmel gefallen sind (dasselbe gilt auch für die Verse 34 bzw. 35). Anders formuliert: Die Bedeutung von ἀδελφοί wird durch die An- oder Abwesenheit von ἀδελφαί determiniert, wenn letztere genannt werden, sind erstere als Brüder zu klassifizieren, wenn nicht, handelt es sich um Geschwister, die dann auch als solche zu übersetzen wären (was etwa die Zürcher 2007 auch tut). Hier wäre der Luther-Revision mehr sprachliche Sorgfalt zu wünschen gewesen, zumal der Text Mk 3,31-35 qua metaphorischer Übertragbarkeit Aussagen über die Jesusbewegung insgesamt macht und nicht einfach nur auf Jesu Familie zu beziehen ist (für die allerdings ebenfalls gilt, dass sie neben einer Mutter und Brüdern auch Schwestern enthielt, vgl. auch Mk 6,3).

Ein vergleichbares Problem lässt sich an einer anderen Stelle der Übersetzung des Markusevangeliums beobachten: In Mk 3,14 gibt es eine textkritisch äußerst zweifelhafte Stelle, in der „die Zwölf" mit den *apostoloi* gleichgesetzt werden; in den neueren griechischen Textausgaben sind hinreichend textkritische Warnzeichen vorhanden. Luther 2017 übersetzt hier: „Und er setzte Zwölf ein, die er auch Apostel nannte, dass sie bei ihm sein sollten und dass er sie aussendete zu predigen". Die Passage „die er auch Apostel nannte" fehlt im Luther-Text von 1545. Textkritisch hatte Luther selbst natürlich eine andere Ausgangslage als wir heute, doch lässt sich plausibel argumentieren, dass es sich beim den „Aposteln" in Mk 3,14 um einen Einschub handelt, der das lukanische Apostelkonzept in das Markusevangelium einträgt und damit die „Apostel" auf eine rein männliche Zwölfergruppe einschränkt, wofür sich sonst keine Indizien im Text des Markusevangeliums finden lassen. In der Übersetzung findet sich bedauerlicherweise kein Hinweis auf die auch textkritische Problematik dieser Ergänzung, er wird als Normaltext wiedergegeben (textkritische Hinweise werden an anderen Stellen durchaus gegeben, vgl. etwa Mk 16,9ff; Joh 5,3f; 7,53ff).

Christologisches

Auch die Christologie ist ein Thema feministischer Exegese; kritisiert wurde u.a. eine einseitige „Vermännlichung" Jesu Christi. Als Beispiel mögen hier nur zwei Stellen des Johannesprologs als eines christologischen Grundtextes dienen. Joh 1,14 ist in der neuen Luther-Version durch Fettdruck hervorgehoben (in Luther 1984 war dies nur der erste Teil) und lautet: „Und das Wort ward Fleisch und wohnte unter uns, und wir sahen seine Herrlichkeit, eine Herrlichkeit als des eingeborenen Sohnes vom Vater, voller Gnade und Wahrheit". Der „eingeborene Sohn" entspricht den älteren Luther-Fassungen von 1545 und 1984; problematisch ist hier jedoch, dass im Griechischen der Sohn schlicht fehlt, es steht dort lediglich eine Form von μονογενής. Nach Ausweis der Lexika bedeutet μονογενής entweder „einzig" oder „einzigartig"; es ist zudem eines jener griechischen Adjektive, die im Maskulinum und Femininum gleichlautend sind. Problematisch ist die Übersetzung „eingeborener Sohn" auf zwei Ebenen: Einerseits suggeriert sie, dass es hier exklusiv um Söhne geht (als hätte, provozierend gesagt, Gott auch noch drei Töchter haben können), zum anderen lässt ein „Eingeborener" in meinem sprachlichen Assoziationsfeld eher an Indianer oder Aborigines denken als an die wohl gemeinte

Einzigartigkeit oder Einmaligkeit.[4] Hier trägt die Treue zum Luthertext von 1545 nicht zur Klarheit der Übersetzung bei, zumal der Ausdruck „eingeboren" in Zeiten eines kritischen psotkolonialen Diskurses anders gelesen wird als dies im 16. Jahrhundert der Fall gewesen sein dürfte, dasselbe Wort also nicht mehr dasselbe bedeutet.

Ein zum vorherigen gegenläufiger Fall findet sich am Ende des Prologs, wo gegen Luther 1545 geändert wurde, womit allerdings ein neues Problem auftaucht. Joh 1,18 lautet in der neuen Übersetzung: „Niemand hat Gott je gesehen; der Eingeborene, der Gott ist und in des Vaters Schoß ist, der hat es verkündigt". Zum Vergleich der Text von 1545: „Niemand hat Gott je gesehen / der eingeborne Son / der in des Vaters schos ist / der hat es uns verkündiget". Abgesehen vom Problem der im Griechischen fehlenden Objekte im letzten Satzteil (der griechische Text lautet nur ἐκεῖνος ἐξηγήσατο, Luther 1984 hat: „der hat ihn uns verkündigt", also eine andere Ergänzung), taucht hier auch der rätselhafte „Eingeborene" wieder auf – und, und das ist der entscheidende Punkt, im Gefolge der textkritischen Entscheidung neuerer Auflagen von Nestle-Aland hat sich der „einzige Sohn" (μονογενὴς υἱός) in einen „Gott" verwandelt. Die etwas umständliche Formulierung „der Eingeborene, der Gott ist" rekurriert auf das Griechische μονογενὴς θεός, das sich in neueren Textausgaben findet, allerdings mit guten Gründen angezweifelt werden kann. Wörtlicher wäre zu übersetzen: „Niemand hat Gott jemals gesehen; der einzige Gott, der im Schoß des Vaters ist, jener hat verkündigt." Ein einigermaßen verwirrender Satz, der zur Meditation über die Anzahl der in diesem Vers genannten Götter einlädt – vermutlich hat hier im Laufe der Textüberlieferung ein „dogmatisches Upgrade" vom „Sohn" zum „Gott" stattgefunden, die relevanten johanneischen Handschriften stammen eben aus der Zeit der dogmatischen Auseinandersetzung um solcherart christologischer Fragen.[5] An dieser Stelle hätte die Treue zur Lutherübersetzung von 1545 Einiges für sich gehabt.

Als vorläufiges Fazit ist festzuhalten, dass die neue Revision der Luther-Übersetzung dazu geeignet ist, gemischte Gefühle auszulösen. Die Gratwanderung

---

[4] Zur Diskussion vgl. Silke Petersen, „... wieso sagt ihr: ‚Du lästerst', weil ich gesagt habe: ‚Sohn des Gottes bin ich'?" (Joh 10,36) – oder: Wie „göttlich" ist der johanneische Jesus? in: Kerstin Schiffner / Steffen Leibold / Magdalene L. Frettlöh / Jan-Dirk Döhling / Ulrike Bail (Hg.), Fragen wider die Antworten. FS Jürgen Ebach, Gütersloh 2010, 470–485.

[5] Ich schließe mich hier an die bei Bart D. Ehrmann, The Orthodox Corruption of Scripture. The Effect of Early Christological Controversies on the Text of the New Testament, New York/ Oxford 1993, 78–82.265f, breit dargebotene textkritische Argumentation an.

zwischen Treue zum Ausgangstext, Treue zum Luther-Duktus und für heute verständlicher Sprache scheint nicht immer gelungen. Und es sieht so aus, als hätte sich die neue Fassung in Fragen der Gendersensibilität nur soweit bewegt, wie unabdingbar erforderlich, ein entsprechendes Programm aber keineswegs konsequent umgesetzt. Bedauerlich erscheint vor allem, dass die Übersetzung streckenweise immer noch hinter der Qualität der Lutherübersetzung von 1545 zurückbleibt, obwohl es laut Werbung im Internet ihr erklärtes Programm ist, „das Original" zu präsentieren,[6] was im Hinblick auf eine Bibelübersetzung ohnehin ein zweifelhafter Anspruch ist.

Silke Petersen studierte evangelische Theologie in Hamburg, wo sie nach Abschluss ihres Diplomstudiums als wissenschaftliche Mitarbeiterin am Institut für Neues Testament tätig war. 1998 promovierte sie und erhielt in Folge ein Postdoktorandinnen-Stipendium an der Universität Würzburg im Graduiertenkolleg „Zur Wahrnehmung der Geschlechterdifferenz in religiösen Symbolsystemen". Zwei Jahre später ging sie als Hochschulassistentin am Institut für Neues Testament wieder an die Universität Hamburg zurück, wo sie 2005 habilitierte. Sie bekam Lehraufträge an den Universitäten Gießen, Heidelberg, Hamburg und Duisburg-Essen sowie Vertretungen an der Universität Hamburg und der Christian-Albrechts-Universität zu Kiel. Seit März 2011 ist sie außerplanmäßige Professorin an der Universität Hamburg.

---

[6] Im Werbetext finden sich die Schlagworte: „Das Original" – „Der Klassiker" – „Das Kulturgut"; vgl. www.die-bibel.de/shop/bibelausgaben/lutherbibeln/, zuletzt eingesehen am 28.2.2017.

Ida Raming, traducido por Sabine Dievenkorn, Teresa Toldy, Montserat Escribano Cárcel

Carta abierta a Cardinal Gerhard Ludwig Müller

Es cierto que los actuales responsables de la Iglesia evitan interpretar la exclusión de la ordenación como forma de quitar valor a las mujeres ya que el pensamiento democrático de muchos Estados no les permitiría hacerlo. ¡Quienes que definen la esencia y el "papel" de las mujeres son los ministros de la Iglesia al considerar que nos encontramos en una situación de inferioridad! Se hace evidente el argumento más común, por parte de los ministros de la iglesia, cuando sostienen que la exclusión de las mujeres de la ordenación no constituye una discriminación.

The exclusion of women from ordination to priesthood is based on a severe, long lasting discrimination against women which can be proven by many sources in church history and tradition. This history remains closed to honest reappraisal by church-leaders even in our own times, and therefore the discrimination remains in place to the present day.

Esta carta fue enviada a principios de julio del año 2015 al Cardenal Gerhard Ludwig Müller, Prefecto de la Congregación de la Doctrina de la Fe. La recepción de la carta fue confirmada, pero aún no ha sido respondida. Por eso, he tomado la decisión de hacerla pública.

Dª en teología Ida Raming
Diciembre 2015

Al Prefecto de la Congregación de la Doctrina de la Fe
Cardinal Gerhard Ludwig Müller
Palazzo del Sant'Uffizio
00120 Città del Vaticano

Excelentísimo Señor Cardenal:

Me dirijo a usted en su calidad de Prefecto de la Congregación de la Doctrina de la Fe, porque estoy preocupada por las actuales directrices negativas

Ida Raming, traducido por Sabine Dievenkorn,
Teresa Toldy, Montserat Escribano Cárcel
Carta abierta a Cardinal Gerhard Ludwig Müller

en la Iglesia Católico-romana que contrarían radicalmente el espíritu de Jesucristo.

Permita que empiece presentándome. Soy una teóloga católica, doctorada en Teología, en el año de 1970, por la Facultad de Teología de la Universidad de Münster. Fui también testigo activa del Concilio Vaticano II (petición al Concilio en 1963, conjuntamente con la Dra. Iris Müller, fallecida en 2011).

En mi disertación doctoral (publicada en el año 1973, segunda edición en el 2002, traducida al inglés en el 1976, segunda edición en el 2004) me dediqué al tema del lugar y de la relevancia de la mujer en la Iglesia Católica, haciendo hincapié respecto a los argumentos para su exclusión del ministerio diaconal y sacerdotal. Mi supervisor (fallecido en 1988) fue un especialista reconocido tanto en Historia del Derecho canónico como en Derecho canónico.

Desde mi doctorado he seguido atentamente el desarrollo intraeclesial de este tema y he publicado varios libros, así como bastantes artículos científicos. Mi investigación académica constante de esta temática me ha permitido tener un conocimiento profundo sobre la larga historia de la discriminación de la mujer en la tradición católica. Me encontré no solo pasajes discriminatorios en la Biblia sino también afirmaciones de los Padres y doctores de la Iglesia por ejemplo Agustín de Hipona o Tomás de Aquino y otros, en los que reinaba la idea de que las mujeres son inferiores tanto por naturaleza biológica/genética como, moralmente. Por eso, ellas están remetidas a un estado de sujeción (*status subjectionis*). Por consecuencia, la similitud de la mujer con Dios también queda cuestionado o completamente negada, y como resultado de este la capacidad de la mujer para ser ordenada ministerialmente es negada (Véase la argumentación de Tomas de Aquino, entre otros, acerca del *status subjectionis* y de la ordenación de las mujeres).

Los textos referidos han constituido las fuentes del derecho en el *Corpus Iuris Canonici* [CIC] y están a la base de la supuesta incapacidad de la mujer para recibir la ordenación ministerial, formulada canónicamente en el CIC/1917 c. 968 parágrafo 1: La sagrada ordinación solo recibe válidamente un varón bautizado.

Esta ley, a pesar de protestas fundadas, de resoluciones de mujeres católicas y de la existencia de investigaciones académicas contrarias, fue asumida sin modificaciones por el CIC/1983 c. 1024.

Como consecuencia resulta que la exclusión de las mujeres de la ordenación presbiteral radica en una fuerte y centenaria discriminación que, gracias a las fuentes testimoniales, puede ser claramente documentada.

Esta historia de discriminación continua no se ha trabajado críticamente por la jerarquía eclesiástica y por ello, aún continua sin ser superada. Es cierto que los actuales responsables jerárquicos de la Iglesia evitan interpretar la supuesta desvalorización de la mujer, como motivo de su exclusión para la ordinación – el pensamiento moderno en los estados democráticos no les permite hacerlo – pero subyacente a todos los argumentos presentados hasta hoy por el magisterio de la Iglesia para excluir a las mujeres de la ordenación se encuentra la discriminación aun no superada de la mujer:

- El Magisterio de la Iglesia se remite a la supuesta voluntad "libre" de Jesucristo al escoger solo 12 hombres para el ministerio apostólico (*Ordinatio Sacerdotalis* [OS] N° 2).

Pero este argumento excluye completamente la situación/ la posición r de las mujeres en el tiempo de Jesús (su incapacidad contractual, su exclusión de la posibilidad de ser testigos en el tribunal y de enseñar en público!). Jesús nunca podría haber llamado a las mujeres para el grupo de los "Doce": Como mujeres, no podrían haber enseñado públicamente en las sinagogas y ni haber dado testimonio público de Jesús, una tarea encomendada a los apóstoles hombres y varones! Tampoco hubiera sido posible para Jesús incluir en este grupo de los Doce a un esclavo (sin capacidad contractual) a la hora de, por ejemplo, exigir la liberación de esclavos.

Es evidente que un Magisterio eclesial sin la integración de la evolución sociocultural e histórica lleva necesariamente a conclusiones y enseñanzas erróneas.

Los representantes de la doctrina de la Iglesia invocan "el ejemplo de Cristo" y "el plan de Dios para su Iglesia" (OS N° 1). No temen hacer al propio Dios responsable de la exclusión de las mujeres. Al hacerlo de este modo, ofenden, sin vergüenza alguna, la justicia y la santidad de Dios, colocando barreras patriarcales a la libertad de Dios.

- El Magisterio de la Iglesia se refiere también al "ser diferente" y "al rol diferente de la mujer" diciendo, por ejemplo, que solo un hombre varón puede representar el "novio" Jesús, frente a la "novia-Iglesia" (*Inter insigniores* N° 5 y OS N° 2) como fundamento para la incapacitad de la mujer para recibir el ministerio sacerdotal ordenado.

Pero quién define la esencia y el "papel de la mujer"? Son los ministros de la Iglesia frente a los cuales las mujeres se encuentran en una posición inferior!

Así se desenmascara el argumento de los ministros de la iglesia, cuando dicen que la exclusión de la mujer de la ordenación no constituye una discriminación o un prejuicio de la mujer (por ejemplo OS N° 3).

Es esto que dicen los ministros dominantes como argumento para apaciguamiento de los oprimidos – ¡para esconder la injusticia creada por ellos! Pero la verdad es: que solo aquellos y aquellas que sufren la injusticia y la exclusión – las mujeres – pueden expresar lo que ellas consideran la discriminación. No así, aquellos que ostentan el poder (los ministros de la Iglesia)!

Al contrario de las declaraciones de los ministros eclesiales que la Iglesia no recibió "poder" de Jesús/Dios para autorizar la ordenación de las mujeres, véase por ejemplo OS N° 4), subrayo yo:

La Iglesia o los ministros eclesiales tienen autoridad divina para permitir el acceso de las mujeres a la ordenación sacramental, al diaconado y al presbiterado. Se puede, con toda seguridad fundamentándose en los siguientes textos bíblicos:

- 1Cor 12,11: Pero todo lo realiza el mismo y único Espíritu repartiendo a cada uno como quiere...[1] – es decir: Dios no se deja limitar a llamar únicamente a varones al servicio presbiteral. Las mujeres se levantan contra esta forma de actuar por parte de la jerarquía de la Iglesia, contraria a la libertad del Espíritu de Cristo. Ellas dan testimonio público de su vocación sacerdotal con respeto y obediencia al poder del Espíritu de Dios, el cual no puede ser oprimido!
- Gal 3,26-28: Porque todos sois hijos e hijas de Dios por la fe porque todas y todos los que habéis sido bautizados en Cristo, de Cristo estáis vestidos. No hay Judío, ni Griego; no hay siervo, ni libre; no hay varón, ni mujer (ni masculino ni femenino): porque todos vosotros y todas vosotras sois uno/una en Cristo Jesús...

Estos textos aún no han sido reconocidos y aplicados! Es el apego de la jerarquía eclesiástica a un non-Espíritu que impide su realización – para daño de la Iglesia. Es su poder usurpador que contradice totalmente el espíritu de servicio de Jesús, bloqueando las reformas, urgentes y necesarias, con respecto al lugar de las mujeres en la Iglesia – es decir, bloqueando una renovación de la Iglesia de acuerdo con el espíritu de Jesucristo.

---

[1] Traducción de la versión de la autora.

Ida Raming, traducido por Sabine Dievenkorn,
Teresa Toldy, Montserat Escribano Cárcel
Carta abierta a Cardinal Gerhard Ludwig Müller

Mi esperanza y mi fe es: Que el Espíritu vivo y santo de Dios guíe la Iglesia, aún a pesar de la resistencia de los que gobiernan la Iglesia, hacia la verdad plena (Jo 16,13), también respecto al lugar y a la valoración de la mujer!

Saludos en la fe en este "Espírito de verdad".
   Ida Raming

Isabel Gómez Acebo

Comunidades de la Reforma pioneras en la concesión de ministerios a las mujeres: La tradición común

El propósito de este artículo es demostrar que desde una tradición común se ha llegado a lecturas diferentes en lo que respecta a la ordenación femenina. Partimos de los textos de Pablo, que hablan del silencio de las mujeres, para ofrecer una visión de la realidad en las distintas comunidades cristianas. Allí, descubrimos órdenes de vírgenes, viudas, diaconisas, algún testimonio epigráfico sobre mujeres sacerdotes e incluso obispos y en la baja Edad Media, encontramos abadesas sometidas a ceremonias de ordenación. Pero todo este protagonismo muere por varias razones: la sospecha de impureza femenina, la adopción del concepto aristotélico de subordinación de la mujer y la composición de una sociedad que daba prioridad a los varones ¿Cómo iban a reaccionar los líderes reformistas a esta situación? Suprimieron la figura del sacerdote, convirtiéndole en un pastor que basa gran parte de su labor en la predicación, y las mujeres, silenciadas por el mandato de Pablo, quedaban ausentes de ese rol. Pero algunas comunidades dieron un cambio de rumbo a principios del siglo XVIII, abriendo otras posibilidades. Analizaremos el Brüdergemeine en Moravia, los cuáqueros, shakers, metodistas wesleyanos y el Ejército de Salvación porque supieron hacer otras lecturas cristianas, antes del feminismo, y sembraron las semillas que dieron fruto en el siglo XX.

The purpose of this article is to show, from a common tradition, different lectures in respect to the ordination of women. It starts with texts from Paul, ordering the silence of women in church, to show a vision of reality in different Christian communities, discovering orders of virgins, widows, deaconesses, some epigraphic documents with the existence of women priests including bishops, and, in the low Middle Ages, abbesses submitted to ordination ceremonies. But all this prominence died for various reasons: the suspicion of feminine impurity, the adoption of the Aristotelian principle of the subordination of women and the composition of a society that gives priority to males. How were reformed leaders going to react to this situation? They transformed the figure of the priest into a shepherd who spends a significant part of his work preaching, and the women, silenced by Paul's order, became absent from this category. But at the beginning of the XVIII century, some communities took a turn opening other possibilities. The Brüdergemeine in Moravia, the Quakers, Shakers, Wesleyan Methodists and the Salvation Army all provided different Christian lectures, before feminism, and planted the seeds that gave fruit in the XX century.

Todos nacemos en contextos culturales que se han ido formando, capa a capa, con las aportaciones de las generaciones previas a la nuestra y la religión no se escapa de la norma. En el caso del cristianismo, lo referente al protagonismo femenino de los primeros siglos se fue tapando porque no interesaba mostrarse diferente de las costumbres del Imperio Romano en el que crecía. Hoy, que no asusta, se pide un reconocimiento oficial de la valoración, dignificación y promoción de la mujer en la Iglesia, de modo especial en la liturgia, para lo que se han sacado y se sacan del olvido las tradiciones positivas sobre el sexo femenino.[1]

Aunque Pablo aboga por el silencio de las mujeres en las asambleas (1Cor 14,34), tiene otros textos que parecen contradictorios, en los que nombra muchas colaboradoras suyas en diferentes roles. A Junia la reconoce como apóstol (Rom 16,7) y en Tim 5,36 se habla de un orden de viudas cuyas acciones eran rezar, instruir teológicamente, ungir a los recientemente bautizados, atender a los enfermos. En Rom 16,1-2, habla de Febe a la que titula *diákonos* de la Iglesia de Céncreas, un término semejante al que utiliza para los varones que desempeñan el mismo cargo. En 1 Tim 3,8-11, hablando de los diáconos, dice que: "las mujeres igualmente deben ser dignas, no calumniadoras, sobrias, fieles en todo".

En los comienzos del siglo III un texto sirio, la *Didascalia Apostolorum*, nos habla de las funciones que cumplían las viudas y las diaconisas; en el Concilio de Nicea (325) se alude a estas últimas y en las *Constituciones Apostólicas* sirias (380) aparece la primera referencia a la liturgia de su ordenación que no plantea diferencias con la de los varones pues comprendía la imposición de manos en presencia de los presbíteros, de los diáconos y de las diaconisas. Contrariamente a lo que pudiera parecer, los Padres de la Iglesia[2]

---

[1] Se han escrito innumerables obras sobre el protagonismo femenino en los primeros siglos del cristianismo: Roger Gryson, *The Ministry of Women in the Early Church* (The Liturgical Press: Collegeville 1980); Karen J. Torjesen, *When Women were Priests. Women's Leadership in the Early Church and the Scandal of their Subordination in the Rise of Christianity* (Harper: New York 1995); John Wijngaards, *The Ordained Women Deacons of the Church's First Millennium* (Canterbury Press: Norwich 2011); Kevin Madigan y Carolyn Osiek, *Ordained Women in the Early Church (*The John Hopkins University Press: Baltimore 2005).

[2] He tomado estas notas de Fernando Rivas, "Diaconado de las mujeres en la Iglesia. Perspectiva histórica", en: *Vida Nueva* 2989 (mayo 2016), 21-27, donde se puede consultar la lista de los Padres de la Iglesia que mencionan la existencia de las diaconisas.

multiplican las referencias a estas mujeres ordenadas en los siguientes siglos, fundamentalmente en la iglesia oriental.

En el siglo XI en una carta del papa Benedicto VIII al obispo de Oporto le confirma la concesión de ordenar diaconisas, práctica que mantienen sus sucesores Juan XIX y León IX, aunque ya se habían proferido quejas sobre la impureza femenina. Las diaconisas permanecieron hasta el siglo XIII en ambientes conventuales y de manera marginal en algunas Iglesias orientales como la maronita[3]. Esta tradición antigua hizo que Harnack en 1905 reconociera que las mujeres tuvieron un papel como viudas, diáconos, profetisas y maestras en los dos primeros siglos hasta que a raíz de "la confrontación contra el gnosticismo y montanismo se les prohibió ejercer toda actividad en la Iglesia".[4]

Lo más curioso de los estudios recientes es que se han encontrado referencias epigráficas y escritos (*Testamentum Domini*), sobre la existencia de mujeres presbíteros e incluso obispos aunque no les faltaron controversias que saldó Epifanio tachando a estas comunidades de montanistas. Parece que existieron mujeres activas en el presbiterado hasta el siglo IV en Asia Menor, Egipto y Grecia mientras que en el oeste se han encontrado evidencias epigráficas de mujeres sacerdotes y obispos en Sicilia y Yugoslavia desde el siglo IV al VI.[5]

Una larga serie de abadesas anglosajonas fueron nombradas mediante ritos de ordenación en el templo. El obispo les imponía las manos, les colocaba la estola, les autorizaba a predicar, a guiar la comunidad y a ejercer jurisdicción sobre el territorio de la abadía. En la liturgia de las abadesas del monasterio de las Huelgas (España) se afirmaba que Dios no hacía distinción entre los sexos, *non est discretio sexuum*. Estas mujeres tenían poderes omnímodos pues gozaban de permiso para bautizar, confesar, excomulgar, predicar.[6] También las hubo con amplios poderes en algunas abadías francesas e italianas.

Algunas comunidades heterodoxas se apartaron de la línea oficial de la Iglesia. Un caso singular fue el de Guillerma, que vivió a finales del siglo XII y a la que sus seguidores, los guillermitas, identificaron con el Paráclito. Su

---

[3] Rivas, "Diaconado de las mujeres", 27.
[4] Adolf von Harnack, *Expansion of Christianity in the First Two Centuries*, dos volúmenes (Putman and Sons: New York 1904-1905), 230.
[5] Ute E. Eisen, *Women Office Holders in Early Christianity. Epigraphical and Literary Sources* (The Liturgical Press: Collegeville 2000). Ver los capítulos que hacen referencia a las presbíteras (116-142) y a las obispas (199-216).
[6] Del fundador del Opus Dei, José María Escrivá de Balaguer, *La abadesa de las Huelgas* (Rialp: Madrid 1974).

portavoz Maifreda, muerta la fundadora, aseguraba que "nuestra señora me ha mandado que os diga que ella es el Espíritu Santo y yo os lo digo, a pesar de los muchos tomases, a pesar de tanto incrédulo".[7]

Una herejía que contó con muchos adeptos en el sur de Francia, zona del Languedoc, fueron los cátaros también conocidos como albigenses porque eran mayoritarios en la ciudad de Albi. A principios del siglo XIII configuraron una comunidad muy semejante en organización a la Iglesia pues contaba con obispos y sacerdotes. Una de las diferencias, en cuanto al sexo femenino, era que las mujeres podían recibir el *consolamentum*, un orden semejante al sacerdocio, que les daba las mismas prerrogativas que a los varones con la única salvedad de que no podían ascender al episcopado aunque en sus manos quedaba ordenar a sus compañeras e impartir el *consolamentum* a los moribundos.[8]

La llegada de la reforma
Con esta tradición detrás, aunque desconocían algunos de estos descubrimientos recientes, los grandes reformadores debían decidir sobre el protagonismo de las mujeres en sus comunidades. Suprimieron el sacerdocio ministerial pasando sus dirigentes a considerarse pastores, guías de sus respectivas comunidades, con un acento muy marcado sobre la predicación. La gran importancia que dieron a la Biblia, que todavía no había perdido la autoridad literal, hizo que el consejo de Pablo, en 1 Cor 14,34, que silenciaba a las mujeres, fuera determinante para el posicionamiento negativo sobre el sexo femenino. No es extraño pues hay que reconocer que la sociedad no estaba preparada para dar el gran salto ya que, en primer lugar, estaba mal visto que las mujeres fueran letradas. De aquí, que otros pasajes bíblicos de mujeres que lideraban a sus comunidades como Débora, las profetisas hijas de Felipe, la mujer samaritana o María Magdalena, a la que Jesús pidió que le anunciara, o las predicadoras junto a Pablo, no fueran relevantes. La esposa del pastor se debería limitar a ser una buena ama de casa, un cuidado que ampliaría a la rectoría y las demás mujeres debían seguir su ejemplo.

Tenemos que ser conscientes de que la dejación de la obediencia a Roma produjo una revolución en la sociedad europea, tanto política, como social y

---

[7] Para profundizar sobre el tema de esta curiosa mujer ver Luisa Muraro, *Guillerma y Manfreda. Historia de una herejía feminista* (Omega: Barcelona 1997).
[8] Anne Brenon, *Les Femmes Cathares* (Perrin: París 1992), hace una buena descripción del protagonismo femenino en sus comunidades.

religiosa. En este último aspecto se rompió la autoridad del Papa y el individualismo multiplicó las sectas y las denominaciones. En este artículo voy a tratar una serie de comunidades pioneras de los siglos XVIII y primeras décadas del XIX que sirvieron de trampolín para que, junto al movimiento feminista de finales del XIX, surgieran iglesias que igualaron a las mujeres en sus comunidades.

Las comunidades pioneras

La iglesia de Moravia

La idea de Lutero de que todas las almas debían conocer a Dios mediante un esfuerzo personal hizo que muchas sectas consideraran que cualquier persona era susceptible de alcanzar la iluminación divina, incluidas las mujeres. Una de estas comunidades es la iglesia de Moravia, que se conoce como la Congregación de los Hermanos, *Unitas Fratrum*, una de las denominaciones protestantes más antiguas ya que empieza su andadura en el siglo XV bajo el reformador Jan Hus.

El movimiento husita fue muy perseguido por el imperio austriaco, cuyos emperadores eran católicos, y se mostraban temerosos de la magnitud que estaban alcanzando los herejes. El 90% de la población de Bohemia practicaba esa fe y, en esta zona, los nobles se levantaron contra el emperador, porque no querían renunciar a sus creencias, pero su ejército fue masacrado en el año 1620.[9] A partir de entonces muchos fieles tuvieron que practicar su religión en secreto o huir y uno de los lugares donde recalaron fue Moravia. Un siglo más tarde de estos acontecimientos un pequeño grupo se instaló en las tierras de Berthelsdorf pertenecientes al conde Zinzendorf, un hombre educado en el pietismo que fue nombrado obispo.

Esta comunidad tendía hacia el igualitarismo y la fraternidad entre todos sus miembros, unas ideas que llevaron a la práctica impartiendo a los dos sexos los mismos ministerios. Con Gálatas 3,28 en mente, en la temprana fecha de 1745, permitieron que las mujeres fueran diáconos y sacerdotes pero no obispos y 15 años más tarde sus anales contabilizan 202 diaconisas y 14 presbíteras. Sus comunidades se dividían en "coros" con distintos pabellones para mujeres y varones, el lado de los hermanos y el de las hermanas. Al espacio de sus reuniones comunales se accedía por puertas distintas y había bancos

---

[9] Se conoce como Segunda Defenestración de Praga.

Isabel Gómez Acebo
Comunidades de la Reforma pioneras en la concesión de ministerios a las mujeres: La tradición común

reservados para cada sexo. La mayor parte del protagonismo femenino giraba en torno a la dirección espiritual y al gobierno de las otras mujeres.

La predicación de estas mujeres, aunque nunca lo hicieran a toda la comunidad reunida, causaba indignación a las otras comunidades protestantes al considerar sus detractores que se rompían las costumbres y el orden establecido por la iglesia y la sociedad. "Esta secta es peligrosa para la profesión de predicador pues la autoridad para hablar en público se daba sin diferencia de género, edad o estudios".[10] La defensa moravia se apoyaba en que, la comunicación de la espiritualidad personal, enriquecía a los oyentes y que a ningún hijo de Dios se le prohibía ser testigo. Consideraban que, en la fe, todos somos iguales aunque limitaban los oficios de gobierno a las mujeres casadas por la prohibición paulina.

Con todo se enfrentaban, como todas las comunidades sucesivas que daban protagonismo a las mujeres, con los textos del Nuevo Testamento y tenían que reinterpretar la Escritura. El conde Zinzendorf admitía excepciones para que las mujeres pudieran aportar sus dones a la comunidad imbuidas por el Espíritu Santo. Pero la feroz confrontación le empujó a alejarse de las otras iglesias protestantes y a mostrarse, cada día, más propenso a imponer su criterio y dejar que las mujeres predicaran. A su muerte en 1760 sus teorías no encontraron valedor y se silenciaron las voces que reconocían la igualdad, el valor y la experiencia de las mujeres pero su influencia perduró, renovada, en los Estados Unidos y en otros reformadores como los hermanos Wesley, fundadores del metodismo.[11]

Los cuáqueros

A mediados del siglo XVII en Inglaterra se crearon muchas sectas protestantes radicales que dejaban predicar a las mujeres, como los ranters, diggers, millenarians, familist, seekers y algunas comunidades baptistas. Se apoyaban en que la luz interna resultaba suficiente para interpretar las escrituras y que todas las almas tenían la capacidad de recibir la iluminación divina. Pero ninguna fue tan abierta para el sexo femenino como los cuáqueros, *Society of Friends* en

---

[10] Afirmaba un profesor de la Universidad de Jena citado en Peter Vogt, "A Voice for themselves: the Moravians", en: Beverly Mayne Kienzle y Pamela J. *Walker* (eds.), *Women Preachers and Prophets through Two Millenia of Christianity* (University of California Press: London 1998), 227-247, aquí 234.

[11] También sobre este movimiento Kenneth G. Hamilton y Taylor Hamilton, *History of the Moravian Church. The Renewed Unitas Fratum 1722-1957* (Moravian Church in America: Bethlehem 1967).

un principio llamados *Hijos de la Luz*, que empezaron su andadura en 1652 y dejaban a las mujeres no sólo predicar, sino profetizar y tener tareas de gobierno lo que hizo pronunciar a Geoffrey Nutall, un estudioso de los movimientos puritanos, que "no conocía existiera previamente una igualdad en esta escala".[12]

Aunque tuvieron diferentes líderes, algunos procedentes de los ranters, se considera fueron fundados por George Fox, que había estudiado el concepto de la igualdad y no lo dejó en meras palabras sino que nombró a Elizabeth Hooton, primera ministra ordenada, lo que le supuso serias discusiones con otros movimientos puritanos como los presbiterianos, baptistas, anglicanos. En la medida que se multiplicó el número de sus fieles, cientos de mujeres tras haber realizado los estudios pertinentes, recibieron el certificado para predicar y Fox tuvo que defender ese derecho femenino que era cuestionado incluso en el seno de la comunidad.

El nombre de cuáqueros les vino de un juez al que Fox advirtió que terminaría temblando delante de Dios y éste respondió que los que iban a temblar eran ellos (quaked). Entre los escritos de Fox se encuentra el lenguaje del alimento donde compara el amor de Dios con el de una madre que amamanta a su bebé, unas imágenes maternas para la divinidad que no eran exclusivas de los cuáqueros pero asombra su frecuencia. Hablaban de la presencia del Espíritu en la liturgia como una experiencia tierna, que generaba sentimientos de amor y compasión entre ellos y para todos los seres humanos.

Al poco tiempo de su fundación fueron perseguidos y encarcelados. Los motivos eran diversos: se les acusaba de negarse a pagar impuestos para sostener a los ministros locales, de no mostrar respeto a los jueces quitándose el sombrero, de interrumpir los servicios religiosos y de no celebrar sus matrimonios por sacerdotes. Pero detrás de este hostigamiento estaba el hecho de que el movimiento puritano colocaba en el varón la última fuente de autoridad en la familia, refrendada por las palabras de Pablo prohibiendo que las mujeres hablaran en la iglesia, lo que veían cuestionado por el protagonismo femenino en esta secta En una controversia pública Fox se defendió diciendo que la iglesia era una casa espiritual, la casa de Jesucristo, donde a diferencia de las que estaban hechas de barro, piedra y madera, las mujeres podían profetizar y hablar.

---

[12] Charles F. Adams, cit. en Margaret Hope Bacon, *Mothers of Feminism. The Story of Quaker Women in America* (Harper & Row: New York 1986), 7.

El fundador encontró la ayuda de una mujer extraordinaria, Margaret Fell, que tuvo que frecuentar la cárcel por sus ideas y se la conoció como la nodriza de los cuáqueros. Margaret Fell, entre rejas por una sentencia de cuatro años de reclusión, escribió un libro con un título muy sugestivo: *Women's Speaking Justified, Proved and Allowed by the Scriptures, all such as Speak by the Spirit and Power of the Lord Jesus*, (La justificación de la predicación femenina, aprobada y respaldada por las Escrituras, para hablar por el Espíritu y poder de nuestro señor Jesucristo), en el que daba las razones, que encontraba en la Biblia, para que las mujeres predicaran.

Hay que reconocer que la primera generación de estas mujeres, llevadas por su entusiasmo religioso, fue excesivamente atrevida. Para llamar la atención se pasearon por las calles desnudas o vestidas con tela de saco y llevando una sartén con carbón encendido sobre sus cabezas con el resultado de que fueron tildadas de locas. Elizabeth Adams se presentó en un juicio con una cazuela por sombrero y cuando la gente le preguntaba su significado respondía: "muchas cosas están cambiando y dándose la vuelta". Aunque algunas se resistían a hablar en público por su condición femenina, el "Reasoner" (¿el Espíritu Santo?), las convencía de que estaban equivocadas pero ceder a sus inspiraciones suponía el abandono de sus hijos, salir a predicar fuera de sus pueblos y temer por sus vidas.[13]

Fox tuvo la intuición de que la forma para conseguir un balance entre la libertad individual y la autoridad del grupo era reunirse, todos juntos, periódicamente. Al principio lo hacían todos los miembros de la comunidad pero cuando crecieron sus órganos de gobierno, las mujeres ya no se juntaron con los hombres en sus asambleas, perdiendo la frescura inicial que habían mostrado, algo a lo que se opuso Margaret Fell, sin éxito. Los argumentos de los opositores eran que las mujeres no se atrevían a hablar en reuniones mixtas y que resultaban más útiles para los intereses de la comunidad cuando se juntaban entre ellas No fue hasta el siglo XX, que volvieron a integrarse los dos sexos en una asamblea.

No desaparecieron, como otras sectas que se desintegraron por su anarquismo interno o por las persecuciones sufridas, porque llevaron sus nuevas ideas igualitarias a las colonias que eran un terreno más propicio. Los cuáqueros misionaron en los Estados Unidos y la llegada a Boston, una comunidad advertida contra sus desmanes, de dos de sus predicadoras escandalizó a sus

---

[13] Creo que el "Reasoner" era el Espíritu Santo y para una relación de todos los problemas que sufrieron estas mujeres. Bacon, *Mothers of Feminism*, 31-40.

habitantes que presionaron para que las condenaran pues los temores en una sociedad reverente para el orden eran que éste se rompiera. No se las autorizó a desembarcar, fueron desnudadas para buscar signos de brujería en sus personas y se confiscaron todos sus bienes. Pero estas mujeres eran el comienzo de la invasión cuáquera de la región y, a pesar de todas las declaraciones de brujería, persecuciones y condenas, como la de Mary Dyer, que fue colgada en 1660, florecieron. Se establecieron comunidades en la región que eran visitadas y apoyadas por personas provenientes de Inglaterra, aunque se estableció un continuo flujo de viajeros en los dos sentidos.

En los Estados Unidos sus anales demuestran que entre los 87 ministros ordenados que fueron a misionar, entre 1656 y 1700, el 33% eran mujeres y en ese número no se cuentan las que viajaban con sus maridos. En los siglos XVII y XVIII, estos viajes podían ser muy peligrosos, pues las enfermedades y las fiebres estaban muy extendidas pero las afrontaban sin miedo. Las cartas de las misioneras dejan ver que se encontraban llenas del Espíritu Santo lo que las producía alegría y gozo aunque sentían temor por estar obrando contra la modestia que "exigía" nuestra condición femenina.

Tenían reuniones mensuales y anuales de las que existen referencias detalladas entre las que se encuentran la atención a los pobres, la responsabilidad de los padres en el cuidado de los hijos y la educación de sus miembros para lo que abrieron colegios que luego ampliaron a personas de otros credos. Las mujeres aprendían las labores propias del sexo femenino pero también las preparaban para el trabajo y de hecho aparecen como directoras de muchos colegios, especialmente de negros y pobres. En Filadelfia en 1754 se abrió el primer colegio para niñas donde aprendían religión, francés, aritmética y los clásicos. Un siglo más tarde un moralista cuáquero, Jonathan Dymond, sostenía "no veo ninguna razón para que la educación de las mujeres sea diferente, en lo básico, de la de los varones. Son parte y contribuyen a la riqueza e inteligencia de la familia humana".[14]

En los Estados Unidos los cuáqueros prosperaron y hoy cuentan con 115.000 fieles. Hay otros 200.000 esparcidos por todo el mundo y las mujeres les deben agradecer su empeño en la educación pues lo pusieron a favor del fin de la esclavitud, de los derechos de los negros y del sexo femenino.[15] Esta

---

[14] Jonathan Dymond, *Essays in the Principle of morality* (Collins: New York 1825), 251-252.
[15] Para referencias al ministerio ordenado de los cuáqueros veer Lucia K. Beamish, *Quaker Ministry 1691-1834* (Oxford University Press: Oxford 1967), y Christopher Hill, *The World Turned Upside Down* (Penguin Books: London 1972).

labor a favor de los derechos civiles les valió ser acusados de haber abandonado sus creencias religiosas, en pos de una vida más secularizada, pero podemos pensar que su alma se había unido a su inteligencia pues no son magnitudes que tengan que vivir separadas. No nos puede extrañar que, con estos orígenes, las mujeres cuáqueras fueran pioneras en la defensa del voto para el sexo femenino y en las sucesivas reformas de la sociedad para conseguir la igualdad femenina.

Los shakers

Un caso extraordinario lo representan los shakers también conocidos como la Iglesia de la Segunda Aparición de Cristo, que fueron los seguidores de una mujer, Mother Ann Lee. Ann tuvo una visión en 1770, cuando estaba en la cárcel, en la que le pareció que Cristo se había vuelto a encarnar en su persona y que a través suyo hacía milagros, una historia muy parecida a la de los guillermitas. A partir de ese momento se llamó "Ann, la palabra" o "la madre Ann". La idea de que Jesús se encarnaría en una mujer no es nueva, tuvo su origen en franceses protestantes, los *camisards*, que habían huido a Inglaterra pero no sabemos si Lee tuvo contacto con ellos.

La fundadora no se sentía con vocación para contraer matrimonio pero fue obligada por su padre. Dio a luz a cuatro hijos que murieron al nacer, unas muertes en las que vio un signo de que sus seguidores debían vivir célibes, algo en lo que se diferenciaban de los cuáqueros, a los que se parecían por sus liturgias de danzas y cantos.

La iglesia anglicana era muy dura con los que consideraba herejes y un castigo habitual era atravesarles la lengua con un hierro incandescente. Los jueces que vieron la causa de Ann no la condenaron, pues vieron un eximente en su ignorancia, pero a ella le sirvió de advertencia y decidió marchar a tierras americanas con algunos seguidores, no más de doce. Partieron en el barco *Mariah* en mayo de 1774 y por sus sermones condenatorios a tripulación y pasajeros y por sus liturgias desenfrenadas el capitán les amenazó con echarles por la borda. En tierras americanas su lema fue "Poner vuestras manos a trabajar y dar vuestros corazones a Dios" con lo que consiguieron unas comunidades rurales prósperas donde continuaron sus liturgias que consistían en bailar y temblar, de aquí el nombre de shakers, para deshacerse del pecado.

Su llegada a América coincidió con la guerra contra Inglaterra, un momento de efervescencia religiosa pues las personas pensaban en la muerte, temían el juicio final y la condena por sus pecados. Fueron predicadores itinerantes y cientos de americanos se sintieron atraídos por sus creencias en las que el espíritu de Cristo se manifestaba a través de la madre Ann. Llenaban sus reuniones, que celebraban en grandes establos, y los fieles salían reconfortados. Fueron condenados por pacifistas, herejes, sospechosos de brujería y traición, acabando muchos en la cárcel o apaleados por las turbas. Cuando los jueces comprendieron que no eran un peligro para la seguridad nacional les dejaron en paz. Cuando murió la fundadora decidieron vivir en comunidad en el campo para separarse del mundo y redactaron normas de convivencia que prohibían la integración de los dos sexos. Construyeron iglesias sin campanarios para diferenciarse de las que consideraban casas del diablo. Hicieron un gobierno dual formado por un varón y una mujer, Sister Lucy, pero cada grupo, de entre 30 y 90 miembros, contaba con una serie de ancianos, diáconos y administradores de ambos sexos. Un milagro de igualdad si consideramos que lo consiguieron 150 años antes de que a las mujeres se les permitiera ejercer el voto. Pero estas comunidades mixtas estaban sujetas a la maledicencia, con frecuencia impulsada por el esposo abandonado.

Como no tenían hijos decidieron adoptar huérfanos y darles educación pero pocos se incorporaban a sus comunidades y aunque les llegaban muchos adeptos de todas partes del país, no perseveraban. Era una vida rural difícil pues tenían que renunciar a sus matrimonios, familias, bienes y empleos. Todos trabajaban en variedad de ocupaciones y por su interés en la educación generaron muchos inventos, entre ellos las pinzas para colgar la ropa, la mayoría de maquinaria agrícola.

Sus danzas rítmicas en Sabbathday Lake, atraían a muchas personas pues comunicaban la libertad y la alegría de haber vencido a los demonios, al pecado y a las presiones de este mundo. A mediados del siglo XVIII había 18 comunidades divididas en 58 unidades familiares que contaban con 6000 personas en total pero fueron perdiendo fieles,[16] pues la revolución industrial y la falta de vocaciones acabaron con sus comunas agrícolas. La hermana Frances Carr, una de las últimas shakers, murió el 2 de enero de 2017, y a su entierro acudieron muchos simpatizantes que se preguntaban si no estaban asistiendo al funeral de esta iglesia porque sólo quedan otros dos representantes.

---

[16] Para profundizar en los shakers, Ann George Leslie, *Dancing Saints* (Doubleday, Doran and Co: New York 1943), y Flo Morse, *The Story of the Shakers* (The Countryman Press: Woodstock 1986).

Isabel Gómez Acebo
Comunidades de la Reforma pioneras en la comisión de ministerios
a las mujeres: La tradición común

Los metodistas wesleyanos

Detrás de la vida de los hermanos Wesley, John (1703 – 1791) y Charles (1707 – 1788), compositor de himnos, está su madre, Susanna, a la que podemos considerar verdadera fundadora de este tipo de metodismo que se conoce por el nombre de sus hijos. Era una mujer culta pues conocía el latín, griego y francés que se casó con el rector de la parroquia de Epworth, con quién engendró 19 hijos aunque solo vivieron 13. Con su marido en prisión por deudas y poco dinero consiguió montar en su hogar una escuela para sus hijos y como sus vecinos no tenían pastor organizó, también en su casa, unas reuniones en las que leía sermones, rezaba y conversaba con sus rústicos paisanos. Enterado su esposo por sus cartas se indignó con ella "por esta novedad" que condenaba la sociedad.

John Wesley estudió en Oxford y abandonó los libros con un futuro brillante por delante para servir como pastor dos años en la parroquia de su padre. De vuelta a Oxford llamado por el rector del Lincoln College se encontró con un grupo orante que había formado su hermano Charles, el *Holy Club*, al que un panfleto anónimo calificaba de los metodistas de Oxford y de aquí el nombre. Tras este periodo de 6 años, en 1735, se marchó con su hermano Charles de misionero a Georgia donde no fue nada feliz. A su vuelta a Inglaterra en 1737, descorazonado por su experiencia misionera, se encontró con un obispo moraviano, Petrus Boehler (nacido Böhler), y se unió a su comunidad incluso viajando a Alemania para conocer mejor su credo.

A su vuelta fundó una nueva manera de ver el cristianismo, aunque nunca dejó de pertenecer a la iglesia oficial, que incluía predicadores laicos itinerantes que se pasearon por Inglaterra e Irlanda creando grupos pequeños de creyentes. Estos hechos motivaron la persecución de la Iglesia de Inglaterra que controlaba la predicación de las personas que elegía y los templos en los que ejercían.

De alguna manera el acercamiento de John Wesley a la Biblia en donde se encuentra todo lo necesario para la salvación fue distinto al oficial pues veía que la inspiración divina era doble: al escritor y al lector lo que significaba que cada persona, comunidad o contexto cultural, podía encontrar en sus páginas distintas claves de interpretación, siempre que el texto sagrado fuera mirado tras la lente de Jesucristo.

Ni que decir tiene que esta lectura abría enormes expectativas a las mujeres predicadoras que encontraban en las páginas bíblicas un escrito liberador. A John Wesley en principio no le parecía mal que predicaran pero se limitaba a dar una aprobación tácita. Su pensamiento queda claro en lo que escribe a

Sarah Crosby, una de sus fervientes seguidoras: "Reza en privado o en público todo lo que puedas. Si en público, puedes insertar pequeñas exhortaciones dentro de la oración, pero aléjate de lo que se conoce por predicar."[17] En su iglesia conocida, como *Society of Friends,* "no se niega la prohibición de hablar de las mujeres, como hacen los cuáqueros, porque aparece claro en la Biblia, pero admitimos excepciones" escribió el fundador.[18]

Sarah refleja en su diario, una recomendación que Wesley hacía a sus seguidores y que nos permite conocer mejor sus experiencias espirituales. Cuenta que en sus viajes misioneros se encontraba con audiencias de doscientas personas lo que le impedía ejercitar el boca a boca y la multitud la obligaba a hablar en público. Esgrime el ejemplo de la Magdalena y de la Samaritana que no podían ser tachadas de inmodestia "cuando invitaron a todo su pueblo a venir al encuentro de Cristo". Y refleja la vocación de Dios a la que se sintió llamada: "Y me dijo estas palabras a mi corazón: apacienta mis ovejas (Jn 21,17) a lo que respondí: Señor, haré lo que tú hiciste. Llevaré los corderos en mi regazo y trataré suavemente a las ovejas con crías (Isa 40,11)".[19]

En la misma situación se encontraron Hester Ann Rogers y Dinah Evans nombradas profesoras de los cursos espirituales, que el metodismo organizaba todas las semanas, y que las colocaba al frente de cien personas a las que predicaron. Un caso curioso fue el de Elizabeth Wallbridge, una sirvienta que renunció a un puesto bien remunerado por ocuparse de sus ancianos padres en la Isla de Wight donde, mujer ignorante, fundó la primera piedra del metodismo en la isla gracias a su ejemplo.[20]

Las mujeres trataron de empujar a Wesley para que el reconocimiento tácito de su labor como predicadoras pasara a explícito y lo consiguieron mediante sus argumentos. Mary Bosanquet Fletcher (1739 – 1815), una de las seguidoras más importantes de Wesley en los orígenes del metodismo, defendía que si las mujeres pueden profetizar con la cabeza cubierta les sería imposible hacerlo si no emplearan la palabra ¿Cómo profetizaban sin hablar en público?

---

[17] Cita en Abel Stevens, *The Women of Methodism* (Carlton & Porter: New York 1866). Obra reeditada por la Universidad de Michigan, sin año, 82.
[18] Cita en Stevens, *The Women of Methodism*, 64.
[19] Las frases de Sarah Crosby, todavía no publicado en español, vienen en un capítulo de Paul W. Chilcote, "Methodist Women and the Bible. Early Nineteenth Century Engagement with Scripture", que se publicará próximamente en el tomo sobre el siglo XIX de la colección La Biblia de las Mujeres.
[20] De todas estas mujeres predicadoras hay largas reseñas en el libro de Stevens, *The Women of Methodism*.

Estos precedentes están en el hecho de que la *United Methodist Church* fuera una de las primeras iglesias reformadas en conceder la ordenación femenina. En 1880 fue ordenada Anna Howard Shaw y en otra denominación metodista, la *United Brethren Church,* Elisza Niswonger en 1889. A partir de la fusión de estas dos ramas, la iglesia metodista americana concedió en 1956 plenos derechos de ordenación a las mujeres y 21 han sido elevadas al episcopado.

El Ejército de Salvación

El Ejército de Salvación, conocido mundialmente como la Salvation Army, fue fundado por el matrimonio de Catherine Mumford Booth, que se educó en una ferviente familia metodista wesleyana y William Booth, que empezó su carrera como predicador metodista. Aunque el metodismo había dado oportunidades para que las mujeres predicaran, los tiempos habían cambiado y se encontraban con muchas trabas y prohibiciones porque la sombra del texto de Pablo se iba agrandando y las críticas contra nuestro protagonismo arreciaron.

Fue el contacto con predicadores americanos, especialmente de Phoebe Palmer, que no creían que el pecado original hubiera afectado a la humanidad permanentemente lo que liberaba a las mujeres de las culpas de Eva y permitían una lectura no literal de la Biblia, lo que hizo reflexionar a Catherine. En un escrito defendió que, en el relato del Génesis, el varón y la mujer fueron creados iguales y que la subordinación femenina fue la consecuencia del pecado. Admitió diferencias entre los sexos pero precisamente esa desigualdad hacía mejor a las mujeres para la predicación. "Dios ha dado a las mujeres amabilidad en forma, actitud y comportamiento, un lenguaje persuasivo y sobre todo una naturaleza emocional bien equilibrada, lo que a mi parecer resulta muy favorecedor para el discurso público".[21]

Creía que las mujeres, si se sentían llamadas por el Espíritu Santo, tenían plenos derechos para predicar y no debían ser frenadas por restricciones al sexo femenino que habían sido levantadas por los hombres. No veía necesario recibir revelaciones especiales, como las de Mother Ann, sino que cualquier mujer podía sentir esa vocación, de manera que cuando su marido enfermó, estaba preparada y no dudó en subirse al estrado en su lugar para predicar.

---

[21] Catherine Booth cit. en Pamela J. Walker, "A Chaste and Fervid Eloquence. Catherine Booth and the Ministry of Women in the Salvation Army", en: Kienzle y Walker, *Women Preachers and Prophets,* 292.

Pero lo hacía esporádicamente pues tenía el eterno problema de las amas de casa: un hogar con cuatro hijos a los que cuidar y alimentar, no le permitía encontrar tiempo para preparar sus sermones.

En 1865 el matrimonio se mudó a Londres donde reunió a un grupo de fieles que se nominaron la *East London Christian Mission*, más tarde conocida como *Salvation Army*, a la que dieron en 1878 una estructura militar inspirada en el ejército. Catherine nunca tuvo un papel oficial, aunque estaba en muchos comités y predicaba, pero enseguida fue reconocida como "la madre de la armada". Su procesión funeraria tras su muerte en 1890 contó con la presencia de 30.000 personas.

Lo más sorprendente en este grupo es que en 1870 se reconocía a las mujeres el derecho a predicar y ser elegidas para cualquier cargo dentro de la asociación. La organización daba a las mujeres, aunque no tuvieran formación, mucho protagonismo pero también les exigía disciplina. Se podían saltar todas las normas sociales de su época, pues trabajaban en la calle, para llamar la atención. Un ejemplo revela estas prácticas, algunas predicaban con el cabello suelto (soltarse el pelo para una mujer es sinónimo de libertinaje) y vestidas con un simple camisón lo que las convertía en una diana para las mofas y los insultos pero como cristianas convencidas aceptaban los insultos y las persecuciones si con ello conseguían que escucharan sus palabras.[22]

Hoy *El Ejército de Salvación* está en muchos países donde se han convertido en una comunidad que ayuda a los más necesitados no sólo con bienes materiales sino aportando valores espirituales.

Conclusión

Hemos visto a lo largo de estas páginas como hombres y mujeres se adelantaron a los tiempos en los que vivieron y consideraron injusta la condición en la que la iglesia y la sociedad sometían a las mujeres. Leyeron la Biblia con nuevos ojos, pusieron las primeras piedras de la igualdad femenina con sus escritos y con su ejemplo, fundaron comunidades en las que las mujeres predicaban o lideraban, una senda que las generaciones posteriores siguieron y llevaron a término. No les fue fácil y sufrieron persecuciones pues defender el protagonismo femenino en la sociedad, nunca lo ha sido, pero perduraron en su empeño.

---

[22] He tomado muchas de las ideas de la obra de Pamela J. Walker antes citada.

Tras sus inicios en Europa se trasladaron a los Estados Unidos donde florecieron en una sociedad más nueva, más permeable y menos asustadiza por llevar a cabo cambios. Unas comunidades se mantuvieron durante más años y otras, por sus condiciones específicas de vida, desaparecieron antes pero a todos estos pioneros les debemos dar las gracias pues han allanado el camino por el que nosotras hemos caminado. Ese agradecimiento es el que ha motivado la publicación de estas páginas.

Isabel Gómez Licenciada en Ciencias Políticas y en Teología por la Universidad de Comillas. Preside y dirige la Fundación Sagrada Familia, entidad dedicada a residencias de ancianos. Miembro fundador de la Asociación de Teólogas Españolas, ATE y de la Asociación Europea de Mujeres para la Investigación Teológica ESWRT. Ha dirigido y participado en la colección de teología En Clave de Mujer editada por Desclée de Brouwer de la que se han publicado 25 títulos, algunos traducidos al portugués y al italiano. Sus últimas publicaciones son una Guía de lectura al evangelio de Lucas, EVD, Estella 2008 y una novela histórica Francisco. El pañero de Asís, Khaf, Madrid 2013.

BOOK REVIEWS – REZENSIONEN – RECENSIONES

Vanessa Götz-Meiners, *Treue und Untreue in der Partnerschaft. Historische Entwicklungen – Moraltheologische perspektiven,* (Aschendorff Verlag: Münster 2016).

Faithfulness and Unfaithfulness in partnership is, at first glance, not a theological issue. In our days, it seems to belong in the sphere of private decisions taken at least among two adult people living together in what current terminology calls "partnership". And, in our times, it is also a well-accepted fact, that faithfulness does not seem to be a natural construction for human beings. In so called modern societies, the time is over in which unfaithfulness has been considered a public issue. For men, it has almost always not been such a norm as it has been – and still is – for a woman. Even into the last century, faithfulness and unfaithfulness were being dealt with within the system of law, such as in the context of divorce. For instance, the final sentence of "divorced guilty" or "divorced not guilty" had only been abolished in West Germany less the 50 years ago, removing unfaithfulness from the list of social crimes. In current day Europe, where prostitution has become an almost normal job and sex workers fulfil nearly every demand – with or without the support of health insurance – the word "faithful" sounds old-fashioned. The right of having sex and all social constructions surrounding this axiom of mostly male life, seem to be the counterpart of the traditional value of faithfulness.

Today's moral of marriage is no longer irreversibly connected with faithfulness. As far as faithfulness still plays a role in relationships and partnerships at all, it is in the context of having sex or making love. Of course, abiding with the social demand of faithfulness had often been reached by way of keeping silent when unfaithful. The first part of Vanessa Götz-Meiners' book is a profound historical excursion into faithfulness and unfaithfulness with the change of times. The geographical background is Europe and its social systems in ancient Rome, Greece and the Land of Israel. In part 2 the author tries to provide an ethical evaluation of faithfulness and unfaithfulness; and in part 3 she outlines some perspectives in ethical and theological dealings with faithfulness and unfaithfulness. Considering the fact that the book contains almost 600 pages, her discussions are far from superficial.

The second chapter in the first part confronts these ancient traditions with theological decisions and the influence of the Church. Here, one could miss a focus on secular developments and legal issues that point out the connection between the religious demand for women's virginity at marriage and the power of inheritance afforded to men. The power relation between "his" inheritance and "his" making sure that it goes without any doubt to "his" sons, and the religiously supported norm and proof of "her" virginity, would help put the category of faithfulness in a broader social and legal context.

In not making social need into the most essential condition for faithfulness, the author enters the field of love and desire, possession and choice, wanting and having:

> Ein häufiges Argument in den spätantiken Diskursen ist die Bedeutung der Treue für die moralische Integrität der Person, genauer gesagt ihre Funktion als Bewährungsfeld spezifischer Ansprüche auf ein Ethos der inneren Reinheit und der Selbstkultivierung durch den kontrollierten Umgang mit der eigenen Sexualität.[1]

This idea refers to norm and control as if they were law and order. It goes hand in hand with the ideal of human beings for which human *ratio* always determines emotional life:

> Die Begierden zu kontrollieren und Stärke im Umgang mit körperlichen Regungen zu zeigen wird als Merkmal des erstrebenswerten Männlichkeitsideals gewertet. Die Frau gilt hingegen als die Schwächere und den körperlichen Begierden eher ausgeliefert als der Mann. Dennoch wird sie nicht aufgefordert, ihre Lüste zu beherrschen, sondern bei ihr steht vielmehr die Abwehr fremder Begierden im Vordergrund.[2]

---

[1] p. 416. "A frequent argument in late ancient discourse is the importance of faithfulness for a person's moral integrity, or more precisely, its function as testing-field for specific claims to an ethos of inner purity and self-cultivation through the controlled handling of one's own sexuality" (here and hereafter, my translation from German).

[2] p. 517. "To control the desires and to show strength in dealing with physical signs of attraction is regarded to be a characteristic of desirable masculinity. The woman, on the other hand, is weaker and more prone to physical desires than the man. Nevertheless, she is not called upon to dominate her lust, but rather, more importantly in her description, she has to push away the desires of others."

At crucial junctions in this historic perception that still influences our lives, the reader could miss a feminine and feminist point of view. Of course, each and every one can discover for him- and herself that history is made by the powerful. Of course, it is at second glance visible that our political, legal and ideological construction of society, culture and religion is arranged around the power of male desire. However, it is still not unnecessary to state loud and clear: prostitution, for instance, has not become a phenomenon in human history because women have been looking for a newer, nicer job. It is male need and power that made this business possible. And the satisfying of male desire by the use of prostitution services does not generally count as unfaithfulness, but with deeper social challenges such as this, the author leaves us to our own devices.

Faithfulness, concludes Götz-Meiners in observing our modern handling of the issue, is no longer exclusively bound to monogamous life. Faithfulness is finally defined as all that gives the relationship stability. It might be sexual, it might be emotional, it might be both. For the author, the main category underlying the discussion of our times and its dealing with faithfulness or unfaithfulness is the happiness in a partnership, however long it may be. The factor of time is not mentioned here, but could nevertheless be enriching in this reflection of marriage, affairs, partnerships, couple counselling, and separations.

> Ein positives Verständnis der Treue, das den Schwerpunkt auf den Erhalt beziehungsstabilisierender Faktoren legt, welche in einer relationalen Beziehungskultur, in Verlässlichkeit, Vertrauen und Solidarität zur Geltung kommen, kann freilich keine Garantie für das konfliktfreie Gelingen von Partnerschaften geben. Es kann jedoch Hilfestellung sein, die Voraussetzungen für ein Beziehungsleben zu schaffen, das sich in den heutigen Herausforderungen der pluralen Lebensbezüge zu bewähren vermag.[3]

Thus ends the book. So, Vanessa Götze-Meiners' final answer to the question: "Why to be faithful?" is that faithfulness should be our daily attitude and personal commitment to and within any partnership because this way of life and love provides us with what we need: stability. One could nevertheless wish

---

[3] p. 547. "A positive understanding of faithfulness focusing on the maintenance of stabilising factors, which, in a relationship culture, are expressed in reliability, trust and solidarity, can of course not guarantee the conflict-free success of partnerships. However, it can help to create the prerequisites for a life-in-relationship, which can withstand today's challenges of the many dimensions of life."

Book Reviews
Rezensionen
Recensiones

that in this impressive compilation, the author would have dedicated some discussion to dilemmas and challenges of the magnitude of "To whom should I be faithful?" A Jewish – as well as Christian – answer across many theologies could be: "To yourself!" And here, I think, a very fruitful theological debate may begin.

Sabine Dievenkorn

Carol P. Christ and Judith Plaskow, *Goddess and God in the world. Conversations in Embodied Theology*, (Fortress press: Minneapolis 2016).

Göttin und Gott in der Welt – Dialoge in Gestalttheologie. Mit dem Gespräch zwischen Carol P. Christ und Judith Plaskow, der in dem vorliegenden Buch niedergelegt ist, eröffnet sich der theologisch interessierten Leserin und feministisch arbeitenden Wissenschaftlerin ein bemerkenswerter Diskurs. Ausgehend von der traditionellen Theologie, mit der wir zu Beginn alle konfrontiert sind oder waren, folgen wir in dem vorliegenden Gespräch zweier Kolleginnen, Theologinnen, Freundinnen und Wissenschaftlerinnen, die aus unterschiedlichen Gründen gezwungen sahen und sehen, Theologie neu zu gestalten. „People who reject the popular image of God as an old white man who rules the world from outside it often find themselves at a loss for words when they try to articulate new meanings and images of divinity."[4] Damit beginnt der Diskurs, der vielmehr eine Reise durch die Geschichte der feministischen Theologie wird. Oberflächlich betrachtet scheint es ein historischer Abriss mancher formalen Eckdaten und Ereignisse, mit denen sich die Etablierung feministischer Theologien und Lehrstühle in den USA verknüpft. In der Tiefe sind die Gespräche, an denen die Leserin teilhat, die Eröffnung eines eigenen inneren biographischen Ablaufs in der persönlichen Geschichte der je eigenen Entwicklung feministischer Theologie. Und hier ist die Leserin eingeladen zwischen beidem oszillierend sich selbst zu begegnen. Sei es formal in Zustimmung oder Ablehnung präsentierter Entwicklungsströmungen us-amerikanischer feministischer Theologie oder aber in der inneren Antwortsuche auf die eigenen persönlichen Entscheidungen, die uns mal nöher oder mal ferner sein ließen, von bestimmten theologisch, feministischen Positionen.

Carol P. Christ begann konsequent als christliche Theologin im Corpus traditioneller Theologie nach den Freiräumen für weibliche, feminine Spiritualität

---

[4] p. xi.

zu suchen. Diese, ihre Beharrlichkeit gepaart mit dem hohen akademischen Anspruch in feministischer Hermeneutik, lassen die christliche Thologin in der Spannung zwischen Exegese und Eisegese verantwotlich dort nach Wegen suchen, wo es Neuland zu erschließen galt. Lesend wir man Zeugin, wie die Theologin und Wissenschaftlerin ihre Forschung nicht von ihrem Selbst zu trennen bereit ist. Behutsam ist die Leserin eingeladen, dem einerseits zu folgen: „I found it dishonest to ignore the violent aspects of the biblical story of God as a liberator of the oppressed. [...] Even though I still considered myself Christian, I could not adapt the paradigm of God as a liberator to a feminist context."[5] Andereseits eröffnet sich ein neuer Horizont, wenn den eigenen Erfahrungen, Begrenzungen, Machtlosigkeiten und Kompromisse lesend mit eingebracht werden. Ist ist die Frage, wie weit sich die Leserin eingerichtet hat in dem christichen Weltbild, des männlich beschriebenen Gottes, der von außen die Welt regiert. Wie viel Raum blieb angesichts dieser Prämisse für weibliche Spiritualität wirklich? Wie viel habe ich? Es wird deutlich, dass sich die formale Frage der Forschung mit der persönlichen Wagnis verknüpft.

Im Dialog mit Judith Plaskow, einer Jüdin, die christliche Theologie studiert, und die andesichts dieses biographischen Umstands auf eine ganz andere Weise feministisch theologische Identität und Klarheit ringt, wäre es zu kurz gegriffen, wenn man meinte, hier am gelungenen feministen Dialog zweier Weltreligionen beteiligt zu sein. Wesentlich ist jenseits dessen, die Einsicht, dass feministische Theologie Gestalt in der eigenen Biographie gewinnt. Dass Biographie und Theologie auf einen Weise miteinander verwoben sind, die Lebensentscheidungen erfordern, in Frage stellen, erzwingen oder verhindern. Es ist Judith Plaskow, die als promovierte Theologin und aktive feministische Wissenschaftlerin sich selbst wieder findet in der Rolle der Ehefrau eines Rabbiners, die einen kosheren Haushalt führt und ihre Lebensgestaltung mit den Normen der Halacha in Einklang bringt. Die junge Frau, die Rabbinerin sein will, studiert Protestantische Theologie und wird Feministin. Sie hört Naomi Weisstein sagen: „Women grow up wanting to be doctors and lawyers and ministers and end up being doctors' wives and layers' wives and ministers' wives." Und sie führt aus: "I was a girl who had grown up wanting to be a rabbi and who now was married to one, and I felt as if she had punched me into my stomach."[6]

---

[5] p. 78.
[6] Naomi Weisstein, *Kinder Küche, Kirche as scientific Law*, quoted p. 52.

Book Reviews
Rezensionen
Recensiones

Die Verbindung von Theologie und Autobiographie ist eine Herausforderung, die all diejenigen trifft, die Spiritualität als einen Teil gestalteter, gelebter verkörperter Theologie betrachten. Gestalttheologie mag dafür ein passender Ausdruck sein. Zeigt es doch die Verwobenheit an, die zwischen Theologie und Biographie sichtbar wird, wenn es um Lebensgestaltung in der traditionellen Spannung von Zuspruch und Anspruch geht, in der Beruf und Berufung im reformatorischen und altdeutschen Wortsinn wieder zusammen gedacht und gelebt – eben gestaltet werden.

Goddess und God in the World ist ein dialogisches Buch, ein gestalttheologisches Buch. Ob die Lesierin dabei ebenfalls mutig Entwürfe zu einer neuen *Thealogie* wagt und einbringt ist dabei nebensächlich. Entscheidend und bereichernd ist es zuzulassen, dass der biographische Weg und Werdegang Teil des feministisch-theologischen Ziels ist. Maricia Falk ist nur zuzustimmen, wenn sie urteilt: „The engaging narratives and conversations in *Goddess an God in the World* brilliantly model the authors' conviction that divinity is to be found within our lives and in our shared experience. Carol P. Christ and Judith Plaskow have given us a unique gift: the record of a long and evolving friendship between two of our foremost feminist foremothers. I am thrilled with this book"[7].

Sabine Dievenkorn

---

[7] Marcia Falk, *The books of Blessings*, quoted p. ii.

EUROPEAN SOCIETY OF WOMEN IN THEOLOGICAL RESEARCH

EUROPÄISCHE GESELLSCHAFT VON FRAUEN IN THEOLOGISCHER FORSCHUNG

ASSOCIACÍON EUROPEA DE MUJERES EN LA INVESTIGACIÓN TEOLÓGICA

President – Präsidentin – Presidenta
Prof.[in] Dr.[in] Kristin de Troyer, Salzburg, Austria

Vice-President – Vize-Präsidentin – Vicepresidenta
Prof.[in] Dr.[in] Agnethe Siquans, Viena, Austria

Secretary – Sekretärin – Secretaria
Dr.[in] Gertraud Ladner, Innsbruck, Austria

Vice-Secretary – Vize-Sekretärin – Vicesecretaria
Prof.[in] Dr.[in] Isa Breitmeier, Freiburg, Germany

Treasurer – Schatzmeisterin – Tesorera
Prof.[a] Dr.[a] Montserrat Escribano Cárcel, Valencia, Spain

Vice-Treasurer – Vize-Schatzmeisterin – Vicetesorera
Dr.[in] Luise Metzer, Bielefeld, Germany

Networking
Dr.[a] sc. Jadranka Rebeka Anić, Split, Croatia

Journal – Jahrbuch – Revista
Prof.[in] Dr.[in] Sabine Dievenkorn, Kiryat Tivon, Israel

Homepage of the ESWTR
http://www.eswtr.org